THE BLACK MAN'S BURDEN

THE
BLACK MAN'S BURDEN

The White Man in Africa
from the Fifteenth Century
to World War I

by E. D. Morel

Modern Reader Paperbacks
New York and London

First published in 1920 in Great Britain
ISBN 978-0-85345-115-0

Library of Congress Catalog Card Number: 74-81792

Manufactured in the United States of America

10 9 8 7 6 5 4

DEDICATION

To My Friends,
W.A.C. and E.H.C.
This Book is Dedicated with many grateful thoughts.

INTRODUCTION

The purpose of this volume, which was suggested to me by Mr. George Lansbury, is a dual one. It seeks to convey a clear notion of the atrocious wrongs which the white peoples have inflicted upon the black. It seeks to lay down the fundamental principles of a humane and practical policy in the government of Africa by white men.

We stand on the threshold of a new era. The moment is propitious for the birth of an international conscience in regard to Africa. Great social changes are in process of development among the white peoples of the earth. The seat of power is shifting from the propertied classes to the producing masses. The latter will find themselves invested before long with executive duties in many spheres of government, with whose problems they are not familiar; among them the administration of dark-skinned peoples. Upon the new Democracy in Britain, in particular, will be laid immense tasks in this respect. These tasks constitute in fact the greatest moral responsibility which the Democracy of tomorrow will have to face. They cannot be set aside. The spirit in which they are approached will be, perhaps, for the new Democracy of Britain, the supreme test of character.

For many reasons the peoples of Africa should make a special appeal to all that is generous and just in the forces which are swiftly marching to the conquest of political power in Europe. Those reasons are set forth in the pages which follow. The rising generation knows little of the evils wrought in Africa by its forbears. This book will help to recall them. Public opinion does not appreciate how great are the evils which are being perpetrated in many regions of Africa to-day; nor the graver evils which loom threateningly upon the African horizon. It ought to do so, for the honour and the interest alike of the white peoples are directly involved—particularly in those European States which are governing States in Africa. This book may assist in the diffusion of that necessary knowledge.

It does not profess to be a connected history of Europe's dealings with Africa. There are many such histories, and they serve their object more or less well. But their object, in the main, is to recount the exploits of Europeans in Africa, many of them worthy of admiration. Mine is to show the sufferings which Europe has inflicted upon Africa. To have attempted a comprehensive survey of Europe's relations with Africa from that point of view in a volume of this size, would not, I think, have left any very definite impression upon the average reader's mind. I have, therefore, adopted the method of selection. Apart from a chapter on the Slave Trade, indispensable to my main purpose, I have sectionalised the determining impulses to which European intervention in Africa has responded, and I have provided specific examples under each section. Each example thus constitutes a complete story in itself. This method of treatment may serve to create a really living interest in the subject and to arrest attention, where the alternative method might have failed. At least that is the author's hope.

A subsidiary purpose of the volume is to impress the reader with the remarkable manner in which the political history of Europe during the past half century has been affected by the reflex action upon European affairs of the proceedings of European Governments in Africa. Those

INTRODUCTION

to whom history appeals as a long chain of inter-connected links, who believe that wrong-doing by men and nations brings its inevitable aftermath, and that human records are stamped all over with the proofs of it, may be forgiven, perhaps, if they are tempted to see in the desolation and misery into which Europe is plunged, the Nemesis of Europe's actions in Africa.

. . . . . .

In order to avoid the use of frequent and elaborate footnotes to which I am partial, with, I am told, exasperating effects upon many readers, I have on this occasion adopted the method of giving a short bibliography of references at the conclusion of most chapters. I have to express my best thanks to Mr. John H. Harris, the secretary of the Anti-Slavery and Aborigines Protection Society, who has done so much to enlighten the public on the policy and actions of the Chartered Company, for kindly placing at my disposal a number of documents upon which I have partially drawn in compiling Chapters IV. and V.

December, 1919.   E. D. MOREL.

Since this book was completed the British Government has taken a grave reactionary step in West African economic policy by decreeing that 90 per cent. of the palm kernel nuts exported from West Africa must be shipped to British ports. This is the sequel to the measures adopted during the war with a view to destroying Germany's considerable share in this trade—a share which was of direct economic benefit to the British West African dependencies. The policy is bad from every point of view. It will restrict output, and to that extent diminish the prosperity of the West African dependencies. It will involve us in disputes with France and the United

INTRODUCTION

States, which have the means of retaliating. France has already done so. It raises the price of soap, salad oil and margarine in all of which palm kernel oil is a constituent, to the British consumer, in the interests of a combination of manufacturers. On these and other points a good deal might be said. But the chief objection to the step is its injustice to the West African producer, and the reversal to the policy of trade monopoly within the Empire which it embodies. It limits the native producers to a single market for the disposal of the fruits of their labour, thus virtually creating a monopoly which can control prices. It imposes upon our African protected subjects, who are powerless to resist it, a system which sacrifices their interests to a handful of capitalists in the Mother country. When Britain has once more an honest Government in power not amenable to the pressure of vested interests, one of the first duties of that Government should be the repeal of legislation which marks a lamentable declension in our West African policy.
E. D. M.

January, 1920.

CONTENTS

	PAGE
FRONTISPIECE	
DEDICATION	v.
INTRODUCTION BY THE AUTHOR	vii.

EXPLANATORY

CHAPTER I.—THE WHITE MAN'S BURDEN ...	3
„ II.—THE BLACK MAN'S BURDEN	7

PART ONE
FIRST PERIOD.—The Slave Trade

„ III.—THE STORY OF THE SLAVE TRADE ...	15

PART TWO
SECOND PERIOD.—Invasion, Political Control, Capitalistic Exploitation

A.—Episodes in the Struggle for the Soil

FOREWORD	27
CHAPTER IV.—THE STORY OF SOUTHERN RHODESIA	29
„ V.—THE STORY OF SOUTHERN RHODESIA (continued)	37
„ VI.—THE STORY OF GERMAN SOUTH-WEST AFRICA	66

B.—Episodes in the Establishment of Political Control

FOREWORD	71
CHAPTER VII.—THE STORY OF MOROCCO ...	73
„ VIII.—THE STORY OF TRIPOLI	87

CONTENTS

	PAGE
C.—Episodes in Capitalistic Exploitation.	
FOREWORD	105-107
CHAPTER IX.—THE STORY OF THE CONGO FREE STATE	109
„ X.—THE STORY OF THE FRENCH CONGO	127
„ XI.—THE STORY OF ANGOLA AND THE "COCOA ISLANDS"	149

PART THREE

THIRD PERIOD.—Reparation and Reform

CHAPTER XII.—THE LAND AND ITS FRUITS	163
„ XIII.—ADMINISTRATIVE PROBLEMS AND THE LAND	197
„ XIV.—WHAT A LEAGUE OF NATIONS COULD DO TO PROTECT TROPICAL AFRICA FROM THE EVILS OF CAPITALISTIC EXPLOITATION AND MILITARISM ...	215

EXPLANATORY

CHAPTER I.

THE WHITE MAN'S BURDEN.

THE bard of a modern Imperialism has sung of the White Man's burden. The notes strike the granite surface of racial pride and fling back echoes which reverberate through the corridors of history, exultant, stirring the blood with memories of heroic adventure, deeds of desperate daring, ploughing of unknown seas, vistas of mysterious continents, perils affronted and overcome, obstacles triumphantly surmounted.

But mingled with these anthems to national elation another sound is borne to us, the white peoples of the earth, along the trackless byways of the past, in melancholy cadence. We should prefer to close our ears to its haunting refrain, stifle its appeal in the clashing melodies of rapturous self-esteem. We cannot. And, as to-day, we tear and rend ourselves, we who have torn and rent the weaker folk in our Imperial stride, it gathers volume and insistence.

What of that other burden, not our own self-imposed one which national and racial vanity may well over-stress; but the burden we have laid on others in the process of assuming ours, the burden which others are bearing now because of us? Where are they whose shoulders have bent beneath its weight in the dim valleys of the centuries? Vanished into nothingness, pressed and stamped into that earth on which we set our conquering seal. How is it with those who but yesterday lived free lives beneath the sun and stars, and to-day totter to oblivion? How shall it be to-morrow with those who must slide even more swiftly to their doom, if our consciences be not smitten, our perception be not responsive to the long-drawn sigh which comes to us from the shadows of the bygone?

. . . .

These contemplations are not a fit theme for lyrical outpourings. These questions are unbidden guests at the banquet of national self-laudation. They excite no public plaudits, arouse no patriotic enthusiasms, pander to no racial conceits. They typify the skeleton at the imperial feast.

But this is a time of searching inquiry for the white races; of probing scrutiny into both past and present; of introspection in every branch of human endeavour.

And these questions must be asked. They must be confronted in the fullness of their import, in the utmost significance of their implications—and they must be answered.

I respectfully ask the reader to face them in these pages.

. . . . . .

My canvas is not crowded with figures. One figure only fills it, the figure which has incarnated for us through many generations the symbol of helplessness in man—the manacled slave stretching forth supplicating hands.

The figure on my canvas is the African, the man of sorrows in the human family.

And the reason he alone is represented there is that the question of " native races " and their treatment by the white races, centres henceforth upon the Black man, as the African is called, although few Africans are wholly black. The statement needs amplifying, perhaps.

Wherever, in Asia, in Australasia and in America, the invading white man has disputed with the aboriginal coloured man the actual occupation and exploitation of the soil, the latter has either virtually disappeared, as in Northern America, the West Indies, and Western Australia; or is rapidly dying out; or is being assimilated and absorbed; the two processes operating in combination in Southern America, while in New Zealand assimilation is the chief factor.

On the other hand where, in Asia, the white man is political over-lord, as in Hindustan, Indo-China, and the East Indies, the problem of contact is not one in which the decay and disappearance of the Asiatic is even remotely problematical. Taking into account the incalculable forces which events are quickening throughout the East, the problem is whether the days of white political control south of the Great Wall are not already numbered. Europe's delirious orgy of self-destruction following the unsuccessful effort of her principal Governments to apportion China among themselves; "the most stupendous project yet imagined," has set vibrating chords of racial impulse, whose diapason may yet shake the Western world as with the tremors of approaching earthquake. For, conceding every credit to force of character, innate in the white imperial peoples, which has enabled, and enables, a handful of white men to control extensive communities of non-white peoples by moral suasion, is it not mere hypocrisy to conceal from ourselves that we have extended our subjugating march from hemisphere to hemisphere because of our superior armament? With these secrets of our power we have now parted. We have sold them to Asia, to an older civilisation than our own. We thrust them, at first under duress and with humiliation, upon brains more profound, more subtle, more imitative, more daring perhaps than our own. Then, for lust of gain, we admitted into partnership those we earlier sought to subdue. Nay more. We have invited our apt pupils to join with us in slaughtering our rivals for-the-time-being; bidden them attend the shambles, inspect the implements, study at their ease the methods of the business.

And so, to-day, after long years of furious struggle with some of its peoples, long years of rough insolence towards others, White imperialism finds itself confronted with a racial force in Asia, which it can neither intimidate nor trample underfoot. Equipped with the knowledge our statesmen and capitalists have themselves imparted to it, this racial force faces us with its superior millions, its more real spiritual faith, its greater homogeneousness, its contempt of death. As the mists of fratricidal passion lessen, our gaze travels eastwards and vainly strives to read the purpose which lurks beneath the mask of imperturbable impassivity which meets us. Do we detect behind it no more than an insurance against white exploitation, or do we fancy that we perceive the features of an imperialism as ruthless as our own has been, which shall mould to its will the plastic myriads our own actions have wrenched from age-long trodden paths of peace? Do we hope that the "colour line," we ourselves have drawn so rigidly and almost universally, may operate between brown and yellow; that the ranges of the Himalayas and the forests of Burma may prove a national barrier to a more intimate fusion of design than the white races have yet shown themselves capable of evolving?

The answer to these riddles lies hidden in the womb of the future. But to this at least we may testify. In Asia the question is no longer, "How have we, the White imperial peoples, treated the Asiatic peoples in the past?"; nor is it, even, "How do we propose to treat them in the future?" It is, "How will they deal with us in their continent, perchance beyond its frontiers, in the days to come?"

CHAPTER II.

THE BLACK MAN'S BURDEN.

IT is with the peoples of Africa, then, that our inquiry is concerned. It is they who carry the " Black man's " burden. They have not withered away befcre the white man's *occupation*. Indeed, if the scope of this volume permitted, there would be no difficulty in showing that Africa has ultimately absorbed within itself every Caucasian and, for that matter, every Semitic invader too. In hewing out for himself a fixed abode in Africa, the white man has massacred the African in heaps. The African has survived, and it is well for the white settlers that he has.

In the process of imposing his political dominion over the African, the white man has carved broad and bloody avenues from one end of Africa to the other. The African has resisted, and persisted.

For three centuries the white man seized and enslaved millions of Africans and transported them, with every circumstance of ferocious cruelty, across the seas. Still the African survived and, in his land of exile, multiplied exceedingly.

But what the partial occupation of his soil by the white man has failed to do; what the mapping out of European political "spheres of influence " has failed to do; what the maxim and the rifle, the slave gang, labour in the bowels of the earth and the lash, have failed to do; what imported measles, smallpox and syphilis have failed to do; what even the oversea slave trade failed to do, the power of modern capitalistic exploitation, assisted by modern engines of destruction, may yet succeed in accomplishing.

For from the evils of the latter, scientifically applied and enforced, there is no escape for the African. Its destructive effects are not spasmodic: they are permanent. In its permanence resides its fatal consequences. It kills not the body merely, but the soul. It breaks the spirit. It attacks the African at every turn, from every point of vantage. It wrecks his polity, uproots him from the land, invades his family life, destroys his natural pursuits and occupations, claims his whole time, enslaves him in his own home. Economic bondage and wage slavery, the grinding pressure of a life of toil, the incessant demands of industrial capitalism—these things a landless European proletariat physically endures, though hardly. It endures—as a C8 population. The recuperative forces of a temperate climate are there to arrest the ravages, which alleviating influences in the shape of prophylactic and curative remedies will still further circumscribe. But in Africa, especially in tropical Africa, which a capitalistic imperialism threatens and has, in part, already devastated, man is incapable of reacting against unnatural conditions. In those regions man is engaged in a perpetual struggle against disease and an exhausting climate, which tells heavily upon child-bearing; and there is no scientific machinery for salving the weaker members of the community. The African of the tropics is capable of tremendous physical labours. But he cannot accommodate himself to the European system of monotonous, uninterrupted labour, with its long and regular hours, involving, moreover, as it frequently does, severance from natural surroundings and nostalgia, the condition of melancholy resulting from separation from home, a malady to which the African is specially prone. Climatic conditions forbid it. When the system is forced upon him, the tropical African droops and dies.

Nor is violent physical opposition to abuse and injustice henceforth possible for the African in any part of Africa. His chances of effective resistance have been steadily dwindling with the increasing perfectibility in the killing power of modern armament. Gunpowder broke the effectiveness of his resistance to the slave trade, although he continued to struggle. He has forced and, on rare occasions and in exceptional circumstances beaten, in turn the old-fashioned musket, the elephant gun, the seven-pounder, and even the repeating rifle and the gatling gun. He has been known to charge right down repeatedly, foot and horse, upon the square, swept on all sides with the pitiless and continuous hail of maxims. But against the latest inventions, physical bravery, though associated with a perfect knowledge of the country, can do nothing. The African cannot face the high-explosive shell and the bomb-dropping aeroplane. He has inflicted sanguinary reverses upon picked European troops, hampered by the climate and by commissariat difficulties. He cannot successfully oppose members of his own race free from these impediments, employed by his white adversaries, and trained in all the diabolical devices of scientific massacre. And although the conscripting of African armies for use in Europe or in Africa as agencies for the liquidation of the white man's quarrels must bring in its train evils from which the white man will be the first to suffer, both in Africa and in Europe; the African himself must eventually disappear in the process. Winter in Europe, or even in Northern Africa, is fatal to the tropical or sub-tropical African, while in the very nature of the case anything approaching real European control in Africa, of hordes of African soldiery armed with weapons of precision is not a feasible proposition. The Black man converted by the European into a scientifically-equipped machine for the slaughter of his kind, is certainly not more merciful than the white man similarly equipped for like purposes in dealing with unarmed communities. And the experiences of the civilian population of Belgium, East Prussia, Galicia and Poland is indicative of the sort of visitation involved for peaceable and powerless African communities if the white man determines to add to his appalling catalogue of past misdeeds towards the African, the crowning wickedness of once again, as in the day of the slave trade, supplying him with the means of encompassing his own destruction.

Thus the African is really helpless against the material gods of the white man, as embodied in the trinity of imperialism, capitalistic-exploitation, and militarism. If the white man retains these gods and if he insists upon making the African worship them as assiduously as he has done himself, the African will go the way of the Red Indian, the Amerindian, the Carib, the Guanche, the aboriginal Australian, and many more. And this would be at once a crime of enormous magnitude, and a world disaster.

. . . .

An endeavour will now be made to describe the nature, and the changing form, which the burden inflicted by the white man in modern times upon the black has assumed. It can only be sketched here in the broadest outline, but in such a way as will, it is hoped, explain the differing causes and motives which have inspired white activities in Africa and illustrate, by specific and notable examples, their resultant effects upon African peoples. It is important that these differing causes and motives should be understood, and that we should distinguish between them in order that we may hew our way later on through the jungle of error which impedes the pathway to reform. Diffused generalities and sweeping judgments generate confusion of thought and hamper the evolution of a constructive policy based upon clear apprehension of the problem to be solved.

The history of contact between the white and black peoples in modern times is divisible into two distinct and separate periods: the period of the slave trade and the period of invasion, political control, capitalistic exploitation, and, the latest development, militarism Following the slave trade period and preceding the period of invasion, occurs the trade interlude which, indeed, had priority of both periods, as when the Carthagenians bartered salt and iron implements for gold dust on the West Coast. But this interlude concerns our investigations only when we pass from destructive exposure to constructive demonstration.

The first period needs recalling, in order to impress once more upon our memories the full extent of the African's claim upon us, the white imperial peoples, for tardy justice, for considerate and honest conduct.

Our examination of the second period will call for sectional treatment. The history of contact and its consequences during this period may be roughly sub-divided thus:

  (a) The struggle for supremacy between European invading *Settlers* and resident African peoples in those portions of Africa where the climate and other circumstances permit of Europeans rearing families of white children.

  (b) *Political action* by European Governments aiming at the assertion of sovereign rights over particular areas of African territory.

(c) *Administrative policy*, sanctioned by European Governments, and applied by their local representatives in particular areas, subsequent to the successful assertion of sovereign rights.

These sub-divisions are, perhaps, somewhat arbitrary. The distinctiveness here given to them cannot be absolutely preserved. There is, for instance, a natural tendency for both *a* and *b* to merge into *c* as, through efflux of time, the originating cause and motive of contact is obscured by developments to which contact has given rise.

Thus racial contention for actual possession of the soil, and political action often resulting in so-called treaties of Protectorate thoroughly unintelligible to the African signees, are both landmarks upon the road leading to eventual administrative policy: *i.e.*, to direct government of the black man by the white.

Nevertheless administrative policy in itself has assumed a peculiar character and precision in certain extensive regions of Africa, irrespective of the antecedent events which led up to it. When this has occurred, as in the Congo and French Congo, for instance, issues have been raised which call for special and separate treatment.

The next chapter is concerned with the period of the slave trade.

PART I
FIRST PERIOD---The Slave Trade

CHAPTER III.

THE STORY OF THE SLAVE TRADE.

The Slave trade, started by the Portuguese in the middle of the 15th Century closely followed by the Spaniards, and at a longer interval (1562) by the British, then in quick succession by the Dutch (about 1620), the French (about 1640), the Swedes, Danes and Prussians, attained the full extent of its terrible activities in the 18th Century.

The earliest beginnings of the traffic were marked rather by an admixture of religious bigotry and love of adventure than by sordid motives. The passion for geographical discovery which inspired the famous Henry the Navigator of Portugal, great grandson of our Edward III., was the originating cause of a hideous and protracted tragedy. The captains of two of Prince Henry's exploring caravels brought back with them to Lisbon in 1442 a dozen Africans, whom they had captured on the West Coast in the course of a wholly unprovoked attack upon an African village. Further exploits of a similar kind followed. The ancient Portuguese chronicles recording them resemble the literature of the Crusaders. The African was a heathen, and as such fair game for the prowess of the noble Christian Knights who opposed their steel breast-plates, tempered swords and cross-bows, to his bare chest and primitive spear. Here is a typical account of one of these predatory forays:

> Then might you see mothers forsaking their children and husbands their wives, each striving to escape as best he could. Some drowned themselves in the water, others thought to escape by hiding under their huts; others stowed their children among the sea-weed, where our men found them afterwards, hoping they would thus escape notice. . . . And at last our Lord God, who giveth a reward for every good deed, willed that for the toil they had undergone in His service they should that day obtain victory over their enemies, as well as a guerdon and a payment for all their labour and expense; for they took captive of those Moors, what with men, women and children, 165, besides those that

perished and were killed. And when the battle was over, all praised God for the great mercy He had shown them, in that He had willed to give them such a victory, and with so little damage to themselves. They were all very joyful, praising loudly the Lord God for that He had deigned to give such help to such a handful of His Christian people.

Thus did Europe first bring the "glad tidings" to the African. It did not take long to ascertain that the spiritual consolation derived from converting the African to Christianity had its utilitarian counterpart. He made an excellent labourer. Thenceforth every newly-returned caravel brought its quota of miserable captives, and a brisk traffic grew up, Lagos in Southern Portugal becoming the principal slave mart.

That was the first stage. The second began with the discovery of America by Columbus, and of gold in the Island of Haiti, which the Spaniards termed Hispaniola. The aboriginal Caribs and Aranaks proving either intractable or useless as labourers, the Spaniards contracted with the Portuguese for supplies of Africans. Thus, in the opening years of the 16th Century, the black man was transported across the Atlantic and flung into that "New World," where he was fated to suffer such unspeakable agonies and which he has fertilised to such purpose, and for ultimate ends still concealed from the vision of prophecy, with his blood and tears and sweat.

For some years the Spaniards continued to employ the Portuguese as intermediaries for their African slaves. But with the extension of their conquests in the West Indies and on the American mainland, the demand for additional human material to exploit the natural riches of the country, gold and silver, precious stones and spices, waxed incessantly. The Spanish Sovereigns thereupon inaugurated a system of special contracts ("Assiento") which became of international significance, and under which they bestowed from time to time the monopoly of the supply of Africans for their American possessions upon foreign nations, corporations, or individuals, who in turn employed sub-contractors.

In 1562 the first British sub-contractor appeared on the scene in the person of John Hawkins, and with Queen Elizabeth as sleeping partner, embarked on his career of murder and brigandage in the good ship "Jesus," lent him by his Royal confederate. Ten years later Elizabeth knighted him as a reward for his persistent energies—

THE STORY OF THE SLAVE TRADE 17

contemporaneously described as "going every day on shore to take the inhabitants with burning and spoiling their towns."

The century which followed saw the breakdown of Spain's attempted imperial monopoly of the Americas, and of Portugal's attempted imperial monopoly of the African Seas; nascent British and French Empires rising across the Atlantic; adventurous spirits of many nationalities hastening towards the New World, and British, French, Danes and Dutch disputing for mastery at countless points on the West African Coast. And throughout that period the trade in African flesh and blood grew steadily in volume. Towards the middle of the 17th Century the British became direct exporters, both from the West Coast through "The African Company," and from the Mediterranean Coast of Morocco through "The Company of Barbary Merchants," among whose directors were the Earls of Warwick and Leicester. The French, Dutch, and Danes were then exporting considerable numbers of slaves from the settlements they had founded on the West Coast to their respective possessions in the West Indies and on the mainland, to work the sugar and coffee plantations. The Swedish effort at slave trading was short-lived as was the Prussian. A curious, isolated attempt on the part of one of the German Baltic Barons also came to nothing.

One can only speculate as to the total number of unfortunate Africans torn from their homes between 1442 and 1700, or as to the number that perished in the course of transportation on the slave ships—the "middle passage" of infamous memory—when:

> the slaves could not turn round, were wedged immovably, in fact, and chained to the deck by the neck and legs . . . not infrequently would go mad before dying of suffocation . . . in their frenzy some killed others in the hopes of procuring more room to breathe . . . men strangled those next to them, and women drove nails into each others' brains.

These horrors were intensified a thousandfold when the trade became an international offence.

It is computed in American records that the British were responsible in the twenty years, 1680-1700, for importing 300,000 Africans into the West Indies and the mainland.

But with the dawn of the 18th Century the trade assumed gigantic proportions. It had been thrown open

two years previously "to all British subjects," and a
swarm of speculators competed to meet the ever-
increasing demand from the American plantations, which
were now yielding enormous quantities of tropical produce,
thanks entirely to this African slave labour. The risks
for those engaged in the actual operations were not inconsiderable: but the profits were correspondingly large.
Thenceforth the slave trade "occupied the very foremost
part in English policy," and became a predominant concern of our foreign policy. This was clearly shown in the
Treaty of Utrecht which closed, in 1713, the needlessly
prolonged war of the Spanish Succession in which England, Austria, and the United Netherlands opposed
Louis XIV. and Philip V. The part of the Treaty which
gave "unqualified and unanimous satisfaction at home"
was the "Assiento" compact, whereby England secured
from Philip, in accordance with the practice of the
Spanish Sovereigns referred to above, an "absolute
monopoly of the supply of slaves to the Spanish Colonies."
The monopoly was conferred by the British Government
upon the South Sea Company. The "immense amount
of guilty wealth acquired through the 'Assiento' Treaty
did much to compensate for the great pecuniary sacrifices of the war." The generation which concluded it
came to regard the "extension of the slave trade as a
capital object of English commercial policy," and it
became the "main object" of national policy to
"encourage the kidnapping of tens of thousands of
negroes and their consignment to the most miserable
slavery." In fact the Peace which brought a precarious
and short-lived truce to Europe, brought war, war of the
most atrocious and desolating character, and on a scale
until then unimagined, to Africa, and "made of England
the great slave trader of the world."

The tradition persisted all through the century. Chat-
ham made the development of the trade a main object
of his policy, and "boasted that his conquests in Africa
had placed almost the whole slave trade in British
hands." Even Pitt, after the war with France which
broke French sea-power, annihilated the French slave
trade, shattered the French Colonial Empire and made
us its heirs, went back upon the position he had
precedently assumed [under the influence of Wilberforce]
in the teeth of the opposition of three of his colleagues

THE STORY OF THE SLAVE TRADE

supported by George III. The result was that "in consequence of the British conquests and under the shelter of the British flag, the slave trade became more active than ever," and that under Pitt the English slave trade "more than doubled."

A considerable number of statistics are available from various sources covering the activities of the trade during the 18th Century and the closing years of the 17th, which give some idea of the stupendous havoc wrought in Africa—almost entirely Western Africa—during that period. The following have been selected from the most reliable authors, but they are only approximately consecutive:

1666-1766.—Number of slaves imported by the British alone into *British, French* and *Spanish American Colonies*—three millions (quarter of a million died on the voyage).
1680-1786.—Slaves imported into the *British American Colonies*—2,130,000, Jamaica alone absorbing 610,000.
1716-1756.—An average of 70,000 slaves *per annum* imported into *all the American Colonies*, or a total of 3,500,000.
1752-1762.—Jamaica alone imported 71,115 slaves.
1759-1762.—Guadeloupe alone imported 40,000 slaves.
1776-1800.—An average of 74,000 slaves *per annum* imported into *all the American Colonies*, or a total of 1,850,000. (Annual average: by British 38,000; Portuguese, 10,000; Dutch, 4,000; French, 20,000; Danes, 2,000.)

Some notion can be formed of the profits of the trade by taking selected cases. From about 1730, Liverpool began for various reasons to eclipse both London and Bristol as the chief English centre of the trade. In the eleven years, 1783-1793, 921 Liverpool ships were employed in the convoying of slaves. They carried 303,737 slaves of the total value of £15,186,850. After deducting 15 per cent. under divers heads, the net return to Liverpool in those eleven years amounted to £12,294,116, or an average of £1,117,647 per annum. The net profit to those actually engaged in the trade was £2,361,455 6s. 1d., or an average of £214,677 15s. 1d. per annum.

There was, of course, a double profit upon the value of the slave when sold in the West Indies, and upon articles of British manufacture—largely cotton goods—disposed of in Africa for the slave's purchase: Manchester merchants largely profited from the latter. It is computed that from 1750 to 1800, one-fourth of the ships

belonging to the port of Liverpool were employed in the
slave trade: Liverpool monopolised five-eighths of the
British slave trade, and three-sevenths of the total slave
trade of the world.

These figures do not, of course, convey any true impression of the horrors and of the devastation involved in
securing the slaves in Africa, or of the cruelties attending
their treatment in the West India Islands and on the
mainland of America. The trade had grown so large
that mere kidnapping raids conducted by white men in
the immediate neighbourhood of the coast-line were quite
insufficient to meet its requirements. Regions inaccessible to the European had to be tapped by the organisation of civil wars. The whole of the immense region from
the Senegal to the Congo, and even further south, became
in the course of years convulsed by incessant internecine
struggles. A vast tumult reigned from one extremity to
the other of the most populous and fertile portions of the
continent. Tribe was bribed to fight tribe, community
to raid community. To every native chief, as to every
one of his subjects, was held out the prospect of gain at
the expense of his neighbour. Tribal feuds and individual
hatreds were alike intensified, and while wide stretches
of countryside were systematically ravaged by organised
bands of raiders armed with muskets, " hunting down
victims for the English trader whose blasting influence,
like some malignant providence extended over mighty
regions where the face of a white man was never seen,"
the trade put within the reach of the individual the means
of satisfying a personal grudge and of ministering to a
private vengeance.

The direct loss of life which this perennial warfare inevitably necessitated must have been enormous in itself,
to say nothing of the indirect loss through the destruction
of crops and granaries incidental to it, and the consequent
starvation ensuing. The transport to the coast by land
and water of an incessant stream of shackled captives,
over distances extending to many hundreds of miles, must
have been even more ruinous. It has been estimated
that something like 30 per cent. of the captives perished
before reaching the coast, where the exhausted and
emaciated survivors were crowded like cattle in barracoons waiting for a slave ship, whose arrival meant for

them the still more terrible agonies of the "middle passage."

Throughout the century did this imported hurricane make furious havoc in the forests, plains and valleys of Western Africa, flinging the human wreckage upon the distant shores of the " New " Continent. Arrogantly and savagely did England's rulers oppose the multiplying evidence of aversion exhibited by the North American colonists at the black flood which England poured upon their country, a policy persisted in until the eve of the War of Independence. "We cannot allow," declared Lord Dartmouth, the Secretary of State for the Colonies, in reply to one of these remonstrances, in 1775, " the Colonies to check or to discourage in any degree a traffic so beneficial to the nation."

Lord Dartmouth was merely giving expression to what, since the Peace of Utrecht, had become the fixed national policy. He was supported by the spirit of the time. The monarchy, the aristocracy, the commercial world, and ecclesiasticism, alike, defended the slave trade and directly benefited therefrom.

Queen Anne saw no objection, it is said, to increase her dowry, like her celebrated predecessor, from its operations. A statute of King William of pious memory affirms that " the trade was highly beneficial to the kingdom "; another of George II. declares it to be " very advantageous to Great Britain," and " necessary to the plantations," while the " Society for propagating Christianity," including half the episcopal bench, derived, as masters, from the labour of their slaves in the West Indies, an income which they spent in " teaching the religion of peace and goodwill to men."

England continued to be "the great slave trader of the world," until a handful of her sons, humane and determined men, compelled her to gaze into the depths of the Hell the greed of her ruling and trading classes had done so much to create.

The treatment of the transported African varied considerably. There is a concensus of opinion that he fared best under the Portuguese, the Danes, the French and the Spaniards, and worse under the Dutch and the British. The abuses, the immoralities, the tortures practised upon the slaves, and the fierce outbreaks to which

they occasionally gave rise, fill hundreds of volumes.
They seemed to have reached the height of their intensity
in Dutch Guiana and the British West Indies. "For
a hundred years slaves in Barbadoes were mutilated,
tortured, gibbeted alive and left to starve to death, burnt
alive, flung into coppers of boiling sugar, whipped to
death."

It would be beyond the scope of this volume to deal
with the long struggle waged by Clarkson, Sharp, Wilberforce, and others against the trade, the gradual awakening of the public conscience to its infamies, and the final
triumph of the reformers. To Burke, more than to any
man, is probably due the changed mental attitude of
England towards the rights and the wrongs of coloured
peoples, which ultimately enabled the efforts of Wilberforce and his colleagues to attain fruition. In Sir Charles
Dilke's incessant labours for the same ends during the
closing years of the 19th, and the opening years of the
20th Century, a later generation will perceive more
vividly perhaps than does the present one, the persistence
of a Parliamentary tradition which has helped to undo
something of the evils of official England's African record,
and caused her in recent years to give to the colonising
Governments of Europe as good an example, on the whole,
as the bad one she so long personified. But neither the
vigour which Britain showed in the early part of last
century in stamping out the slave trade which had con-
duced so largely to her prosperity in the previous one
nor her condemnation of its revival in inverted form on
the Congo, nor the comparatively better treatment she
has meted out to her coloured subjects during the past
half century would qualify her, in view of her terrible past
performances, to exercise the functions of judge in relation
to the offences of her contemporaries.

Nor are Britain's hands wholly clean to-day. The
hands of every European Power which has had dealings
with him is stained deep with the blood of the African.
For any such Power to approach the African problem on
the morrow of the Great War otherwise than with a consciousness of past sins, would be to proclaim itself
hypocrite in the eyes of the world. What Britons may
legitimately hope for from their rulers is that British
policy, devoid of pharisaism, may be directed patiently,

THE STORY OF THE SLAVE TRADE 23

strenuously and unselfishly to the task of providing for the long persecuted black man and his descendants a future of hope, promise and assured security.

BIBLIOGRAPHY.

" The Story of Africa and its Explorers." Brown.
" Liverpool and Slavery." Bowker.
" Life of Wilberforce." Murray.
" The Discoveries of Prince Henry." Major.
" The Negro in the New World." Sir Harry Johnston.
" The Chronicle of the Discovery and Conquest of Guinea." Hakluyt Society.
" Description of Guinea." Barbot.
" Coast of Guinea." Bosman.
" A New Account of Guinea and the Slave-Trade." Snelgrave.
" History of the Conquest of Peru." Prescott.
" History of England in the Eighteenth Century." Lecky.

PART II

SECOND PERIOD—Invasion, Political Control and Capitalistic Exploitation

A—EPISODES IN THE STRUGGLE FOR THE SOIL

FOREWORD

The story of Southern Rhodesia and of German South-West Africa is the story of conflict between white invaders and African peoples for the possession of the soil in the colonisable area of the Southern Continent. That conflict of a kind should ensue from such racial contact is as inevitable as contact itself. It is, nevertheless, pure sophistry to contend that the crimes and treacheries which have stained the history of contact in South Africa might not have been avoided. They were unnecessary and, in the main, they were provoked by the white man's conduct. The validity of the white man's excuse for this kind of wrong-doing decreases progressively with his cultural advance. That which was pardonable in a ruder age becomes unpardonable in our own. Yet between the exploits of the 16th Century Spaniard in the West Indies and South America, and those of the 19th Century Dutchman, Anglo-Saxon, and Teuton in South Africa, there is little material difference.

CHAPTER IV.

THE STORY OF SOUTHERN RHODESIA.

The portion of the Continent south of the Zambesi is—with some exceptions—suitable for settlement by white races, so far as the climate is concerned. The exceptions are the vicinity of the Zambesi itself, the desert and waterless coast regions of Damaraland, and a fairly wide belt of Portuguese territory on the East Coast. The whites are, however, incapable, save in a very limited degree, of performing the more arduous forms of manual labour. The actual development of the country, both agricultural and mineral must depend, therefore, either upon African labour or upon imported Asiatic labour—to which the whites are opposed for various reasons, which need not here be discussed.

For a century the healthy tablelands and plateaux of this region have been the scene of the kind of racial conflict which occurs when an invading race, of a higher culture than the aboriginal population and possessed of superior offensive and defensive weapons, disputes with the latter for the occupation of the land. Natural man presently finds himself threatened in his liberties. Civilised man is filled with the terror which comes from the knowledge of overwhelming odds. Mutual fears inspire reciprocal cruelties.

An unusual amount of light has been thrown upon the incidents of this racial strife in South Africa, because of the contest and rivalry between various sections of the invading whites: between the Dutch and French Huguenot element on the one hand—known to us as "Boers"—and the British on the other, and between British and German. This rivalry has engendered a natural desire on the part of the warring sections to advertise and accentuate the shortcomings of the other, thus adding to the sum of general knowledge. Other causes have also contributed. Before Southern Africa became a political and international storm-centre, and the Mecca of large financial interests, when the troubles between colonists and aborigines were looked upon by the Home Government as a nuisance, British Secretaries of State were disposed to display a sense of impartiality in judging of such troubles and a freedom of expression in commenting upon them to which the present generation is quite unaccustomed. The older British Blue Books dealing with these native wars and the part played by the colonists in provoking them, are marked by a vigorous candour inconceivable in these days, except when it is a matter of State policy to paint the black records of an opponent even blacker than they are. Thus Lord Glenelg on the earlier "Kaffir" wars:

"The Kaffirs had ample justification of the war into which they rushed with such fatal imprudence . . . urged to revenge and desperation by the systematic injustice of which they had been the victims . . . the original justice is on the side of the conquered, not of the victorious party."

Twenty years later we find the Committee of the Privy Council speaking of the warfare against the South African native peoples as "revolting to humanity and disgraceful to the British name." And thus the late Earl Grey in 1880:

"Throughout this part of the British Dominions the coloured people are generally looked upon by the Whites as an inferior race, whose interest ought to be systematically disregarded when they come into competition with their own, and who ought to be governed mainly with a view to the advantage of the superior race. And for this advantage two things are considered to be specially necessary: First, that facilities should be afforded to the White colonists for obtaining possession of land heretofore occupied by the native tribes; and secondly, that the Kaffir population should be made to furnish as large and as cheap a supply of labour as possible."

That judgment is as true to-day as it was then.

No detailed narrative of the struggle between white and black in the colonisable parts of the Southern Continent is possible here. It is stained, so far as the British are concerned, with pages almost as dark as those which disfigure our earlier Indian records. Unhappily there has been no Burke to gather up the sinister threads, and weave them by his sublime eloquence into the national conscience. Lord Morley once said of our treatment of the native races of South Africa that:

THE STORY OF SOUTHERN RHODESIA 31

It is one of the most abominable chapters in the history of our times; one of the most abominable chapters in the history of our dealings with inferior races.

Few who have really studied the history of South Africa will be disposed to quarrel with this tremendous indictment by a statesman of ripe experience and wide knowledge, not prone to the use of extravagant language. And few who are acquainted with the splendid South African work of Sir George Grey, Sir Marshall Clarke, and Sir Godfrey Langdon, can fail to realise how different that history might have been if men of their stamp had controlled its more decisive phases.

I propose to recall two recent and typical examples illustrating the particular Section of the history of contact we are now examining. The first is concerned with Rhodesia, the second with German South-West Africa.

. . . .

Between the Zambesi and Limpopo rivers stretches a country some 148,000 square miles in extent, *i.e.*, just about three times the size of England. It is now known as Southern Rhodesia. In 1911 it contained 23,606 whites, 744,559 African natives, and 2,912 Asiatics and other " coloured persons " In the twenty-four years, 1890-1913, it yielded 6½ million ounces of gold, valued at £25¼ millions sterling.

In the middle of last century this country was occupied by a ruling African people, calling themselves the Amandebele (since corrupted into Matabele) " the naked men with shields." They had conquered and incorporated other tribes, the Mashonas and Makalakas, who were the descendants, or the successors, of many ancient peoples inhabiting the country when the Phœnicians [or as some think, Arabs of the pre-Islamic period] were drawing from it large quantities of gold, and covering it with those remarkable monuments which still continue to be a fertile subject for scientific disputation.

When, at a later date, it became necessary in the interests of certain parties, to paint the Matabele in the light of brutal conquerors, much was heard of the cruel treatment inflicted by them upon the Mashonas. An impartial authority has, however, placed it upon record that under the Matabele, the Mashonas increased both in numbers and in cattle, always a sure sign of the prosperity of a South African people. " They say themselves," he adds, "that they preferred the Matabele rule to ours, because under them they were troubled but once a year, whereas now their troubles came with each day's rising sun."

The story which follows is the story of what befell the "naked men with shields" at the hands of the clothed men with guns seeking for "concessions."

In the 'seventies and 'eighties of last century, British, Boer, Portuguese, and German adventurers began wandering about the Limpopo River. Boers and British had been in touch with the Matabele since the early 'fifties and competed to acquire political influence over the then ruler of this people, by name Lobengula. They made unpleasant remarks about one another. "When an Englishman once has your property in his hands," wrote the Boer Joubert to Lobengula in 1882, "then he is like an ape that has his hands full of pumpkin seeds: if you don't beat him to death he will never let go." But Lobengula was partial to the British. Between his father and the famous missionary, Dr. Moffat, a real friendship had existed. The link was perpetuated in the person of Lobengula and Dr. Moffat's son, a British official in the adjoining territory of Bechuanaland, over which a British Protectorate was established in 1884. These personal relations determined Lobengula's final choice. In February, 1888, at his capital, Buluwayo, he signed a treaty with Moffat acting for the British Government, in which he undertook to hold no communications with any "foreign State or Power." It was stipulated in the treaty that "peace and amity shall continue for ever between Her Britannic Majesty, her subjects, and the Amandebele people."

The knowledge that the country over which Lobengula held sway, was passing rich in gold, had been gradually permeating South Africa. The signing of this treaty had been preceded, and was followed, by numerous efforts on the part of rival corporations to secure special privileges from its ruler. In the October following the conclusion of this bond of friendship, Messrs. Rudd, R. Macguire, M.P., and Mr. F. R. Thompson, commissioned by Mr. Cecil Rhodes and by Mr. Alfred Beit, succeeded in getting Lobengula to append his signature to a document. By its terms, in exchange for a monthly payment of £100 and material products of European

THE STORY OF SOUTHERN RHODESIA 33

civilisation in the shape of 1,000 Martini-Henry rifles and 100,000 rounds of ball cartridges, they obtained "the complete and exclusive charge over all metals and minerals" in the country, together with "full power to do all things that they may deem necessary to win and procure the same, and to hold, collect and enjoy the profits and revenues, if any, derivable from the said metals and minerals."

This all-embracing instrument became known as the Rhodes-Rudd concession.

The scene now shifts from Buluwayo, the capital of this African community to London, the heart of the mighty Empire over which the sun never sets. In April, 1889, the Colonial Office was approached by certain persons, representing the Bechuanaland Exploration Company on the one part, and the Goldfields of South Africa Company on the other. These corporations proposed to amalgamate their interests provided they could secure a Royal Charter, " in that region of South Africa lying to the north of Bechuanaland and to the west of Portuguese East Africa (*i.e.*, embracing Lobengula's country). On October of the same year the charter was duly granted, the grantees being the Most Noble James Duke of Abercorn (Groom of the Stole, and one time Lord of the Bed Chamber to the Prince of Wales); the Most Noble Alexander William George Duke of Fife (son-in-law of the late King Edward); Lord Gifford (one time Colonial Secretary of Western Australia, and of Gibraltar); Cecil John Rhodes (then a Member of the Executive Council and of the House of Assembly of Cape Colony); Alfred Beit, Albert Henry George Grey (afterwards Earl Grey and Governor-General of Canada), and George Causton. Thus was born the British South Africa Company Chartered and Limited, with an original capital of one million sterling. Its principal objects, as set forth in the charter, were the working of concessions, " so far as they are valid " in the territories affected by the grant, and the securing of other concessions subject to the approval of the Secretary of State. One of the grounds upon which the charter was granted was, that " the conditions of the natives inhabiting the said territories will be materially improved and their civilisation advanced."

The Matabele and their ruler do not appear to have been consulted in respect to this transaction, and I have not been able to discover that they even figured on the list of the company's shareholders. It must, however, be borne in mind that Lobengula stood to acquire £100 a month, not to mention the rifles.

Meanwhile consternation reigned in Matabeleland. Very shortly after Lobengula had affixed his seal to the Rudd concession, the rumour became current among the Matabele that their ruler had been induced to part with his people's rights in their land. Lobengula sent in hot haste for certain British missionaries with whom he entertained friendly relations, showed them a copy of the document, and asked them for their opinion. They appear to have confirmed the popular fears. Whereupon Lobengula caused his Head Counsellor, who had advised him to sign, to be executed as a traitor, and despatched two other counsellors to London on a mission to Queen Victoria, begging her to " send someone from herself," as he had no one he could trust, and he was " much troubled " by white men coming into his country and asking to dig for gold. The messengers reached London in February, 1889. On March 26, a month before receiving the petition for the grant of the charter from the influential personages named above, Lord Knutsford, the Secretary of State, answered Lobengula in the Queen's name as follows:

> Lobengula is the ruler of his country, and the Queen does not interfere in the government of that country. But as Lobengula desires her advice, Her Majesty is ready to give it. . . .
> In the first place the Queen wishes Lobengula to understand distinctly that Englishmen who have gone to Matabeleland to ask leave to dig for stones have not gone with the Queen's authority, and that he should not believe any statement made by them, or any of them, to that effect. The Queen advises Lobengula not to grant hastily concessions of land, or leave to dig, but to consider all applications very carefully. . .

On April 23, Lobengula followed up his first representation to the Queen by a further communication, in which he formally protested against the Rudd concession. His letter contained the following passage:

> Some time ago a party of men came into my country, the principal one appearing to be a man called Rudd. They asked me for a place to dig for gold, and said they would give me certain things for the right to do so. I told them to bring what they would give and I would show them what I would give. A document was written and presented to me for signature. I asked what it contained, and was told that in it were my words

and the words of those men. I put my hand to it. About three months afterwards I heard from other sources that I had given by that document the right to all the minerals of my country. I called a meeting of my *Indunas*,[1] and also of the white men and demanded a copy of the document. It was proved to me that I had signed away the mineral rights of my whole country to Rudd and his friends. I have since had a meeting of my Indunas and they will not recognise the paper, as it contains neither my words nor the words of those who got it. . . . I write to you that you may know the truth about this thing.

Again on August 10, Lobengula wrote to the Queen to the effect that:

The white people are troubling me much about gold. If the Queen hears that I have given away the whole country it is not so.

But these pathetic appeals from an untutored African ruler, victim of trickery, or guilty of misjudgment, had no effect upon the course of events. No scruples as to taking prompt advantage of what was manifestly an action repented of directly its significance became apparent, appear to have been entertained. The white man was determined to assume the "White man's burden," which offered prospects of being an exceedingly light one. The negotiations for the charter went through, and it was in a very different tone to that adopted in his communication of March 26, that the Queen's advisor, Lord Knutsford, replied on November 15—a fortnight after the charter had been conferred upon a company with which the ducal husband of the Queen's granddaughter was intimately connected—to Lobengula's protest. Lobengula was now told that it was "impossible for him to exclude white men," and that it was in the interests of himself and his people to make arrangements "with one approved body of white men who will consult Lobengula's wishes and arrange where white people are to dig, and who will be responsible to the chief for any annoyance or trouble caused to himself and his people." The letter went on to say that the Queen had made inquiries as to the persons concerned and was satisfied that they "may be trusted to carry out the working for gold in the chief's country without molesting his people, or in any way interfering with their kraals,[2] gardens,[3] or cattle."

[1] Counsellors.
[2] Villages. [3] Cultivated fields.

In such fashion were powers of government and administration, involving the establishment of a police force, the making of laws, the raising of revenue, the administration of justice, the construction of public works, the grant of mining and forestry concessions, and so on, in an African country three times the size of England, eventually conferred upon a corporation, whose interest in that country was to make money out of it: and conferred, on the strength of a document construed by the European signees in a manner which its African signee had repudiated in the name of his people.

The events ensuing from the grant of these powers have now to be examined.

CHAPTER V.

THE STORY OF SOUTHERN RHODESIA.—(*Continued*).

For some time the Company's agents avoided direct contact with the Matabele people, confining their activities mainly to the region inhabited by the Mashonas who acknowledged Lobengula's overlordship. Here they proceeded to mine, to lay out settlements, and to build forts. But friction of a minor kind seems to have been constant.

Eighteen months passed. In May, 1891, the British Government, by Order in Council, assumed the powers of a Protectorate "within the parts of South Africa bounded by British Bechuanaland, the German Protectorate, the Rivers Chobe and Zambesi, the Portuguese possessions, and the South African Republic." Matabeleland and Mashonaland were comprised within this area. It might have been assumed that this action would have secured for the native inhabitants of the country the guidance and protection in their external relations to which, as protected subjects of the Crown, they were thenceforth entitled, and which the British Government was morally bound to extend to them.[1] But four months later we find the official representative of the British Government at Buluwayo (Mr. Moffat) an assenting party to a transaction by which the unfortunate Matabele ruler completed his undoing and that of his people. By this transaction, known as the Lippert Concession, Lobengula made over to a German banker of that name settled in the Transvaal, acting in association with an Englishman called Renny-Tailyour:

> the sole and exclusive right, power and privilege for the full term of 100 years to lay out, grant, or lease, for such period or periods as he may think fit, farms, townships, building plots, and grazing areas, to impose and levy rents, licenses and taxes thereon, and to get in, collect and receive the same for his own benefit, to give and grant certificates in my name for the occupation of any farms, townships, building plots and grazing areas.

[1] For some reason, probably because the Order in Council was hardly consistent with the Lobengula-Moffat Treaty, Matabeleland was not specifically mentioned. Nevertheless, Resident Commissioners and Magistrates were immediately appointed, both to Matabeleland and to Mashonaland.

These rights and privileges were to apply only to such territories as were at the time, or might subsequently become, within the sphere of operations of the Chartered Company. The agreement appears to have superseded a precedent agreement with Mr. Renny-Tailyour, the text of which is not available.

It is clear that Lobengula could not have realised and did not, in fact, realise the significance of such an agreement. A careful perusal of the document reveals what was in the mind of the misguided African potentate. His idea was to appoint a reliable European bailiff, who would take the troublesome business of his relations with the white men off his hands, and protect his interests in his dealings with the Chartered Company. The opening passage of the agreement is explicit on this point: ".Seeing that large numbers of white people are coming into my territories, and it is desirable that I should, once and for all, appoint some person to act for me in these respects." The consideration to be paid, " in lieu of the rates, rents, and taxes," which Mr. Lippert was to appropriate, amounted to £500 per annum and to £1,000 cash down. The relative modesty of these sums is a further indication that Lobengula imagined himself to be merely employing an agent who would rid him of the harassing perplexities in which he was becoming increasingly involved, and who would remit a moiety of the revenues to which he was entitled. In point of fact, however, the wording of the agreement was such that the Chartered Company, after having acquired it from Lippert, claimed on the strength thereof ownership over the whole of the land of the Matabele. In due course, Lippert disposed of his privileges to the Mr. Rudd, whose name will be familiar to readers of this story, the said Mr. Rudd promptly disposing of them to the Chartered Company!

It was mainly on the strength of the acquired " Lippert Concession " that twenty-three years later, the Chartered Company was to put forward, officially, its monstrous claim to the whole unalienated land of the country, meaning by " unalienated " land, all land not given or sold to white immigrants, *i.e.*, the whole land of the country. The Judicial Committee of the Privy Council

THE STORY OF SOUTHERN RHODESIA 39

have now declared the Lippert Concession to be valueless as " a title deed to the unalienated land."[1]

Meantime friction increased between Lobengula and the Chartered Company, whose manager in Africa was the famous Dr. Jameson, author of the armed raid into the Transvaal, and eventually Prime Minister of the Union. Lord Knutsford, the Secretary of State for the Colonies, called the attention of the High Commissioner at the Cape to a statement published in London to the effect that everything possible was being done to provoke Lobengula. The trouble was first confined to the Company's dealings with the Mashonas. We obtain some indication of the Company's methods from the fact that the High Commissioner found it necessary to remind the Company's manager that, " no death sentence can be carried out without warrant." The reminder did not appear to inconvenience the Company's officials. Shortly afterwards a Mashona chief and his people having been credited, rightly or wrongly, with stealing cattle belonging to some white settlers, the chief's village was attacked by the Company's armed forces, the chief himself and twenty of his followers killed, and 47 head of cattle " lifted." This affair drew further expostulations from the High Commissioner, and from the Secretary of State for the Colonies : " The punishment inflicted in this case," wrote Sir Henry Lock, " appears utterly disproportionate to the original offence." " There is nothing in the information now before his Lordship," wrote Lord Knutsford, " which affords any justification of Captain Lendy's proceedings. . . The full report by Captain Lendy subsequently received and forwarded, would, in Lord Knutsford's opinion, have justified much stronger terms of remonstrance than were used by the High Commissioner." But neither the High Commissioner nor the Secretary of State demanded this officer's retirement, and his services were retained by the Company.

Events were rapidly maturing for that direct collision with Lobengula which was obviously desired in certain quarters. Complaints of cattle stealing by the natives were rife. What justification there may have been for them we are never likely to know. But cattle lifting was apparently not wholly on one side. Early in 1893 the Company seized cattle from a petty Mashona chief,

[1] 1 July, 1918.

whom it accused of having abstracted some yards of telegraph wire. The cattle taken was the property of Lobengula, who, in accordance with the custom of the country, hired out his herds in which his subjects had a communal interest. The " King's cattle " was a kind of symbol of sovereignty, and any interference with them was an affront not to the King only, but to the tribe. The Company was advised by the High Commissioner's representative at Buluwayo, " to be more careful in their seizures." Two months later Lobengula, apparently at Dr. Jameson's request, sent a body of warriors to punish a Mashona community living in the neighbourhood of the Company's settlement at Fort Victoria, for alleged stealing of " royal " cattle. He notified the Company of his purpose in advance. Acting without orders, Lobengula's men pursued some of the Mashonas into the " communage " of the settlement, and there killed them. Accounts, subsequently ascertained to have been wildly exaggerated, were put into circulation as to the number of Mashonas who lost their lives in this affray. Dr. Jameson thereupon summoned Lobengula's men to retire. As they were retiring he sent a body of troopers after them under the same Captain Lendy. Firing ensued. Thirty Matabele were killed. No member of the Company's force received a scratch. This occurred in July, 1893. Dr. Jameson reported to the High Commissioner that the troopers fired in self-defence. Lobengula denied this. The High Commissioner ordered an investigation. The official charged with this task eventually reported that: " Dr. Jameson was misinformed when he reported officially that the Matabele fired the first shot at the whites . . . the sergeant of the advance guard fired the first shot . . . the Matabele offered practically no resistance."

But this report came long " after the fair." The collision had at last provided the Company with the pretext its representatives on the spot had been seeking, and for which they had provided. The right atmosphere now prevailed for the " smashing of Lobengula." In his history of the smashing process, Major Forbes, who was in chief command, reveals that *on the morning of the day after the collision*, Dr. Jameson produced an elaborate campaign for the military invasion of Matabele-

THE STORY OF SOUTHERN RHODESIA

land. A month later (August 14) Dr. Jameson sent his historic letter to Captain Allan Wilson, the "Officer commanding the Victoria Defence Force." The exact wording of this document was only revealed, in 1918, at the Privy Council Inquiry into the company's claim to proprietorship over the land of Southern Rhodesia, to which allusion has already been made. Its substance had been known in South Africa for some years [together with the creation of a "Loot-Committee" to give effect to its terms after the "smashing" had been duly administered.] Its full text has been published this year by the Anti-Slavery and Aborigines Protection Society.[1]

In this communication, which we are entitled to assume was made without the knowledge of the High Commissioner or of the Secretary of State, Dr. Jameson undertook, on behalf of the company, that every trooper engaged in the forthcoming expedition should receive 3,000 *morgen* (nearly nine square miles) of land. The company retained the right of purchase "at any time" at the rate of £3 per *morgen*. The potential value of the grant was, therefore, £9,000.[2] Every trooper would also be permitted to peg out twenty gold claims. The communication additionally provided that: "7. The 'loot' shall be divided, one-half to the B.S.A. Company, and the remainder to officers and men in equal shares."

As the only lootable property possessed by the Matabele (apart from their land and its minerals) was cattle, "loot" could have referred to nothing else, and large quantities of cattle, as we shall see, were eventually seized. To reckon the potential value of the twenty gold claims and his share of the "loot" together at £1,000 per trooper, would be ridiculously low. But on that basis it will be seen that the incentive to participate in the invasion of this African community, enjoying British protection, was £10,000—£9,000 in land, £1,000 in gold and cattle—per invader.[3] According to Messrs. W. A.

[1] In a pamphlet, published after these chapters were written, in which many of the facts here stated can be verified. ["An Appeal to the Parliament and People of Great Britain, the Dominions and the Dependencies."]

[2] It is now known that much larger grants were made in some instances.

[3] It has just been recorded before Lord Cave's Commission of Enquiry into the claims of the Company that the looted cattle fetched 35s. per head See further on for the numbers looted, in various ways.

Willis and Lieutenant Collingridge,[1] the force which had been gradually got together on the Matabele frontier numbered, at the date of this letter, 672 Europeans and 155 Colonial natives. Although the latter were entitled under this agreement to certain benefits, I will deal only with the Europeans. It will be seen, therefore, that the collective stake amounted to £6,720,000. The land of the Matabele thus confiscated in advance amounted to over 6,000 square miles, being six-sevenths the area of Wales. For a parallel to so comprehensive and cynically calculated a plan of anticipatory spoliation, we must hark back three hundred and sixty-seven years to the famous contract between Pizarro, Amalgro, de Luque and their followers, for the sack of Peru.

While Dr. Jameson was thus perfecting his arrangements for the filibustering enterprise which he was to repeat, with less success, later on against the Boers. Lobengula on the one hand, and the High Commissioner and the Colonial Office on the other, were doing their best to avert war. It cannot be said that the High Commissioner's efforts in this respect were characterised by much vigour. It is fair to bear in mind that he was doubtless hampered by his distance from the scene, and by the ingenious misrepresentation of facts at which th' manager of the Chartered Company was an adept. Th. desires of the Colonial Office were unmistakably expressed by Lord Ripon, who had succeeded Lord Knutsford as Secretary of State:

> It is important—he declared in a dispatch dated August 26 —that the British South African Company should not, by menacing Lobengula, commit themselves to any course of action which I might afterwards have to reverse. Their duty under existing circumstances must be limited to defending their occupied territory and Her Majesty's Government cannot support them in any aggressive action."

But vague threats of this kind were not likely to deter those responsible for the action on the spot of a corporation with the Court and social influence possessed by the British South Africa Company.

Lobengula's attitude seems to have been distinguished throughout by a courage, a dignity and a pathetic trust in the British Government's sense of justice which are remarkable, but by no means unparalleled in the authenticated record of "Barbarism's" clash with "Civilisation."

[1] "The Downfall of Lobengula."

THE STORY OF SOUTHERN RHODESIA

Telegraphing to the Company after the massacre of his warriors by Captain Lendy's troops, he says: " I thought you came to dig for gold; but it seems that you have come not only to dig for gold, but to rob me of my people and country as well." He refused to accept the monthly payments falling due under the Rudd and Lippert Concessions, as it " is the price of my blood." He repeatedly appealed to the High Commissioner:

> Your people have been telling you lies. . . . They speak like this to make an excuse for having killed my people. How many white men were killed! . . . My cattle which were taken by your people have not been returned to me, neither have those taken by the Mashona, whom I sent to punish. Perhaps this is why they have killed my people.

He wrote to the Queen:

> I have the honour respectfully to write and state that I am still keeping your advice laid before me some time ago, *i.e.*, that if any trouble happens in my country between me and the white men I must let you know.

Proceeding to give his version of the events attending and preceding the Lendy episode which, as we have seen, was afterwards corroborated by the official inquiry, he asked:

> Your Majesty, what I want to know from you is, why do your people kill me? Do you kill me for following my stolen cattle, which are seen in the possession of the Mashonas living in Mashonaland? I have called all white men at Buluwayo to hear my words, showing clearly that I am not hiding anything from them when writing to your Majesty.

Lobengula's anxiety to keep the peace and so prevent the slaughter and ruin of his people which he knew must be otherwise inevitable, is vouched for in a number of public statements made at the time, or since, by European residents in Buluwayo: most of them are to be found in the Blue Books. The High Commissioner's dispatches to Dr. Jameson show that he himself was persuaded of the sincerity of the Matabele ruler.

The Company continued imperturbably its preparations for the invasion. On October 18, an incident occurred which must have finally convinced Lobengula of the fruitlessness of his efforts to avert the impending doom of his country. He had despatched three of his Indunas as envoys to the High Commissioner. They arrived at the British camp on a " safe-conduct " pledge. In that camp, on the day of their arrival, two out of the three were " accidentally killed."

The truth was, of course, that the issue of peace and war had never lain with Lobengula. Nor did the issue lie with the Imperial authorities, unless they had chosen to assume a really decided attitude, which they were apparently disinclined to do. It lay with the Chartered Company, whose chief representative in South Africa had already arranged for the " loot " of Matabeleland by the freebooters he had gathered together on the borders, who had sent a false account of the affray with Captain Lendy's troopers to the High Commissioner, and who had been engaged in " working " the London and South African Press, as assiduously as he afterwards did when maturing his plans for raiding the Transvaal.* War had, indeed, already begun, the final pretext being that one of the Company's patrols had been fired upon by Matabele scouts, fore-runners of a great invading army. The " invading army " turned out to be a phantom one, and the alleged firing upon the Company's patrol was never established.

In less than three months the war was over. Thousands of Matabele were killed—one regiment of 700 lost 500 of its number. Many fled towards the Zambesi, where they suffered terribly from fever and famine, as well as from wild animals. It is said that 18 of them were killed by lions in one night, in the dense forest that lies some fifty miles north of Gwelo. Lobengula, a hunted fugitive, had disappeared and was seen no more. One wonders whether in his untutored savage soul he ever puzzled over the message which had reached him, only four years before, from the advisers of that far-off mighty Woman-ruler, whom his missionary friends had taught him to revere, assuring him that the persons who had come to dig for gold in his country could be trusted not to molest him and his people. Buluwayo was a smoking ruin. The " loot " contract was being actively put into execution, the beneficiaries thereof, as a contemporary observer records, " being scattered all over the country, either for themselves or backed by capitalists, in search of the best country and the richest

1 This system of deception was imitated when the Company's plans for raiding the Transvaal had matured. When, in December, 1905, the High Commissioner learned that the Company's police were being concentrated on the Transvaal border, he wired to Rhodes asking what the purpose was. Rhodes replied "For the purposes of economy and to protect the railway." Two days later the Company's forces crossed the border and attacked the Transvaal Republic

THE STORY OF SOUTHERN RHODESIA 45

reefs, until, by the end of January, over 900 farm rights
were issued, and half registered and pegged out, while
nearly 10,000 gold claims were registered during the same
period." The seizure of cattle, too, was in full operation
and yielding excellent results, many herds being driven
over the border into Bechuanaland by their capturers.
The Colonial Office was highly scandalised by these
latter proceedings. Lord Ripon telegraphed to the High
Commissioner:

> According to newspaper telegrams Dr. Jameson is marking
> out townships in Matabeleland, one of which includes the Bulu-
> wayo Kraal; patrols are continuing to seize large numbers of
> cattle from the Matebele; the followers of Lobengula are dying
> of small pox and starvation; and the Matabele are being pre-
> vented from sowing until they surrender their arms. If these
> reports are in substance correct, it would appear that the final
> settlement of the question is being seriously prejudiced, contrary
> to the public declarations and intentions of the Government.
> You should, as soon as possible, communicate with Rhodes,
> representing to him the state of the case, and inviting him to
> give Jameson instructions to moderate his proceedings and to
> take steps to stop the looting of cattle, or to arrange for restor-
> ing it in future to its owners.

The effect of this protest was as nugatory as all similar
official representations had been from the beginning. The
Chartered Company never cared a snap of its fingers for
the Colonial Office. It was too well and too influentially
supported to be in the least discomposed by well-meaning
but faint-hearted remonstrances which came to nothing.

The story of the Matabele's cattle is particularly
instructive. The total, officially estimated at 200,000
head at the time of the invasion, was stated early in 1895
to be 79,500; by December of that year it had fallen still
lower, to 72,930. This appears to have been the actual
number left at that time. Of this total the Company
retained a further 32,000 head, and handed the balance
over to the surviving natives. Thus, assuming native
property in cattle to have been correctly estimated at
200,000 at the time of the invasion, it had sunk to 40,930
in two years! It should be remembered that, for the
Matabele, cattle were not merely a source of riches, but an
essential food product. The beasts were very seldom
killed, but their milk, mixed with mealies, was one of the
staple food supplies of the country. And it is more than
likely, although I have not observed any record of it, that

the manure was used for agricultural purposes, as it is in Northern Nigeria, where the Fulani herdsmen contract with the Hausa agriculturalists for quartering their herds in the dry season upon the latter's fields.

Henceforth the " naked men with shields " became bondsmen to the Company and its shareholders, as the Mashonas, whom the Company claimed to have saved from Matabele oppression, had already become. The gold of Southern Rhodesia had to be won. It could only be won by native labour. But an African people of herdsmen and agriculturists does not take kindly to digging for gold. Moreover, the Matabele, unlike the Mashonas, had a peculiar aversion to working below ground. Such scruples and prejudices could not be expected to carry weight with the members of a superior race. So the Company soon added to the cultural advantages it had already bestowed upon the Matabele a process whereby these backward folk might become conversant with the dignity which comes from work, however uncongenial, performed for the benefit of others.

Forced labour, gradually assuming a more stringent and extensive character as the multifold requirements of the white men grew with the development of the " farms " and the mines, succeeded the conquest of the country. The *Buluwayo Chronicle* of February 22, 1896, recorded that: " The Native Commissioners have done good work in procuring native labour. During the months of October, November, and December they supplied to the mining and other industries in Matabeleland no less than 9,000 boys." On February 27 a letter from the Chief Native Commissioner Taylor to the Buluwayo Chamber of Mines reported that: " The number of natives supplied for labour to the mines and for other purposes from the different districts in Matabeleland totals 9,102." Some hundreds of native police were raised and armed, and, as happens everywhere in Africa where the supervision is not strict, committed many brutal acts. Their principal duty appears to have been " assisting " to procure the needed supply of labour, and hunting down deserters. Their tyranny was even more oppressive among the Mashonas than among the Matabele, owing to the milder character of the former. Writing of these police in 1898 Mr. H. C. Thomson says : " They are the scourge of the country, and, like the *Zapteihs* in Turkey, do more than

THE STORY OF SOUTHERN RHODESIA 47

anyone else to make the lives of the people wretched and to foment rebellion." An official report by Sir Richard Martin, subsequently issued, records that:

> (a) Compulsory labour did undoubtedly exist in Matabeleland if not in Mashonaland;
> (b) That labour was procured by the various native commissioners for the various requirements of the Government, mining companies and private persons;
> (c) That the native commissioners, in the first instance, endeavoured to obtain labour through the *Indunas* (chiefs) but failing in this, they procured it by force.

Compelled to work in the mines at a sum fixed by the Chartered Company, flogged and otherwise punished if they ran away, maltreated by the native police, the Matabele doubtless felt that these experiences, coming on the top of their previous ones (to which a cattle disease had added further perplexities), did not impart such attractiveness to life that the risk of losing it in an endeavour to throw off the yoke was not worth entertaining. In his evidence before Sir Richard Martin, Mr. Carnegie, a well-known missionary, thus interprets the Matabele view of matters by themselves:

> Our country is gone, our cattle have gone, our people are scattered, we have nothing to live for, our women are deserting us; the white man does as he likes with them; we are the slaves of the white man, we are nobody and have no rights or laws of any kind.

So in March, 1896, profiting by Dr. Jameson's withdrawal of his white fighting forces from the country for the purpose of trying the Lobengula treatment upon the robuster constitution of President Kruger, the Matabele rose, and later on the Mashonas also. The risings were spasmodic and not universal. They were accompanied by the usual brutal murders of isolated settlers and their families, and by the usual panic-stricken and indiscriminate slaughter of human beings with black skins by parties of undisciplined volunteers. The *Matabele Times* had some plain words on the subject:

> The theory of shooting a nigger on sight is too suggestive of the rule of Donnybrook Fair to be other than a diversion rather than a satisfactory principle. We have been doing it up to now, burning kraals because they were native kraals, and firing upon fleeing natives simply because they were black. . . . Should the policy of shoot at sight continue it will merely drive the natives more and more into the ranks of the insurgents.

The Matabele rising was represented as the inevitable sequel to the incomplete subjugation of a warlike people, but when the timid Mashonas followed suit it was obvious that no such excuse would suffice. Much light was thrown by missionaries and others upon the treatment meted out to the Mashonas and the Matabele precedent to the outbreak. Sir Richard Martin's report and the publications of the Aborigines Protection Society may be consulted with advantage in this respect. Apart from the general character of that treatment which has been already indicated, many of the details given were of a revolting character. The Rev. John White, Wesleyan minister at Salisbury, in a letter to the *Methodist Times* dated September 30, 1896, cites the case of one of the Company's officials compelling a native chief by threats of punishment to hand him over his daughter as a mistress:

> I brought the matter to the notice of the Administrator and the accused was found guilty of the charge. He shortly after left the country; yet so trivial seemed the offence that within nine months he was back again and held an official position in the force raised to punish the rebels.

It is easy to over-estimate this " social " question, and no doubt exaggerated charges were brought at the time. Sexual relations between native women and white invaders will always be of a loose description; and the break-up of tribal and family authority which follows in the wake of conquest invariably leads to social demoralisation. But, even so, there are recognised decencies, and one incident such as Mr. White describes is in itself sufficient to fire a whole countryside. Nor was it isolated. Assaults upon women by the native police were frequent. Mr. White also relates a shocking story of the slaughter of three chiefs who were arrested when actually on the precincts of a Wesleyan mission station, on the charge of being implicated in the murder of a native policeman. Mr. Thomson says that he made inquiries into the cases referred to by Mr. White, and describes them as of a " peculiarly atrocious character." Wholesale robbing of Mashona cattle seems also to have been rife, Mr. White alleging that " in many districts where previously considerable heads of cattle were to be found, now hardly one exists."

The crushing of the rebellion by the Imperial authorities was attended by great loss of native life and by many terrible incidents, amongst others the dynamiting of the caves in which the Mashonas had taken refuge. For a long time after the back of the rebellion had been broken battues took place all over the country and executions were constant. "When I was in Rhodesia," wrote Mr. Thomson, " native Commissioners and police were out in every direction hunting down these unhappy wretches. Many had already been executed, both in Buluwayo and Salisbury, and the prosecutions were still going on."

. . . .

Since these events took place the Chartered Company, basing its claim to " unalienated " land, in part upon the Lippert concession, which, as already stated, the Judicial Committee of the Privy Council has now declared to be ' valueless " for that purpose, and in part upon military conquest, has pursued the policy of treating the land of Southern Rhodesia as though it had passed entirely out of native ownership and had become the property of the Company's shareholders. It has divided the land into two main categories, " alienated " and " unalienated." Land in the occupancy and ownership of white men is called " alienated " land. Any native living on " alienated " land pays the white occupant and owner £1 *per annum*, and a further £1 *per annum* to the Company as head tax. " Unalienated " land is the land not in the occupancy and ownership of white men, and includes the native " Reserves." Natives living in the Reserves pay £1 per head *per annum* to the Company as tax. Natives living on " unalienated " land outside the Reserves pay £1 per head *per annum* to the Company as tax, and another £1 per head for the privilege of living where they do. Portions of this " unalienated " land outside the Reserves can, apparently, be taken over at any moment by individual white men, provided, of course, that they obtain the Company's sanction. The natives living on such acquired portions are then expected to pay £1 per head *per annum* to the white acquirer, plus the £1 per head they already pay to the Company. The logic of the amazing situation thus created would seem to be this: There would appear to be no obstacle to my, or to any of my readers, going to the Chartered Company's offices in London, and having secured the local services of an agent in South Africa, applying for such or such a specific area of "unalienated" land in Southern Rhodesia. If I am willing to pay the Company's price I can purchase this area, and by making the necessary local arrangements in Africa for the collection of my rent, I can constrain every male native living upon my distant property to hand over annually to my agent the sum of £1. In effect, I buy the human animal as well as the land upon which he dwells, and upon which his ancestors may have dwelt for generations before him.

The net position is this: The native population of Southern Rhodesia possesses to-day no *rights* in land or water. It is allowed to continue to live upon the land on sufferance and under certain conditions, according to the categories into which the land has been divided. The natives have no secure titles anywhere, not even in the Reserves, which are always liable to be cut up and shifted, and from which they can always be evicted upon " good cause " being shown; the " good cause " being the Company's good pleasure. A " Reserve Commission " was appointed in 1917. This is a supposedly impartial body. Its Chairman figured among the beneficiaries of the " Loot " agreement. Its activities, so far, appear to have resulted in enormously diminishing the Reserves. The attitude of the Company towards the native population living on the "unalienated" lands outside the Reserves, and the position of that population, are tersely summarised in the following extract from one of the Company's reports:

> We see no objection to the present system of allowing natives to occupy the unalienated land of the company and pay rent. The occupation is merely a passing phase; the land is being rapidly acquired by settlers, with whom the natives must enter into fresh agreements or leave.

There appears to be no attempt on anyone's part to deny the bed-rock fact that these 700,000 natives have been turned from owners of land into precarious tenants. The defence, such as it is, is merely concerned with points of detail. It is claimed that the Rhodesian Order in Council contains safeguards ensuring a sufficiency of land for the native population, and providing that no evictions shall occur of natives to whom land has been " assigned "

THE STORY OF SOUTHERN RHODESIA 51

without "full inquiry." It is also claimed that the Reserves are adequate. Even if these safeguards were worth the paper they are written on, and even if the second statement were true, the fundamental issue would remain untouched. In point of fact there is only too much reason for doubting the efficacy of the one and the substantial truth of the other. It is true that the Reserves are very large. It is also true, even according to the findings of one of the Company's own commissions, that "in certain Reserves," not only is a "large portion of the soil "poor," but that "water is deficient"; and that certain localities are "wholly unsuitable for human occupation." The Reserves Commission of 1917 put on record the estimate of a responsible official that "85 per cent. of the total area " of Southern Rhodesia was "granite," and gave it as its opinion that the estimate was "not far from correct." The Chartered Company contends that the native prefers the granite soil; to which the Anti-Slavery and Aborigines Protection Society reply that "the natives will pay almost anything rather than go into these territories," and that while the natives had every opportunity of settling upon these granite areas before the advent of the Chartered Company, they "deliberately refrained from doing so."

. . . .

This whole iniquitous policy of spoliation and expropriation does not appear to have been queried by the Colonial Office until 1914. The Government's indifference to the Company's proceedings is the more remarkable when it is borne in mind that the Charter conferred upon the Company, expressly stipulates that careful regard shall be had to native customs and laws, "especially with respect to the holding, possession, transfer, and disposition of lands. . . ."

In 1914 Lord Harcourt, then Colonial Secretary, who took a genuine and sympathetic interest in questions of native rights in Africa, contested the Company's claim to possession of the whole of the "unalienated" land of Southern Rhodesia, and brought it before the Judicial Committee of the Privy Council. The case was argued before Lords Loreburn, Dunedin, Atkinson, Summer, and Scott Dickson in the spring of 1918. The Anti-Slavery and Aborigines Protection Society briefed Mr. Leslie Scott.

K.C., to represent the rights of the native population. Under the judgment the Company lost its claim to ownership of the 73 million acres of " unalienated " land, which was declared to be vested in the British Crown as trustee for the native population, together with its "commercial" claim to the Reserves.

So far so good. But is that judgment to govern policy? And how does the British Crown propose to interpret its trusteeship? Nothing appears to have been changed in the actual position of the natives, which is typically portrayed in a petition recently presented to King George by the family of Lobengula, in the course of which the petitioners say:

> The members of the late King (Lobengula's) family, your petitioners, and several members of the tribe are now scattered about on farms so parcelled out to white settlers, and are practically created a nomadic people living in this scattered condition, under a veiled form of slavery, they being not allowed individually to cross from one farm to another, or from place to place except under a system of permit or pass and are practically forced to do labour on these private farms as a condition of their occupying land in Matabeleland.

. . . .

No such abominable scandal as this story reveals has stained British Colonial records since Burke thundered against the misfeasance of the East India Company. Englishmen have reason to be proud of much that has been done in many parts of Africa by their countrymen in the last quarter of a century. In Nigeria and on the Gold Coast, especially, British Administration has earned, and deserved, great praise. But the perpetuation of the Rhodesian outrage is an intolerable national disgrace.

The very least that can be done in extenuation of the wrongs inflicted upon the natives of Southern Rhodesia is to confer upon the native population living in the Reserves a secure title; to make the Reserves inalienable save for public works of indispensable utility, and then only on the same conditions as those which apply to lands in white occupation; to make the " unalienated " land outside the Reserves equally inalienable wherever native communities are in occupation—such occupation to embrace villages, cultivated fields, grazing lands and water; and to give to those native communities an equally secure title.

THE STORY OF SOUTHERN RHODESIA 53

The Chartered Company should disappear, and before the British tax-payer is mulcted in heavy ' compensation '' sums for the benefit of the Company's shareholders (it seems that among the bills we are to be called upon to pay, there is one of £2,500,000, being the cost of the Company's wars upon the Mashonas and Matabele!), Parliament should insist upon a public and searching investigation into the Company's administrative and financial history.

CHAPTER VI.

THE STORY OF GERMAN SOUTH WEST AFRICA.

A recently published Blue Book has revived the horrible story of the treatment of the Hereros in Damaraland, which caused such an uproar in Germany fourteen years ago, and such fierce Parliamentary denunciation that it seemed likely at one time to kill the whole " Colonial movement." The story needed recalling and no condemnation of it can be too strong. German rule in South West Africa from 1901 to 1906 was abominable and many of its bad features lingered on until the invasion and conquest of the country by General Botha, despite the altered spirit in German Colonial policy which marked the supersession of General von Trotha, and the presence of Herr Dernburg at the Colonial Office. The evils had bitten too deep, the immunity from wrong-doing enjoyed by the settlers had lasted too long, the demoralisation and destruction had been too general and widespread to permit of rapid change. Substantially, of course, reparation was impossible. It is reputed that from one-third to one-fourth of the Hereros—who, at the time of the German occupation were estimated to number 80,000—perished in, or as the result of, the sanguinary fighting with von Trotha. For the campaign assumed all the character of the struggle between the settlers and the North American Indians, between the settlers and the Australian Aborigines, and at one time between the French and the Kabyles of Algeria—*i.e.*, a war of extermination.

The land of the Hereros was confiscated; their herds were partly seized, partly destroyed; the remnant of the people reduced to pauperism and subjected to the brutalities of forced labour. Nor was there any attempt on the part of those actually governing the country on the spot, or directing affairs from home, still less, of course, on the part of the settlers themselves, to conceal the main purpose which inspired the policy, viz., the substitution of the native owners of the soil by German immigrants and the transformation of free men into a landless proletariat of hewers of wood and drawers of water. Herr Schlettwein, a Government representative on the Reichstag's Colonial Budget Committee, delivered himself in 1904 of an essay on the principles of Colonial policy, in the course of which he says, after sundry scoffing allusions to "exaggerated humanitarianism, vague idealism, and irrational sentimentality":

> The Hereros must be compelled to work, and to work without compensation and in return for their food only. Forced labour for years is only a just punishment, and at the same time it is the best method of training them. The feelings of Christianity and philanthropy with which missionaries work, must for the present be repudiated with all energy.

The Blue Book must, however, be read with a sense of perspective. It is more in the nature of a "War Aims" publication than a sober, historical narrative, and has been compiled for a perfectly obvious purpose. The reader is left in entire ignorance of the fact that, as Sir Harry Johnston wrote in 1913, referring to this and other German Colonial scandals, "Germany wisely did not hush up these affairs, but investigated them in open court and punished the guilty." There is no mention of von Trotha's proclamations—which, by the way, are misquoted—being annulled by the German Government. Von Trotha's recall is only referred to incidentally. The barest reference is made to the massacre of many German settlers and the destruction of homesteads; and nothing at all of the heavy losses of the Germans, amounting to 90 officers and 1,321 men killed by wounds and disease. and 89 officers and 818 men wounded, a very considerable total for an African campaign of this kind, showing that the Hereros were by no means so helpless and defenceless as the reader would be led to believe. Neither is there the slightest reason to doubt the perpetration in German South West Africa of many hideous individual outrages, floggings, murder, rape and all the concomitants of unbridled passion which have disgraced the records of the White invaders of colonisable South Africa. But an impartial judgment will not accept without mental reservation the depositions of witnesses testifying to such acts years after the event, especially when the circumstances under which their testimony was obtained is borne in mind. Without minimising in the slightest degree the action of the Germans in South West Africa, we should do well to have at the back of our minds the sort of

THE STORY OF GERMAN S.W. AFRICA

indictment which would have been drawn up by a successful enemy in occupation of Rhodesia and Bechuanaland, desirous of demonstrating our iniquities to the world in order to make out a case for retaining those territories for himself. The treatment of the Matabele and the Mashonas by the Chartered Company would certainly not have appeared less black if it had been supported by affidavits of individual Matabele and Mashonas eager to curry favour with their new masters. Nor would the so-called Bechuana Rebellion of 1895, some of the incidents which distinguished it, the wholesale confiscation of native lands which followed it, and the fate which overtook the 3,000 odd "rebels" who surrendered, make other than excellent reading for a world audience sitting in judgment upon our sins. Between the decrees of a von Lindequist or a Leutwein, the brayings of a Schlettwein *et hoc genus omne*, and the pompous pronouncements of certain leading South African statesmen there is fundamentally little difference.

After the Bechuanaland Rebellion, Sir Gordon Sprigg, then Premier of Cape Colony, referred in a public despatch to the warning he had addressed to the people of Pondoland : " If they were disobedient and raised their hand in rebellion, they would be swept from the country and other people would be planted upon the land." He went on to say that it was the intention of his Government to introduce a Bill " providing for a disposal of this land (the land of the 'rebels') with a view to settling upon it a European population." Mr. Chamberlain having assented in principle, the Bill was duly introduced, its avowed object being " to appropriate lands contained in certain native reserves, the previous occupants having gone into rebellion." It was, he went on to say, " very valuable land, and probably would be cut up into very small farms, so that there might be a considerable European population established in that part of the country." As regards the Langeberg portion of the disaffected districts, he wrote that, " it would be necessary, of course, before anything could be done, that the rebellion should be crushed, and that the natives now occupying it should be destroyed or driven out of the country." It was the same South African statesman, who declared that " The policy of the Government with regard to disloyal, rebellious natives is, and has always been, to deprive them of their land, and so teach them that the course of wisdom lies in obeying the laws of the country." A contemporary issue of the *Cape Times* put the case in a nutshell:

> We Whites want the Black man's land just as we did when we first came to Africa. But we have the decency in these conscience-ridden days, not to take it without excuse. A native rising, especially when there are inaccessible caves for the rebels to retire to, is a very tiresome and expensive affair; but it has its compensations, for it provides just the excuse wanted.

The distinction, and it is an important one, between ourselves and Continental nations in these matters is that, owing to the past labours of Burke and of the leaders of the *ante* Slave trade crusade, there is a public opinion in the homeland—worthily represented by the Anti-Slavery and Aborigines Protection Society, of which Mr. John H. Harris is the able Secretary—which can be appealed to, which genuinely resents the ill-treatment of native races, and which can sometimes intervene to prevent or to mitigate it.

. . . . . .

German intervention in the western portion of the colonisable southern part of the Continent, between the Kunene and Orange rivers, known as Ovamboland, Damaraland and Great Namaqualand with an estimated area of 322,450 square miles, began in 1883 and attained its fullest territorial limits in 1890. The presence of Germans in South Africa is not an event of yesterday. German missionaries were working in Great Namaqualand as far back as the early 'forties of last century, and ever since the British Government settled in Cape Colony the 2,000 Germans of the Foreign Legion, which it had raised for the Crimean War, South Africa has seen a steady trickle of German immigration. This missionary *cum* commercial enterprise was the origin of German political control in the western portion of South Africa [with the exception of Walfisch Bay, the only accessible port on the Western Coast, which Britain annexed]. From time to time the missionaries had complained of ill-treatment from the natives, and the German Government had on various occasions endeavoured to obtain from our Foreign Office a clear statement as to its attitude in regard to the protection of the lives and property of Europeans in the country. This, neither the Disraeli nor Gladstone

Administrations would vouchsafe. Bismarck, who was at first opposed to German oversea adventures, but who had to face a growing popular opinion favourable to them, eventually caused the German flag to be hoisted [in 1883] in the Bay of Angra-Pequena, some 300 miles south of Walfisch Bay. Here a German merchant had bought land with a ten-mile sea frontage from a Hottentot Chief. A full account of the correspondence between the British and German Governments on the subject is given in Lord Fitzmaurice's *Life of Lord Granville*.

Most of the coastwise region of German South-West Africa is a desert of sand and scrub, but inland the country rises, is fertile and healthy. The northern and central part is inhabited by branches of the Great Bantu family—Ovambos and Hereros—to which the Matabele, Mashonas, Zulus, Basutos, etc., belong; interspersed with communities of Damaras (whose origin is doubtful), Hottentots, Bastards (half-breeds with a strong admixture of Boer blood) and primitive Bushmen. The southern region is mainly peopled by Hottentots.

For a number of years after the hoisting of the German flag at Angra-Pequena the German Government took very little direct action in the country, contenting itself with a desultory support of various trading companies which had started local businesses. "My aim," said Bismarck in 1885, "is the governing merchant and not the governing bureaucrat in those regions." He persisted in that view until events forced his hand. The representative of one of these companies, assisted by the missionaries, concluded a number of the usual treaties of amity and "protection" with the native tribes, amongst others with Kamaherero, the chief of one of the principal Herero clans. These the German Government subsequently evoked as political instruments, although it is very doubtful whether the original negotiator had any direct official authority. The Dependency's affairs were, in short, very much in the hands of a few merchants, settlers and missionaries, whose numbers, however, grew with the years. Nor did the German Government show any disposition at first to help them when in difficulties. Thus, in 1888, replying to one such appeal, the German Chancellor remarked that:

it could not be the function of the Empire, and that it lay outside the adopted programme of German Colonial policy, to intervene for the purpose of restoring, on behalf of the State, organisations (order?) among uncivilised people; and, by the use of military power to fight the opposition of native Chiefs towards the not yet established business undertakings of German subjects in overseas countries. He could therefore give no promise on behalf of the Empire that the peaceful pursuit of mining and such like undertakings in South West Africa must be insured by the military forces of the Empire.

In taking up this position the German Government undoubtedly intensified the difficulties its representatives were afterwards to be confronted with and which led to such dire results. An active and overbearing interference succeeded years of complete apathy and indifference, and was entrusted to civilians and military men who were utterly inexperienced in the handling of problems of native administration which were, indeed, wholly new to Germany. The upshot was inevitable. To assume political responsibility for African territory without exercising authority over the acts of local settlers, and providing machinery for the redress of native grievances is always a grave error. In this particular case it was particularly disastrous owing to the unsettled conditions prevailing within the territory.

The German settlers had two chief obstacles to contend with. One was the state of endemic warfare between the Hereros and the Hottentots—the latter of whom, although much fewer in numbers, were better armed and better shots. The struggle between these two races had continued ever since the southern Bantu movement came into contact with the drive northwards of the Hottentots, impelled thereto by white pressure from the South. Between 1864 and 1870 it went on uninterruptedly. It was renewed from time to time between 1870 and 1890, when it broke out again with renewed violence. The other obstacle lay in the fierce competition between the German newcomers and British and Boer colonial traders from the Cape. Probably these men were neither better nor worse than their German competitors; but they admittedly, and with the support of prominent Cape politicians, did everything possible to oppose the Germans both in matters of trade and in matters political. There was a strong party at the Cape which wanted Damaraland and Great Namaqualand annexed to Cape Colony and which bitterly resented the action of the Home Government in not preventing the establishment of German political control over those regions. The natural conse-

THE STORY OF GERMAN S.W. AFRICA

quence of this rivalry was that the natives were used by both parties to attain their several ends, and that a peaceful establishment of German political control was afterwards made more difficult than it would otherwise have been, and the temptation to precipitate and high-handed action was stronger. In the 1864-1870 wars between Hereros and Hottentots, the former were led by English traders. In 1883, the date of the hoisting of the German flag at Angra-Pequena, a party of Transvaal Boers and Cape colonists trekked into Ovamboland and founded the " Republic of Upingtonia," which broke up after the murder of its founder by the natives. In 1888 an English trader and prospector named Lewis, induced Kamaherero to expel the German settlers from his territory. This event was a land-mark in the history of the Dependency, for it destroyed what little authority Bismarck's so-called " Merchant Administration " possessed, and was the propelling cause of German official intervention, and of the creation of the " German South-West Africa " Chartered Company to which large concessions of land and minerals were granted without any regard to pre-existing native rights. No sooner did the company secure its privileges than it demanded Government action, to " assist the spirit of German enterprise by securing peace there " and the establishment of an organised administration, and announced its intention of preparing for the future settlement of the country by German farmers and agriculturists " on a large scale."

In 1890, the German Government, yielding to domestic pressure, resigned itself reluctantly to political action. Its early steps were half-hearted and inefficient. It sent out a single officer, Captain von François, with an escort of 21 soldiers and with instructions to put what order he could into the existing chaos, " to take no sides, but to remain strictly on the defensive." Contemporaneously with his arrival in the country, the Hereros and Hottentots had taken to the field once more, the former under Kamaherero, the latter under Hendrik Witbooi. Von François' first step was to get Kamaherero to renew the " protection " treaty he had repudiated at Lewis' instigation; his next to induce Witbooi to come to terms with his antagonist. In this he was unsuccessful. Witbooi insisted upon prosecuting the war. He had, moreover, attacked and defeated the chief of the Red " Bastards," with whom a similar "protection" treaty had been negotiated, removed a German flag he had found there and taken it to his capital of Hoornkranz. The war dragged on until August, 1892, when Witbooi and his Herero antagonist patched up their differences. The Hottentot chief persistently declined, however, to treat with the Germans and refused to allow German settlers in his country. The Germans thereupon decided to attack him. He was surprised in his stronghold and many of his followers killed, but he himself succeeded in escaping. Two years later, after a vain attempt to come to terms without further fighting, the Germans again moved against Witbooi. Their case against him was that he would not acknowledge German suzerainty and was perpetually raiding his neighbours. Witbooi inflicted further severe losses on the Germans before finally submitting in 1894. From then onwards, until the General Rebellion in 1905, he fought on the side of the Germans against the Hereros and against other Hottentot communities, which were subdued between 1895 and 1903 with as little or as much justification as is habitual in the majority of these African conflicts. Each side accused the other of atrocities, probably with truth. The fact that the Germans found themselves virtually without native support of any kind and were, indeed, confronted with the active enmity of the Hottentots when the general Herero uprising occurred, although the two races had been engaged in internecine warfare for decades, is the best proof of the detestation in which their rule was held.

A general peace with the Hottentots, was arrived at in 1906. By that time, if the early German estimates of the Hottentot population were approximately accurate, their communities had become greatly reduced. Although the decrease in their numbers may have been partially attributable to their perennial affrays with the Hereros, the prolonged struggle with the Germans must undoubtedly be regarded as the principal contributory cause. Palgrave estimated them in 1877 at 18,350, Governor Leutwein and Captain Schwabe at 20,000 in 1894, while the German official census taken in 1911 gives a total of only 9,781.

The fate of the Hereros has now to be narrated. In 1894 Major Leutwein replaced von François. Owing to the peculiar combination of circumstances narrated above,

THE STORY OF GERMAN S.W. AFRICA 63

the Germans started their attempted administration of the country under unusual difficulties. The situation needed firmness and tact in dealing with the natives, and an iron hand over settlers and speculators guilty of oppression and crime. Leutwein was a well-meaning man—so much even the Blue Book allows—who made himself unpopular in the Dependency by refusing to go as far as the settlers wished him to go, but who lacked efficient home support and the necessary strength of character to grasp with firm hands the nettles of muddle and misrule. His assistants were young and totally inexperienced officials and officers trained in the art of Prussian regimentalism, utterly unfitted for the task of administering African peoples, and many of them of indifferent reputation. An impartial account, published in 1908, of the vices of the German colonial system at that time contains the following instructive passages:

> Tradition proved too strong even for Prince Bismarck, and gradually the whole system of Prussian bureaucracy was introduced into each of the Colonies. . . The Germans never went to school in colonial matters They light-heartedly took upon themselves the governing of vast territories and diverse races in the confident belief that the " cameral sciences," which had for generations proved an efficient preparation for local administration at home, would qualify equally well for Africa. . . Instead of studying native law and custom systematically, and regulating administration in each colony according to its peculiar traditions and circumstances, all Colonies alike were governed on a sort of *lex Germanica*, consisting of Prussian legal maxims pedantically interpreted in a narrow, bureaucratic spirit by jurists with little experience of law, with less of human nature, and with none at all of native usages. . . Worse still, the choice of colonial officials has not, in many cases, been a happy one. . . The Colonies were for a long time looked upon as a happy hunting ground for adventurers who could not settle down to steady work at home, or a sort of early Australia to which family failures might conveniently be sent.

The trouble with the Hereros began in 1890 upon the death of Kamaherero, the chief of the Okahandja clan of the Herero tribe. With their usual passion for centralisation, the Germans had treated Kamaherero as the paramount chief of all the Hereros, to which position he had no title in native law. When he died the Germans supported the claim of his younger son, Maherero, to the headship of the clan, as against that of the rightful heir, Nikodemus. Worse still, they persisted in their policy of investing the head of the Okahandjas with the paramount chieftainship, with the idea, apparently, of disintegrating the tribal organisation, and making of it a house divided against itself. The upshot was civil war within the tribe, the Germans siding with Maherero. To this initial impolicy the cattle and land questions added their causes of disturbance. Land and cattle, sometimes one, sometimes the other, sometimes both combined, have been at the bottom of every collision between whites and blacks in South Africa. The Hereros, like the Matabele, were great herdsmen. The Blue Book states that in 1890 they " must have possessed well over " 150,000 head of cattle; that the cattle disease killed off half that number; that " something like 90,000 " were left, and that by 1902 the Hereros retained 45,898, while the 1,051 German settlers then in the country possessed 44,487 between them. It is interesting to compare these totals with the Matabele totals given in the last chapter. No authority is cited for the Herero totals but, accurate or not, it is glaringly evident that from 1894, on one pretext and another, the Hereros were systematically despoiled of their herds. The robbery of cattle went hand in hand with successive encroachments upon the land of the tribe. The land syndicate formed in Germany had applied for an area in the Dependency as large as Wales and had sent out a large number of new settlers for which, in point of fact, it had made no provision. Acting under the pressure of these demands and the incessant disputes between settlers and the natives as to boundaries and cattle grazing, the local Authorities drew up in 1894 a quite arbitrary boundary line, which trenched severely upon native rights. All Herero cattle found beyond the boundary were to be impounded and sold to settlers, the proceeds to be divided between the Administration and Maherero. This suited Maherero and his clan, but naturally infuriated the other clans. Two years later, several thousand native head of cattle were seized despite the protests and tears of their owners. The act was one of sheer robbery. The whole country was convulsed. The settlers were threatened by the exasperated natives and fled to the coast. War seemed imminent. Maherero's people were, however, placated by receiving half the proceeds in accordance with the terms of the agreement. The other clans, and the Khamas—Hottentots who were also affected by the seizure, remained angry and resentful. A meeting between Leutwein and many of the chiefs for the purpose of reopening

THE STORY OF GERMAN S.W. AFRICA 65

the boundary question, failed to secure unanimity. It was characteristically opened on the part of the German Governor with a threat of war, which could result " only in the extermination of one party thereto, and that party could only be the Hereros." It was followed by a summons to the dissatisfied Herero Chiefs and the Khamas to deliver up their arms. The summons meeting with a refusal, the Khamas were attacked by the Germans, aided by the Okahandja Hereros, and " practically exterminated." Nikodemus and another prominent Herero chief were seized and executed as "rebels." Large quantities of their peoples' cattle were confiscated.

The ensuing years witnessed a further whittling down of Herero grazing lands by settlers, and many cases of abuse, extortion, and cruelty on the part of individual settlers. There were no courts to which the aggrieved natives could have recourse. All they could do was to make representations to the nearest official who . . . sided with the settlers. Unable to obtain redress in any direction, incessantly harassed and defrauded of their property, it is little wonder that the Hereros were gradually goaded into that condition of desperation, which it was the deliberate object, at any rate of the settlers, the land and mining syndicates and their backers at home, to provoke.

The last straw was the Credit Ordinance of 1903. The settlers and traders had long been in the habit of giving credit to natives for goods sold. The practice is a common one in many parts of Africa, and much is to be said for it where there are Civil Courts to see justice done between debtor and creditor. But in German South-West Africa no court of any kind had been set up, the system had preceded the Administration, and the Administration had done nothing to regulate it. Governor Leutwein had drafted an Ordinance as far back as 1899, providing for their creation. His proposals had been strongly opposed —a sinister incident—by the settlers and by the syndicates in Germany, who had the ear of the incompetent Foreign Office officials who mismanaged the Dependency's affairs. The creditor preferred being a law unto himself. And still he grumbled. Then came the Credit Ordinance. Creditors were given a year within which to collect their outstanding debts: after that period the debts would not be recognised as valid. No measures whatever seem to

have been taken either to prevent them from attempting
to recover by personal action, or even to supervise them
in the process of doing so, with the inevitable consequence
that seizures of land and cattle; spasmodic before, became
thenceforth systematised. This iniquitous order was
forced upon the Dependency by the vested interests concerned despite the Governor's protest.

It was the final provocation. Profiting by the
Governor's absence in the south in connection with one
of the perennial Hottentot troubles and believing the
report of his death, spread by the settlers by whom he
was hated, for their own purposes, the Hereros, led by
Maherero, rose in a body and fell upon the officials and
settlers, killing as many as they could reach. In a letter
to Governor Leutwein, replying to the latter's remonstrance, Maherero wrote :

> I and my headmen reply to you as follows : I did not commence the war this year; it has been started by the white people; for as you know how many Hereros have been killed by white people, particularly traders, with rifles and in the prisons. And always when I brought these cases to Windhuk the blood of the people was valued at no more than a few head of small stock, namely, from fifty to fifteen. The traders increased the troubles also in this way, that they voluntarily gave credit to my people. After doing so they robbed us; they went so far as to pay themselves by, for instance, taking away by force two or three head of cattle to cover a debt of one pound sterling. It is these things which have caused war in this land. And in these times the white people said to us you (i.e. Leutwein) who were peacefully disposed and liked us, were no longer here. They said to us, the Governor who loves you has gone to a difficult war; he is dead, and as he is dead you also (the Hereros) must die.

Reinforcements were sent out under General von
Trotha, a perfect type of the ruthless Prussian soldier.
Until recalled, owing to the indignation aroused by his
brutalities, von Trotha carried out for twelve months a
war of expulsion and extermination against the Hereros,
who, encumbered by their women, children, and cattle,
driven from place to place, were killed in great numbers,
or perished in the desert regions into which they were
mercilessly hunted. Peace could have been made with
them after their signal defeat in August, 1904. But von
Trotha would not hear of peace. The war degenerated
into wholesale, retail, and indiscriminate slaughter of
both man and beast.

THE STORY OF GERMAN S.W. AFRICA

Thus perished the Hereros—a vigorous, intelligent people, like all the Bantus: to-day a miserable, broken remnant. "The late war, wrote the missionary Schowalter in 1907, has reduced the Herero tribe by more than a quarter. After the battles on the Waterberg the rebels disappeared in the sandy desert, and here the bones of 12,000 to 15,000 men who fell victims to hunger and thirst lie bleaching." Wholesale executions and forced labour on the Coast completed the work of destruction.

The moral of it all—the old, familiar, ghastly story, in all its futility and short-sighted greed, is stated with fluent veracity in the record of a conversation between one of the earlier settlers and some newly arrived German soldiers:

> Children, how should it be otherwise? They (the Hereros) were ranchmen and landowners, and we were there to make them landless working-men, and they rose up in revolt . . . this is their struggle for independence. They discussed, too, what the Germans really wanted here. They thought we ought to make that point clear. The matter stood this way : there were missionaries here who said you are our dear brothers in the Lord, and we want to bring you these benefits—namely, faith, love, and hope : and there were soldiers, farmers, and traders, and they said we want to take your cattle and your land gradually away from you and make you slaves without legal rights. These two things didn't go side by side. It is a ridiculous and crazy project.

"How should it be otherwise?" The question is easily answered. There is room in colonisable Africa for the White man and the Black. There is no necessity for these robberies, these brutalities, these massacres. They are the product of lust, of greed, of cruelty, and of incompetence.

BIBLIOGRAPHY.

"The Life of Lord Granville." Fitzmaurice. (Longman & Co.).
"The Evolution of Modern Germany." Dawson. (Fisher Unwin).
"Germany." Alison Phillips and others. (Encyclopædia Britannica Co.).
"The Colonisation of Africa." Sir Harry Johnston. (Cambridge Press).

B—EPISODES IN THE ESTABLISHMENT OF POLITICAL CONTROL

FOREWORD

In the story of the French seizure of Morocco, and of the Italian descent upon Tripoli, we are concerned with a set of motives determining European action in Africa entirely different from those we have been examining in the last chapters. We now enter the sphere of purely imperialistic undertakings. We chronicle events and policies which are not the outcome of haphazard circumstance, and which do not respond to the immutable laws of racial expansion. They are precipitated and evolved by statesmen, whose actions are propelled in part by nationalistic impulses, and in part by personal ambitions—by the will-to-power. The driving force behind them is essentially imperialistic, the desire for national dominion and world-power. For a time they incarnate this nationalist sentiment. They alternately use, and are used by, capitalistic finance, by a military caste, by associations of individuals—influences expressing themselves through a purchasable Press, by which public opinion is excited. But these personal and collective influences would hardly suffice to bring about the desired ends, without the presence in a considerable section of the population, of the glowing embers of nationalist arrogance ever ready to burst into flames.

The generating motive of these imperialistic adventures must not be sought in local circumstances alone, but in the complicated game of high politics played by diplomatists in Europe. The African peoples and territories affected are pawns on the diplomatic chessboard of Europe, counters in higher stakes.

The French seizure of Morocco and the Italian descent upon Tripoli are first and foremost chapters in contemporary European history. They are links, and powerful links, Morocco especially, in the chain of circumstances which generated the Great War of 1914. Indeed, it was the decision of France, Britain, and Italy in the years immediately preceding the Great War to treat Mediterranean Africa in the light of their own respective nationalist interests; to partition among themselves an extensive region of the earth's surface of notable economic and strategic importance without the slightest regard to the interests of its native inhabitants, and in defiance of formal international treaties, which produced the condition of international anarchy whence the Great War sprang.

The historian who, in his survey of the underlying causes of the most terrible catastrophe which has befallen civilisation, concentrates his view upon the rape of Belgium, and omits the precedent rape of North Africa, is dishonest with the generation he professes to enlighten. The French seizure of Morocco and the Italian descent upon Tripoli made havoc of the moral law of Europe.

The invasion of Belgium was not the inauguration of an era of Treaty-breaking in Europe. It was the culmination of an era.

CHAPTER VII.

THE STORY OF MOROCCO.

CONDEMNATION of European *political* action in Africa is often attributed to the prevalence in the critics of two erroneous conceptions which are held to vitiate their judgment. One of them is the belief, which the critics are supposed to entertain, that native government is without serious blemish, and that the general condition of the population under native government is one of beatitude. The other is the alleged incapacity of the critics to appreciate the automatic and irresistible driving force of modern political and commercial progression, which, it is argued, makes the extension of European political control over these countries simply unavoidable. Now, people are, no doubt, to be met with who do think that it is possible in these days to build a Chinese wall round a certain area of the earth's surface. But those who stress the fallacies of uninformed commentators know perfectly well that they are avoiding the real issue. This is not European political action in itself, but the hypocrisy and injustice which so often distinguish it, the murderous cruelty which so often stains its methods, and the abominable selfishness which usually characterises its objects.

It is sheer cant to apologise for these things on the ground of the expansive commercialism of modern Europe, and it is worse than cant to do so on the ground of native misgovernment. The misgovernment of modern European statesmen has brought Europe to a state of misery and wretchedness unequalled in the history of the world. The social system of Europe is responsible for more permanent unhappiness, affecting a larger aggregate of humanity, than that which any native tyrant has ever succeeded in inflicting.

The story of the French absorption of Morocco has given rise to much of this cant-talk. A disturbed Morocco on the frontiers of French Algeria was an undoubted inconvenience to the French. As with all loosely governed States in a condition much resembling the Europe of feudal times, the central authority at Fez exercised very little power over the nomadic tribesmen of the borders, to whom frontier lines existing on paper meant nothing, as they drove their flocks and herds to fresh pasturages. This state of affairs led to frontier " incidents " in the vague and indeterminate region separating the Morocco and Algerian frontiers. These " incidents " were quite unimportant in themselves, but they gave the military wing of the French Algerian administration the necessary excuses for military action, which professional soldiers will ever, and necessarily, take. These frontier skirmishes were never more than a pretext put forward in Paris and Algiers to cover political designs. If the interminable public professions of amity and friendship towards the Moroccan Government which were the stock-in-trade of French politicians for many years had contained the least germ of sincerity, the fate of Morocco would have been very different—and so, probably, would have been the fate of Europe. France had many opportunities of proving herself a true friend of the Moroccan people. She could have strengthened and purified their Government, developed every legitimate French interest in the country without violence, and gradually established an effective direction over that country's internal affairs. The French Government could have done this while safeguarding the independence of the people and of their institutions. In so doing it might well have succeeded in recreating under the stimulus of French imagination and French genius the latent qualities of a race once great and powerful; revived the glories of an art whose achievements, still exquisite in their partial decay, are among the noblest monuments in the world; given a renewed impetus to that intensive cultivation which in Moorish hands once made of southern Spain the fairest and most fertile spot in Europe. The French Government chose a different path, a treacherous, selfish, and a bloody one, which it concealed as far as possible from its own people and pursued in defiance of repeated protests from the French Chamber. In treading that path the French Government was from 1904 onwards consistently supported by the British Foreign Office. I have told the story at length elsewhere. Here I can but summarise it, and the world-events linked up with it.

In 1898 the last attempt on the part of France to dispute the British position in the valley of the Nile ended with Colonel Marchand's withdrawal, under threat of war, from Fashoda. The direction of France's foreign affairs passed henceforth into the restless and ambitious hands of M. Delcassé. The next year—the year of the Hague Peace Conference—marked the opening rounds of the Boer War, and the year after witnessed the accession of Edward VII. In the state of international anarchy to which the game of high politics and high finance had reduced Europe since the Berlin Congress of 1878, the entanglements of one nation were the opportunity of another. Smarting under the Fashoda rebuff, the French Government felt the need of doing something disagreeable to Britain, which was still the "traditional foe" in the eyes of an active and powerful school of French politicians. It hoped to restore French "prestige" by the same stroke. Successive British Cabinets had strenuously resisted every attempt on the part of France and Spain to acquire an exclusive political footing in Morocco. In defending stubbornly the independence of Morocco from interested encroachments, British official policy was no more altruistic than German, when Germany for her own ends pursued a like one. But in both cases it was a policy which corresponded to the interests of the Moroccan people, whereas the opposing policy took no account whatever of those interests. So long as Britain maintained that policy she was protecting the natives. When she abandoned it in the circumstances presently to be recalled, she sacrificed the interests of the natives to her own purposes. The utilitarian object of the British Government in defending Morocco diplomatically against French aggression was a double one: that of preserving the "open door" for trade; but, above all, that of preventing the Mediterranean coast line of Morocco from falling into the hands of a first-class naval Power. Such an event would, according to accepted strategy, have weakened British naval influence in the Mediterranean by impairing the strategic value of Gibraltar, thereby threatening the route to India. By one of the most subtle exhibitions of diplomatic *finesse* which modern diplomatic annals record,

the British Government subsequently found the means
of reconciling that major interest with the desertion of
Morocco.

This determination on the part of the British Government to prevent the absorption of Morocco ran counter
to French colonial ambitions. The project of a great
North African Empire which should ultimately equal in
importance the lost French Empire of the Indies had long
haunted the imagination of the French Imperialist
school. Algeria and Tunis had already been acquired.
Egypt was henceforth and finally excluded from the
picture. Morocco remained—the richest portion of the
Northern Continent, a great and beautiful country which,
with its favourable climatic conditions, its magnificent
spinal column in the Atlas mountain chains, with their
numerous rivers, varied elevations and fertile soil,
can grow anything from ground nuts to tea, from wheat to
Indian corn, contains valuable mineral deposits, produces
the finest horses in the world, and could sustain
innumerable flocks and herds.

To " jump the claim " while the British were fully
occupied in suppressing the Boer Republics was the
French Government's plan. But Spain, with her long
historical connection and her settlements on the Coast,
could not be set aside. Italy, still sore over Tunis (see
next chapter) must have her pound of African flesh before
France could feel free to move. Then there was
Germany. German interests in Morocco were purely
commercial. Like Britain she stood for the " open
door," and had strongly supported the diplomatic mission
Lord Salisbury sent to Fez in 1892. Her explorers had
made notable contributions to our knowledge of Morocco.
Her Government had maintained direct diplomatic representations with the Moorish Court since 1873, and had
concluded a commercial Treaty with the Sultan. This
Treaty the German Government had submitted before
ratifying it to the signatory Powers of the Madrid Convention of 1880. In short, Morocco was an international
question, and had been since the first International
Conference on its affairs met at Madrid in 1880, the
Convention drawn up on that occasion assuring to all the
Powers represented " the most favoured nation treatment."

THE STORY OF MOROCCO

M. Delcassé set himself the task of removing, so far as possible, the obstacles to his schemes arising out of this situation. If he could " square " Spain, Italy, and Germany he would risk the consequences of confronting Britain, whose unpopularity at that moment was universal, with an accomplished fact. Italy, he disposed of by giving her carte blanche in Tripoli in return for a free hand in Morocco (see next chapter). To Spain he proposed (1901) that Morocco should be partitioned between them. There is some warrant, but no available documentary proof, for assuming that formal assurances were simultaneously given to Germany, guaranteeing the maintenance of the " open door," which was all Germany cared about. Spain's hesitation and British diplomacy combined in frustrating M. Delcassé's first attempt to secure a French Protectorate over the greater part of Morocco. His second attempt was more successful.

The Boer War had left Britain without a friend in Europe. French criticism had been more offensive, if possible, than German. But irritation at the Kaiser's telegram to Kruger on the occasion of the Jameson raid had gone deep. The German Naval Law had further undermined the centuries' old friendship between the two Powers, and had introduced a new element of friction. The temperament and outlook of King Edward and the Kaiser were mutually incompatible. The strenuous, restless, vain nephew alternately annoyed and bored the Uncle—*bon viveur*, affable, frivolous, and shrewd. To Edward VII., as Prince of Wales, Paris had offered attractions in which she specialises. The King preferred the French to his own stock across the Rhine. British diplomacy came to the conclusion that the " Balance of Power " was tilting too much on the side of the Teuton, and resolved to win over France. In the Spring of 1903 King Edward visited Paris and laid the foundations of the Entente. Thenceforth the fate of Morocco was sealed.

· · · · · · ·

While these intrigues for the dismemberment of their country were going on in Europe, the Moors were being alternately cajoled and bullied by the French Government. Alleging the plea of military necessity owing to roving bands on the coterminous frontier, the French Algerian authorities occupied several oases in the South of Morocco over which the Sultan laid claim but exercised no visible authority. The murder of a French subject at Tangier led to the dispatch of a Moorish mission to Paris. This mission resulted in the drawing up of a Protocol, in which arrangements were mutually arrived at with regard to policing the frontier. The Protocol was based upon "respect for the integrity of the Shereefian Empire."[1] An agreement of the same kind was signed in April, 1902. While the French Government was thus assuring the Moorish Government of its disinterestedness, it was pressing Spain to hasten the partition negotiations. At this stage "high finance" appears on the scene. Abdul Aziz, the young, well-meaning, but extravagant Moorish ruler, contracted a loan of £380,000 with some French banking establishments (October, 1902). It was apparently just about this time that British diplomacy realised what had been going on at Paris and Madrid, Pressure was put upon Spain to break off the partition negotiations with France, and a British financial house was found willing to oblige (April, 1903) the Sultan with a sum equal to that which he had secured from the French bankers in the preceding October. Meantime the Moors were becoming uneasy in their dull, ineffective way. The attitude of the French military authorities in Algeria was not calculated to reassure them. The Sultan felt the need of a more explicit recognition of Moorish independence. Learning that the President of the French Republic was to visit Algiers, he sent a special envoy to greet him, hoping to receive from the lips of the head of the French State a formal declaration in that respect. But in response to a speech from the Moorish envoy, framed with that intention, M. Loubet contented himself with a few polite generalisations. Thenceforth the suspicions of the Moors deepened until the events of 1904 converted suspicions into certainties. Those events may now be epitomised.

· · · · · · ·

The Anglo-French Convention of April, 1904, and the Franco-Spanish Convention of October, 1904, completed the diplomatic machinery for the disposal of North Africa, and "slammed the door in the face of the peace-

(1) "You should make the Sultan understand"—wrote M. Delcassé to the French Minister in Tangier—"that it will depend upon himself to find in us friends the surest, the most anxious for the integrity of his person, the most capable of preserving him in case of need from certain dangers. Our loyalty, as also our interests, are guarantees to him that we shall not encroach upon it."

makers in Europe." Diplomacy on this occasion succeeded in coupling treachery towards an African people with treachery towards Europe, and especially towards the European peoples whom it professedly represented. Outwardly, by its published claims, the Anglo-French Convention of 1904 was a Peace instrument which disposed of Anglo-French differences. Inwardly, by its Secret Articles, it prefigured a French Protectorate over Morocco while imposing upon that potential French Protectorate, in the British strategic interest, a permanent Spanish mortgage over the Mediterranean and North Atlantic coasts of Morocco. As such it was a war instrument, because it infallibly involved a rupture with Germany. Outwardly, the Franco-Spanish arrangement consisted in the formal declaration that both Powers " remain firmly attached to the integrity of the Moorish Empire, under the sway of the Sultan." Inwardly, by its secret Convention—to which the British Government was not merely a consenting, but a compelling party—it postulated the French absorption of Morocco when the French purpose could be conveniently executed subject to a Spanish occupation of the Coasts as stipulated in the Secret Articles of the Anglo-French Convention; and it provided for a Franco-Spanish economic monopoly over the whole country.

Thus, to suit their own nationalistic and imperial designs, the French and British Governments—for Spain was used throughout merely as Britain's broker—not only signed away the independence of an African State while publicly professing tender attachment to its preservation. They secretly converted an international issue—so recognised by International Agreement—into an issue affecting their interests alone. And, so far as the economic side of the bargain was concerned, they deliberately violated Article XVII. of that International Agreement—the Madrid Convention—which provided, as has already been pointed out, for the "most favoured nation treatment" to all the Powers represented thereat. The diplomatic leakage ensuing, determined the first German intervention, which, in turn, led to the secret Anglo-French " military and naval conversation," so-called.

The same ethical, national and international offence was repeated when, as the result of the German intervention, another Conference of the Powers solemnly reaffirmed the international character of the Morocco problem in the Act of Algeciras in 1906.

> Now, there is no doubt—as Mr. L. S. Woolf remarks—that the principle insisted upon by Germany in the events which led up to the Conference of Algeciras was that the regulation of the question of Morocco belonged not to any one Power, but to the Powers collectively. The danger of the Morocco question for the peace of Europe was that Foreign Governments would act as isolated Sovereign Powers towards Morocco. The essence of the French case was that France could, and would, so act; the essence of the German case was that the Powers should act collectively. That was why Germany, in 1905, was demanding, and France resisting, an International Conference.

With these secret arrangements for the dismemberment of Morocco in their pockets, the British and French Governments went to the Algeciras Conference and affixed their signatures to the Act, there drawn up " in the name of Almighty God," and "based upon the threefold principle of the sovereignty and independence of His Majesty the Sultan, the integrity of his Dominions, and economic liberty without any inequality." They departed from the Conference and began immediately to give effect to their secret compact. The second German intervention was the result.

Throughout the whole of this nefarious transaction the *peoples* of Britain and France were absolutely deceived as to the cause of German action. It is essential to remember this. For seven years—until the secret arrangements were revealed in 1911—the British people were led to believe that in resisting French encroachments upon Morocco, Germany was trying to upset the Anglo-French Entente. For seven years the French people were led to believe that in supporting their Government against German intervention in Morocco affairs, they were opposing an unwarrantable assault upon their dignity. Neither people had the least idea until the mischief was done and had become irreparable, that their Governments had all along been acting in virtue of a secret and internationally illegal pact; that the German case was intrinsically just, and that Germany had been treated as though her signature at the foot of international treaties could be regarded as a negligible quantity. To do the French justice they tardily recognised the fact:

> Could we affect to ignore—said M. Deschanel, President of the French Parliamentary Committee on Foreign Affairs, when

THE STORY OF MOROCCO 81

defending the ratification of the Franco-German Convention of November, 1911—the efforts of Germany in Morocco for half a century, the travels of her explorers, the activity of her colonists, her agricultural and mineral enterprises, her steamship lines, her post-offices, and especially that movement of ideas which gravitated towards the Shereefian Empire. . . .

But no such admission was ever made by a leading British authority. To this day, owing to deliberate misrepresentation and suppression of the facts, nine Englishmen out of ten are utterly ignorant of the part played by the Morocco affair in international politics, and deem Germany's action throughout to have been totally unjustifiable.

Another distinguished Frenchman, Baron d'Estournelles de Constant, speaking in the French Senate on February 6, 1912, uttered an outspoken denunciation of the whole wretched intrigue :

> The French Parliament by an abuse morally, if not constitutionally, unpardonable, was kept in ignorance of this policy. . . Far from ensuring general Peace, the arrangements of 1904 tended to compromise it. . . Why was the French Parliament told only half the truth when it was asked to give its opinion upon our arrangement with England? Why was it not allowed to suspect that this arrangement had as its complement and corrective some secret clauses and other secret Treaties? It is this—*it is this double game towards Parliament and the world which becomes morally an abuse of trust.* . . Now the whole effect of the arrangement of 1904 appears to-day in its truth and in its vanity. It was a Treaty of friendship with England recognising the freedom of our political action in Morocco, and also proclaiming our will to respect the integrity of that country; that was what the public knew and approved. But the public was ignorant that at the same time, by other Treaties, and by contradictory clauses hidden from it, the partition of Morocco between Spain and France was prepared, of that Morocco whose integrity we had guaranteed. There existed two irreconcilable French policies in Morocco, that of public arrangements, i.e., a policy of integrity which was not the true one; *and that of secret arrangements postulating a Protectorate and the partition of Morocco.*

When the European anarchy had become uncontrollable, largely as the result of this " double game " played over Morocco, a few days only before the final outbreak, and before his own foul murder, one of the few outstanding figures in Europe, Jean Jaurés, laid an unerring finger upon its origins :

> In so grave an hour—said Jaurés, speaking at Vaise a fortnight before the Great War—so full of peril for all of us, for all our countries, I shall not indulge in an elaborate search after

responsibilities. We have ours; and I claim before history that we (Socialists) had foreseen and announced them. When we declared that to penetrate into Morocco by violence, by force of arms, was to *inaugurate in Europe* an era of ambitions, covetousness, and conflicts, we were denounced as bad Frenchmen, but it was we who were concerned for France. There, alas! is *our* share of responsibility.

. . . . .

Given *carte blanche* by British diplomacy, the French Government thenceforth advanced by rapid steps to the goal of its desires. It knew, although the British and French people did not, that French generals were bending, in community of association with their British colleagues, over war maps and strategic combinations, while British and French naval commanders were working out in concert the disposition of their respective fleets. Trampling upon public obligations, Moorish rights, and German susceptibilities alike, the French politicians of the "forward school," dragging a reluctant Chamber behind them, marched to the conquest of Morocco. Within five years of the signing of the Act of Algeciras, the independence and integrity of Morocco had gone by the board, tens of thousands of Moors had been killed, Morocco was a French Protectorate, and official Germany, baffled and enraged, feeling herself diplomatically humiliated, nursed her sores, while her Emperor, " whose personal influence had been exercised in many critical circumstances in favour of the maintenance of peace,"[1] had been " brought to think that war with France was inevitable."[2]

In March, 1907, the French occupied the first Moorish town, Udja, on the pretext of the murder of a French subject by Moors. They promised to withdraw, but remained. M. Pichon, the Foreign Minister, denied that this action was a " step towards Fez." In September a Franco-Spanish syndicate, in constructing a railway at Casablanca, deliberately desecrated a Moorish burial ground of great antiquity. A collision between the employees of the French railway contractors and the populace ensued, in the course of which several of the former lost their lives. A French fleet thereupon bombarded Casablanca, the helpless Moors being slaughtered in thousands amid the indignant protest of British and

(1) French Yellow Book. French Ambassador in Berlin to French Minister for Foreign Affairs. (No. 6).
(2) Idem.

other European residents. Following the bombardment, the French landed a large body of troops, permanently occupied Casablanca and Rabat, and gradually overran the whole of the Shawiya district where, for three years, incessant military expeditions, dispatched in every direction, prosecuted the task of "pacifying" the country, causing "much blood to flow."[1] With supreme irony the French Government called upon the already impoverished Moorish exchequer to meet the expenses involved in these acts of "peaceful penetration," and forced an "indemnity" of £2,400,000 upon the Moorish Government. Taxed beyond endurance to meet these demands, and infuriated by the inability of their ruler to protect them against French encroachments, the Moors deposed Abdulaziz, and proclaimed his brother, Mulai-Hafid, Sultan, but not before a civil war had intensified the internal chaos into which the country was rapidly drifting. Instantly international finance, used by the French Government as a convenient lever, dug its talons afresh into the dying Moorish State. Mulai Hafid was compelled to contract a loan. He was not even consulted about it. All liabilities incurred by Abdulaziz since the consolidated French loan of 1904, were merged into a new £4,040,000 loan—secured upon various sources of Moorish revenue, including the remaining 40 per cent. of the Customs—by an international banking syndicate, in which France held the lion's share. On being requested to sign the document embodying the transaction, Mulai Hafid refused. France thereupon presented him with an *ultimatum* and he had perforce to give way. It was not really a loan at all. The Sultan could not touch the capital because it had already been earmarked by the bondholders to pay off Morocco's previous debts. Nor could he meet the interest upon it except by imposing more direct taxes upon his subjects, seeing that he had been deprived under its terms of the remaining sources of indirect taxation. The "loan" was, in fact, an enforced tribute for the benefit of cosmopolitan finance, which was cosmopolitan and not merely French *only* because some other countries were interested, either politically or financially or for both reasons, in preventing the French from securing complete financial control of Morocco's resources. Thus, while

[1] Augustin Bernard.

the French share in the " loan " was 40 per cent., the
German was 20 per cent., the British 15 per cent., and
the Spanish 15 per cent. The same kind of consideration
had, doubtless, inspired the divers international groups
which had been formed to exploit the mineral and other
natural products of Morocco, such as the *Union des
Mines*, which included several of the big French and
German armament firms, Mr. A. E. Harris, of Harris
Dixon, Ltd., London, Mr. W. B. Harris, correspondent
of the *Times* at Tangiers, and Mr. Bonar Law. It is
instructive to note that the plundering of the Moors went
hand in hand with the plundering of the home public.
Thus the participating French banks were allowed to take
up the bonds of the new " loan " at 435 francs, while in
the afternoon of the day of issue the bonds were driven
up to 507 francs.

This tribute levied upon the Sultan, the Sultan could
only meet by levying tribute upon his tribesmen. The
latter, driven to desperation by exactions and cruelties
incidental to the process, flung off the last vestiges of
his authority, rose in revolt and besieged him in his
capital, Fez. This result had, of course, been foreseen.
Instantly there arose a bogus clamour, scientifically
arranged beforehand, and subsequently denounced in the
most scathing terms by the most distinguished of French
journalists then living, M. Francis de Pressenssé, that
the Europeans in Fez were in danger. A French force
of 30,000 men was found in convenient readiness, set off
to Fez, occupied it after a skirmish and . . remained
there. And that was the end of Morocco in one sense.
But not in another.

. . . . . .

The narrow, irregular streets of a Moorish town, into
which shells from warships riding on the sparkling blue
waters of the western Atlantic are falling in an incessant
and murderous hail, smashing the white-walled, flat-
roofed houses and splashing them all over with the blood
of the white-clad inhabitants who sprawl in mangled
heaps at the doors of their homes—between such a scene
as this and the pitted, scarred battlefields of Europe
to-day with the blasted stumps which once were trees,
and the piles of masonry and timber which once were
towns and villages, there appears at first thought no
connecting link of circumstance.

Yet it was the violence done to Casablanca which furnished the first direct incentive to that "era of ambitions, covetousness and conflicts in Europe," whose fruits the people of Europe have been reaping for the past five years.

Africa has always repaid her exploiters.

BIBLIOGRAPHY.

"International Treaties and Conventions and Agreements from 1880 to 1911."
"Ten Years of Secret Diplomacy." E. D. Morel. (National Labour Press).
"White Books and Yellow Books."
"French Parliamentary Debates."
"L'affaire Morocaine." V. Berard.
"Morocco and Armageddon." E. D. Morel. (National Labour Press).
"The Policy of the Entente, 1904-1914." Bertrand Russell. (*Idem*).
"The Belgian Diplomatic Despatches, 1911-1913."
"The European Anarchy." Lowes Dickinson. (Allen and Unwin).
"Our Ultimate Aim in the War." Armstrong. (*Idem*.)

CHAPTER VIII.

THE STORY OF TRIPOLI.

From 1835, until the events narrated in this chapter, Turkey held an internationally recognised suzerain power over that portion of the North African Coast line and interior roughly designated as Tripoli which at various periods in the world's history has been claimed by the Phœnicians, Carthaginians, Romans, Spaniards, Arabs, and the Knights of St. John. It was wrested from the latter by the Turks in the middle of the 16th century.

Tripoli is inhabited by a population of agriculturists and herdsmen, mostly nomadic in character owing to the scarcity of water. The bulk of it is Berber, Arabs coming second in number. There is, too, a large sprinkling of Negroes from West Central Africa, whose presence is due, in part to the old trans-desert Slave trade, and in part to the still existing but now much reduced trans-desert trade, with Northern Nigeria particularly, in ostrich feathers, gold and skins. Many thousands of Berbers and Arabs from Algeria fled into Tripoli to escape French rule. The phenomenon was repeated when the French occupied Tunis in 1881. Amongst these immigrants was the Algerian Sheikh, Senussi-el-Mejahiri, who founded the famous religious fraternity which bears his name, and which gradually spread all over the country, uniting Berber and Arab in a common spiritual bond. The Senussi were most numerous and influential in the province of Barca (Cyrenaica), the eastern promontory of the Tripolitan territory, whose seaport is Benghasi, near the supposed site of the Garden of the Hesperides. Although the founder himself successively moved his headquarters into regions more and more remote from contact with Europeans, the influence of the Order was paramount in Cyrenaica. The Turkish Governors of the Province recognised it themselves, and at Benghasi the dispensation of civic justice, which in all Mohammedan communities is based upon the Koran, was entrusted not to the official of the Sultan, but to the representative of the Order. The policy of the Senussi has been described as anti-European. It is so in the sense that they have done their best to get out of the European's way, and that they have preached to their adepts a voluntary exile from territory ruled by the European. But in no other. They had never pursued an aggressive policy. When the Mahdi raised the Eastern Sudan against us and invited el Majahiri to join him, the latter refused. Senussiism has been primarily an intellectual, moral and spiritual force which has spread through its numerous schools, and by the spiritual purity of its teachers, a religious, not a political movement, aiming at the centralisation of the orthodox Islamic sects in a theocracy free from secular interference. It has covered the province with monastical centres of learning and made waste places fruitful. In recent years, Mr. Hogarth, who has studied its work in Cyrenaica generally, and Mr. Vischer, in his famous journey across the desert from Tripoli to Nigeria, have testified in its favour. The latter says:

> I have seen the hungry fed and the stranger entertained, and have myself enjoyed the hospitality and assistance enjoined by the laws of the Koran. My own experiences among the Senussi lead me to respect them as men, and to like them as true friends, whose good faith helped me more than anything else to accomplish my journey. . . ."

These particulars were necessary to make it clear that in invading Tripoli, Italy was not only wresting from Turkey the last of her African Dependencies: she was committing an unprovoked attack upon native peoples and was additionally assaulting Islam in Africa. This serves to explain at once the fierce and prolonged resistance which Italy experienced from communities who had no particular love for the Turk; the appeals to a "Holy War," issued by certain Italian bishops, whose utterances the Vatican felt called upon to repudiate, and the anger aroused among Mohammedans all over the world, notably in India, against "this war of aggression unparalleled in the history of modern times "—to quote the manifesto of the London All-India Moslem League.

The predatory imperialism of modern Europe has never been revealed with such revolting cynicism as when Italy, profiting by the acute tension between France and Germany over Morocco in the autumn of 1911, issued.

like a bolt from the blue, her *ultimatum* to Turkey. In this document the Italian Foreign Minister, after recapitulating in the vaguest terms a list of grievances, which even if they had been well founded, were of the most trivial, indeed, puerile character, calmly announced the Italian Government's intention of occuping Tripoli and Cyrenaica by military force, and summoned Turkey within twenty-four hours to express acquiescence in this burglarious proceeding. It shocked even the most *blasé* of our imperialist leader writers.

The consummation of Italian unity which had awakened such generous sentiments and such high hopes, opened up avenues of the highest endeavour for the exploration of Italian statesmen. The poorest, the most heavily taxed, and, in the South, one of the most uneducated and half-fed populations in Europe constituted a paramount claim upon its rulers. But a number of Italians thought otherwise.

> Italy, as soon as she is independent . . . will have in turn to think of that need of expansion eastwards and southwards which all Christian people feel. . . Whether it be to Tunis or to Tripoli, or to an Island, or to any part of the European Continent matters not.

Thus the author of *Delle speranze d'Italia*. In fact Italian unity had hardly been attained when the fever of imperialism seized hold of Italy's governing classes, and the country in Europe which, perhaps, could least afford it, plunged headlong into oversea adventures

The seed of the Tripoli "raid" was sown at the Berlin Congress which met in June, 1878, ostensibly to revise the Treaty of San Stefano concluded between Russia and Turkey at the close of the Russo-Turkish War. The Congress arose through the British Government's threat of war upon Russia if the Treaty were ratified, on the ground that it affected certain provisions of the general European Settlement at Paris in 1856 and must, therefore, be first submitted to a European Conference. The real reason was the fear of British diplomacy, that if the provisions of the Treaty stood, Russia, using Bulgaria as a cat's-paw, would be in a stronger position to attain the goal of her Tsars' secular ambitions—Constantinople. Everything about the Congress and its preliminaries was fraudulent. The very day after it met, indiscreet disclosures revealed that the diplomatists concerned had already made secret arrangements with one another on the issues at stake. The rôle of the Congress consisted in pronouncing a benediction upon decisions which had been reached before it met. Every Government was pursuing in characteristic fashion its own nationalistic and imperialistic designs and bluffing its home public. Every plenipotentiary was intriguing behind the backs of his associates. As Count Corti, the Italian ambassador at Constantinople, sarcastically observed: "Everybody was telling everybody else to take something which belonged to somebody else." Disraeli was the master-mummer of them all. While spending millions of national money on loudly-advertised preparations for war, he was negotiating with Russia under cover of them. He got Cyprus out of Turkey before the Congress met, in exchange for a promise to guarantee the Sultan's possessions in Asia, which promise he never had the slightest intention of carrying out. He proposed at the Congress that Austria-Hungary should occupy the Turkish provinces of Bosnia and Herzgovina, having secretly agreed to the step beforehand. After the Congress he secretly urged France to seize Tunis, Bismarck taking the same line, and her ultimate action in doing so inaugurated the rape of North Africa.

Meantime Italian imperialism knocked vainly at the door of the Congress and retired empty and chagrined. It had largely itself to thank. In the preceding March, the British Cabinet had proposed to the Italian ambassador "an exchange of views," directed to the formation of a Mediterranean League to maintain the *status quo*. Italy had declined the overture, and Disraeli had no plums for her when the Congress met, although Lord Salisbury is reported by the Italian delegate to have casually remarked, in course of conversation with him at the Congress, that Italy might eventually console herself in the direction of Tripoli for the British acquisition of Cyprus, and for the Austrian occupation of Bosnia. Three years later the French Government took steps to apply the "free hand" in Tunis, which Disraeli had graciously undertaken to secure for it. On the flimsiest of pretexts the French picked a quarrel with the Bey—who was a nominal vassal of the Sultan of Turkey—invaded the country, forced a Protectorate upon it, and

THE STORY OF TRIPOLI

after a year's fighting reduced the Tunisians to submission. The ground had been well prepared, in much the same manner as it was even then being in Egypt, and was to be in Morocco twenty years later. An extravagant native ruler, encouraged in his extravagancies by European financial sharks; bondholders, whose exigencies had to be met and interests safeguarded; finally, control of the native Government's finances by European Powers. In the case of Tunis, the financial Commission of Control, which had been formed in 1869, was composed of Britain, France, and Italy; and Italian imperialism had gradually come to regard Tunis as the promised land. Italian emigration was encouraged and Italian commercial undertakings were financed. Before the Berlin Congress, the independence of Tunis was a British diplomatic interest. After the Berlin Congress it ceased to be. Thenceforth the British Government wiped Tunis off its diplomatic horizon, and when France pounced and Franco-Italian relations became strained to breaking-point, it gave Italy a pretty strong hint to keep quiet. So, "Mancini begged and entreated at Vienna and Berlin, and finally succeeded in persuading the two Empires to recognise Italy as an ally."[1] Italy joined the Teutonic group of Powers in May, 1882.

Shortly afterwards there came the turn in Egyptian affairs which ultimately brought about the British occupation. The reluctance of France to join us, led to the British Cabinet suggesting to Italy, first a triple intervention, and, in the ultimate resort, if France persisted in her refusal, direct Anglo-Italian co-operation. The French Government refused the first suggestion and getting wind of the latter, told the Italians (according to Baron Blanc, afterwards Italian Foreign Minister) that ' France would look upon it as an act of hostility on the part of Italy if that Power should take in Egypt the position which belonged to France, and occupy, without France, any portion of Egyptian territory.'' The French Government also threatened to extend its occupation of Tunis to Tripoli. The upshot was that the Italian Government declined the British proposal, a rejection which seems to have irritated the British Cabinet, for the ensuing year it promptly vetoed Italian

(1) Crispi's Memoirs.

aspirations in New Guinea towards which, among other regions of the earth's surface, Italian imperialism had momentarily cast its gaze. This restless hunt for overseas territory on the part of a Government whose subjects left its shores by tens and hundreds of thousands, was next directed to the independent African State of Abyssinia. Reviving a questionable claim to Assab Bay on the Somali Coast, the Italian Government successively extended its occupation to a long stretch of littoral which formed the seaboard outlet for Abyssinia. This brought it into immediate and disastrous conflict with the Abyssinians. Later, the internal affairs of Abyssinia becoming complicated, the Italian Government made a Treaty with the new ruler Menelik. Subsequently on the strength of a vaguely-worded clause about "mutual protection," it declared Abyssinia to be an Italian Protectorate. The final clash with the Abyssinians came in 1895 when an army, partly composed of Italian regulars, partly of native levies, was sanguinarily defeated by Menelik's warriors, and Italy was compelled by Treaty to recognise Abyssinian independence. The Abyssinian adventure was to have constituted in the view of the then Italian Premier: "An indemnification, a reparation as it were, for the disappointments Italy had suffered in the Mediterranean." If from the hecatombs of dead in the Great War there should arise a new International Order and the practice of slaughtering masses of innocent men, women and children to serve the nationalistic and imperial ambitions entertained by statesmen and by a relatively minute section of the community, should become obsolete; one can imagine the kind of judgment which will be passed by a generation from whom the threat of war is removed, upon the proceedings of their forbears who sought "reparation" for wounded vanity by assaulting communities who were absolute strangers to the cause of the wound!

Abandoning its attempt upon the independence of the sturdy Abyssinians, Italian imperialism thenceforth concentrated upon Tripoli, for whose absorption it had long prepared. Very instructive and typical of the immoralities of secret diplomacy is the history of the diplomatic steps taken by Italy to effect her objects. The first accessible document which illustrates them is an

Italian memorandum to Lord Salisbury dated February 12, 1887, which preceded by a few days the first renewal of the Triple Alliance. This document, together with most of the others hereinafter mentioned, form part of the fœtid secret diplomatic history of Europe which investigation of the archives of the Russian, Austrian and German Foreign Offices by the Revolutionary Governments is now bringing to light. It will be salutary for the moral purification of the world if Labour Governments in Britain and France complete the process later on, and examine their own national cesspools "high-piled with the droppings of two hundred years," and clean out "the dead pedantries, unveracities, indolent, somnolent impotencies and accumulated dung mountains there," which Carlyle truly declared seventy years ago to be "the beginning of all practical good whatsoever."

Italy's object in joining the Triple Alliance was primarily to protect herself against France. She subsequently endeavoured to use it for her own ends as a lever to pursue her general imperialistic designs. Disappointed with the results, she gradually went over to the Anglo-Franco-Russian camp, while continuing down to the very moment of the outbreak of war to remain officially a member of the "Triplice." Then, after a frantic bargaining bout with both sides, she elected not only to abandon her old Allies, but to make war upon them. This by the way.

The writer of the Italian memorandum to Lord Salisbury, Count Corti (then Italian ambassador in London), proposed an understanding based upon the preservation of the *status quo* in the Mediterranean, Adriatic, Euxine and Agean. But he also tried to pin Lord Salisbury down to recognise a potential Italian protectorate over Tripoli. "Great Britain," runs Corti's memorandum. "on her side is prepared to support, in the case of invasions by a third Power, the action of Italy on any other part of the North African Coast line, notably in Tripoli and Cyrenaica." But while Lord Salisbury was willing to come to terms with Italy in order to check French designs on Morocco, he was not at all disposed to lend himself to Italian adventures. His policy really was the *status quo*. So he declined, at least in writing, to be drawn. While expressing satisfaction at the prospect of Anglo-Italian co-operation for the main purpose specified, he says nothing in his reply about Tripoli, and contents himself with the following guarded indication of his views:

> If owing to some calamitous events it becomes impossible to maintain the *status quo*, both Powers desire that there shall be no extension of the domination of any other great Power over any portions of these coasts.

Nevertheless, on the strength of this exchange of Notes [the Notes were formally adhered to a month later by Austria-Hungary in an exchange of Notes between Count Karolyi and Lord Salisbury] Italy succeeded in getting her partners to give an extension and a new significance to the Triple Alliance quite at variance with its original character. The renewal took place on February 20, 1887. A separate agreement with Austria attached to the Treaty provided that if either Italy or Austria were compelled to modify the *status quo* by a temporary or permanent occupation of territory in any of the regions affected by the Treaty, they would come to a preliminary and mutual agreement " based upon reciprocal compensation." By a separate agreement with Germany, likewise attached to the Treaty, it was provided that if France should occupy Tripoli or Morocco, and if as a result of such action Italy should feel it necessary "in order to safeguard her position in the Mediterranean " to herself take action in those territories, or even in French territory, and should war result, Germany bound herself to support Italy in arms. [Article IX.]

Then Italian statesmen turned to Spain, and in an exchange of Notes on May 4 (1887) Spain undertook not to conclude with France any political arrangement affecting North Africa "aimed directly or indirectly against Italy, Germany, Austro-Hungary, or one or other of them." This agreement was renewed in May, 1891.

In the years which followed, the weathercock of Italian policy veered round more and more to the French side. Indeed, as far back as 1890, the year before the second renewal of the Triple Alliance, Crispi was apparently willing to change camps . . . for a consideration. Writing to the Italian Ambassador in Paris on September 2, he says:

> M. Ribot's attempts to discover our intentions in regard to the renewal of the Triple Alliance are unworthy of a statesman. In politics it is impossible to foresee anything at a distance of a year and a half. . . . Before inquiring as to our intentions concerning the renewal of the Triple Alliance, Ribot should

seek to place us in a position where we might be able to dispense with it; he should provide us with a guarantee that, our obligations to the two Empires once cancelled, France would not renew her Tunisian venture in other regions, that she would never again betray us in our own peninsula by means of the Vatican, and that she would undertake to ensure our independence. But up to the present nothing has been done to persuade us that the French people and their Government desire to become our serious and loyal friends.

Sincerity and loyalty are strange words in the mouth of an adept in a profession whence the exercise of the human virtues is rigidly excluded. A year before that letter was written, the Italian Government, fearing an attack by France, had made urgent representations to Berlin and London, and in July, 1900, Lord Salisbury, marking a considerable advance upon his attitude in 1887, had told the Italian Ambassador that Italy must occupy Tripoli, " that the Mediterranean may be prevented from becoming a French lake "—but not at that precise moment!

By 1901-2 Italy and France—or rather the diplomatists of those countries—had concluded their little " compensation " deal. Delcassé's plans for Morocco were maturing and Italy's benevolent neutrality was secured at the price of a free hand in Tripoli. The alliance between thieves was complete. In January 30, 1902, Italy squeezed a similar consent out of Austria in the shape of a declaration by Baron Posetti, the Austrian ambassador, that his government, " having no special interests to safeguard in Tripoli and Cyrenaica," would do nothing to prevent Italy taking such action therein as might seem to her appropriate.

Incredible as it may appear, the third renewal of the Triple Alliance, which took place five months later (June 28, 1902), contained a repetition of the same anti-French provision on Italy's behalf in the separate but attached agreement to which allusion has already been made! Through such septic processes was imperialism in North Africa promoted.

Thenceforth the ripening of the Tripoli plum was merely a matter of time and opportunity. It shaped well when the Russian Tsar and the Italian King signed a secret pact at Racconigi on October 24, 1909, the last paragraph of which reads as follows: " Italy and Russia bind themselves to adopt a benevolent attitude, the former in the interests of the Russian Straits question, the latter in the interests of the Italians in Tripoli and Cyrene (Cyrenaica)." It was judged to be rapidly approaching the right condition in the summer of 1911. It was declared fully ripe by the *ultimatum* of September 26. But here, too, a certain amount of preparatory manuring of the soil had been found necessary. The two most important banks in Italy, the Banco di Roma and the Banco d'Italia, which enjoyed the highest connections in State and Church, found it in their interest to start operations in Tripoli, playing the politico-financial rôle of the Banque de Paris et des-Pays Bas in the Morocco affair, and of the Russo-Chinese Bank in Manchuria. The Banco di Roma financed a large esparto-grass mill, a sponge factory, a steamboat service, and an oil and soap factory, besides speculating in real estate. Italian archæological expeditions became increasingly numerous. Glowing reports about (non-existent) phosphate deposits and sulphur mines; about vast potential granaries and cotton fields; about fertile lands only waiting for Italian peasants to blossom like a rose; filled the Italian papers, which are mainly run by powerful private interests, or owned by trusts. "Travellers" brought back alluring reports of the brilliant future in store for Tripoli under European management. A mass of nationalistic literature sprang up like magic. Corradine's "L'ora di Tripoli" was typical of these lyrical outpourings. After insisting upon the need for Italy to preserve and increase "her position in the Mediterranean against the Powers which dominate over the same sea," it goes on to predict that: "Twenty years hence all Italy will be imperialistic and the nation should then begin an extraordinary revolutionary action against things and persons which cannot at present be named." Patriotic associations placarded the walls of Rome with devices in flaming rhetoric: "A people is great only on the condition that it accomplishes a great and saintly mission in the world." One final demonstration was required to place impending events beyond the possibility of doubt, viz.: a declaration on the part of the Italian Government that an aggression upon Turkey was remote from its thoughts. This had been duly supplied by the Marquis di San Guiliano, Italy's Foreign Minister, in June: "Our policy," he had then declared in the Chamber, "like that of the other Great Powers has for its foundation the integrity of the Ottoman Empire." By July, army contractors were working full time. By September, the Turkish papers teemed with accounts of military and naval preparations. On September 26 the *ultimatum* was launched. The Turks sent a conciliatory and dignified reply on September 29. On September 30 [1911] Italy declared war.

Italy had what the French call a " bad Press " all over Europe, which pained and surprised the Italians very much. Questioned in the House of Commons as to whether the British Government was aware of Italy's intention beforehand, the spokesman for the Foreign Office declared that the Italian declaration of war was the first intimation of Italian intention which it had received. This statement was certainly untrue in substance if not in form. It is unlikely, to say the least, that the Italian Government would have taken action without advising both France and Germany. It is equally unlikely that under the circumstances of the moment France would have kept the information from the British Government, her partner in the Morocco deal. M. Lucien Wolf declared at the time that a few days after the Franco-German negotiations over Morocco began, the French ambassador at Rome was informed that if the French Protectorate over Morocco was acknowledged, Italy would occupy Tripoli. A French paper published a detailed story to the effect that the signal for Italy to move came from the British Foreign Office itself at the moment when the Franco-German negotiations had reached an acute stage. A Reuter's telegram from Rome, referring to Italian resentment at British Press criticisms, reported Italian assurances that all the European Governments were informed, " many weeks in advance " of Italy's plans. In any case, as the secret diplomatic documents referred to in this chapter bear witness, Italy's share in the rape of North Africa had been acquiesced in long before France's performance in Morocco. In the course of a bitter indictment of Europe, Ahmed Riza, the President of the Turkish Legislature, declared " Italy is not the sole culprit. The other Powers are her accomplices, as the blow that was struck had been prepared by them."

It is no longer open to doubt—remarked the *Manchester Guardian* on September 29th—that the Italian Government meditates the crime of making unprovoked war on a friendly Power . . . it is definitely shown that the Italian Government contemplates the violence, naked and unashamed, which was first attributed to it some days ago. There can surely be few parallels in history to the indifference towards the opinion and conscience of civilised States which the aggressor has shown in entering on this quarrel.

But was the aggressor more culpable than the accessories before the fact, who, for their own selfish ends, acquiesced in the "crime?"

The *Daily News* editorial of September 30 added prophecy to its outspokenness:

> Thus opens—it said—the first war which French action in Morocco has launched upon Europe; the first, but who knows whether it will be the last?

It was the precursor of Armageddon, but when Armageddon came the *Daily News* forgot, and concluded that it was a holy war.

Meantime enthusiasm ran high in Italy. Patriotic demonstrations were held in many of the principal cities. Bishops issued pastoral letters declaring the war necessary to uphold the national prestige and honour. But these sentiments were not altogether universal. The Prince of Teano, Deputy of Rome, who knew more of Tripoli than any living Italian, denounced the Government's proceeding as "an act of criminal political brigandage, which would cripple the prosperity of the nation for the exclusive advantage of a few clerical capitalists." Mario Borsa, the well-known journalist, described it as a "raid pure and simple, not excused by the shadow of a pretext; it is an act of military violence." How the Italian *ultimatum* impressed foreigners residing in Tripoli, may be estimated from the letter which Mr. Richard Norton, the director of the American excavation party at Cyrene, wrote to the *Times,* in the course of which he said:

> The reasons which Italy gives to show that she has suffered desperate wrongs at the hands of the Turks have been greeted in Tripoli with the ridicule they deserve. . . No, Sir, let the Italian Government grab Tripoli if they are able, but let them at least cease to steal the laurels of Gilbert and Sullivan by such lists of grievances as they have put before us.

In the opening days of October, the Italian fleet bombarded Tripoli town and Benghasi. At the former place practically no resistance was offered and little damage was done, the Turkish garrison retiring inland. At Benghasi the bombardment killed some three hundred civilians. The Turkish Government sent telegrams of protest to all the Parliaments of the world, to the various

Peace and Arbitration Societies, to the Hague Tribunal, and to King George. In the course of the month the Italians landed some 25,000 troops in the town. From the first the Italians had been told that they had merely to set foot on shore and all resistance would collapse. The tactics of the Turks in leaving the capital as the invaders entered it, seemed to confirm the accuracy of these forecasts. But the Italians were quickly undeceived. They imagined they were only fighting a few Turkish soldiers. They found, in due course, that they were fighting the whole population, both in Tripoli proper and in Cyrenaica. Strange as it no doubt appeared to the Italians, even Arabs and Berbers object to being slaughtered for no other reason than that the country they inhabit is coveted by another party. The unexpected resistance they met with appears to have given the Italians "nerves." That is the most charitable interpretation which can be placed upon the policy they pursued after the occupation of the town. I do not propose to narrate again in detail the ghastly story of the Tripoli massacres. Those who care to refresh their memories on the subject may be referred to Mr. McCullagh's book, and to the contemporary reports which appeared in the British, Austrian, Italian, French and German Press. But the bare facts may be recalled.

On the outskirts of Tripoli town is a fertile oasis. It goes by the name of the Mechiya and is several square miles in extent. It consists, or rather consisted, of a wide and scattered belt of palm trees, among which nestled many a beautiful Arab home, where the wealthier inhabitants of the town resided, embowered in gardens, luxuriating in myrtles, oleanders, and oranges. The Italian troops, marching through this oasis on October 23, were attacked in front by the Turks and in the rear by a force of Arabs. They lost heavily. There appears to be no doubt that the Arab tribesmen who participated in the fight were not the actual residents of the oasis, but formed part of the Turkish force. It is possible that a few of their countrymen within the oasis assisted them, but this view is not, I believe, now held by Italians who, at a later date, impartially investigated the evidence. Alleging "treachery," the Italian command decreed a "purge" of the oasis. This process lasted several days and was commendably thorough, so thorough, indeed, that the Italian military authorities adopted the most drastic steps to prevent the facts from reaching the outer world. For three days the oasis was given over to massacre in wholesale and detail. Some 4,000 men, women and children perished in the course of it—the vast bulk of whom were certainly innocent of any participation whatever in the Italian defeat. They were murdered in the streets, in their houses, farms, gardens and, according to a peculiarly horrible narrative by a British officer serving with the Turkish forces, in a mosque, where several hundred women and children had taken refuge. Thousands more were deported by sea. All the newspaper correspondents were in agreement as to the main facts. Englishmen and Americans united with Frenchmen, Austrians and Germans in indignantly censuring them. Several of them handed in their official papers to the Italian commander-in-chief by way of protest. The feelings of these eye-witnesses may be gathered by the following brief expressions culled from a copious literature:

> Tripoli has been the scene of one of the reddest dramas in the history of wars. It was a week of atrocities, a mad rush of assassins, a hecatomb of aged people, women and children—executions in groups. (Correspondent of *Excelsior*, Paris).
>
> A perfect nightmare of horror . . . a veritable carnival of carnage. (Correspondent of the *Daily Express*).
>
> We must have passed the bodies of over one hundred persons on this one high road, and as similar scenes were enacted throughout the length and breadth of the oasis, some estimate of the numbers of innocent men, women, and children who were butchered, doubtless with many who were guilty of attacking the Italian troops in the rear, may be appreciated. (From the statement signed, at the request of the British Consul at Tripoli, by the representative of *Reuter's Agency*, of the *Morning Post* and of the *Daily Mirror*).
>
> The Italians having set themselves to cow the Arabs, the floodgates of blood and lust were opened. . . . One hardly knows to what limits the elasticity of the phrase "military exigencies" will be stretched in the 20th century. (Correspondent of the *Times*.)
>
> Parties of soldiers penetrated every portion of the oasis, shooting indiscriminately all whom they met without trial, without appeal. (*Reuter's* Correspondent).
>
> For three days the butchery went on. . . Cripples and blind beggars have been deliberately shot; sick people whose houses were burned were left on the ground and refused even a drop of water. The Arab quarter was over-run by crazy soldiers armed with revolvers, who were shooting every Arab man and woman they met. (Mr. Francis McCullagh, Correspondent for the *Daily News*, *Westminster Gazette*, and *New York World*).

Mr. McCullagh afterwards lectured in London, supported by some of his brother correspondents, and his book is the best and fullest account of these horrible deeds—" pacification by depopulation," as Mr. Abbott terms it. The correspondents of the Austrian and German papers expressed themselves with equal vigour. At Benghasi the Italian military authorities expelled the correspondents in a body as the result of the *Figaro* correspondent's protest against the bombardment of that place. The Italian Government endeavoured to minimise what had been done, and several tame correspondents were sent out from England, after the event, to whitewash the Italian command. One Italian paper, the Turin *Stampa*, gave its readers the truth at the time. Later on the admissions of Italian soldiers in letters to their relatives, which far exceeded in picturesque details of horror the accounts sent from the newspaper men, were collected and published by Signor Ghisleri in his pamphlet, " The Libyan War and the Law of Nations."

So far as Turkey was concerned the war went on for a year, when it was brought to an end by the Treaty of Ouchy (October 18, 1912) by the terms of which the Turkish Government undertook to withdraw its troops, leaving Italy in nominal possession. At that time Italian control did not extend more than six miles into the interior from any part of a coast-line of about 200 miles held by Italian troops; and the war was estimated to have cost forty million sterling. Several fierce engagements took place with the Senussi in 1913, and when the Great War broke out Italy's hold over Tripoli was not much more effective than when the last Turkish soldier departed two years before. According to reports which have reached me recently, the area of Italian occupation is even more restricted to-day.

BIBLIOGRAPHY.

"The Life of Sir Charles Dilke." Gwynne & Tuckwell. (Murray).
" The Memoirs of Francesco Crispi." (Hodder & Stoughton).
" Géographie Universelle." (Réclus).
" The Turco-Italian War and its Problems." Barclay. (Constable).
"Italy's War for a Desert." McCullagh.
Documents extracted from the Austrian State archives [*Pribram*].
Documents extracted from the Tsardom's archives [*Pravda*].

C—EPISODES IN CAPITALISTIC EXPLOITATION

FOREWORD

We have now to record the operations of a System which Conan Doyle has described as the "greatest crime in all history"; Sir Sidney Olivier as "an inversion of the old Slave-Trade"; the British Primate as a matter "far transcending all questions of contemporary politics"; and a British Foreign Secretary as "bondage under the most barbarous and inhuman conditions, maintained for mercenary motives of the most selfish character." These are quotations taken from a mass of similar utterances. It would be an easy matter to fill an entire volume with similar denunciations by men of many countries and of all classes and professions, which resounded in Legislative Chambers, from platform, pulpit, and throughout the world's Press for over a decade. And it is undeniable that all the misdeeds of Europeans in Africa since the abolition of the over-sea slave trade, pale into insignificance when compared with the tragedy of the Congo. Indeed, no comparison is possible as regards scale, motive, and duration of time alike.

There is much that is removed from the merely covetous in the ambitions of statesmen to extend their country's *dominion* over alien peoples and territory, and in the imperialistic impulses of nations from which statesmen derive the necessary support for their actions. A restricted section of the community may, and does, benefit pecuniarily, but lucre is not usually the originating influence.

The clash between civilised and uncivilised man for *possession of the soil* may lead to injustice and cruelty which a wider vision would recognise as short-sighted and unnecessary, and a wise statesmanship avoid. But the driving forces are those of instinctive and uncontrollable racial movements.

No such considerations apply in the case of the Congo. There, the motive from first to last was despicably sordid. Whatever may have been King Leopold's original purpose in seeking to acquire a vast African demesne, the acquisition of wealth and of power through its systematised pillage soon became his fixed design. The capitalists he gathered round him and who shared his spoils never had any other. The extension of this System to the French Congo was the result of a combination of circumstances. Venality in French political circles made its extension possible. Once introduced, a vested interest was created which proved too strong for every successive Minister who spent a precarious and short-lived tenure at the Colonial Ministry, and which gradually obtained entire mastery over administrative policy. This can be doubted only by those who are unaware of the part which *la haute finance* plays in French internal politics.

FOREWORD

and who are unacquainted with the evidence of it in this particular case. When indications of the inevitable consequences of the System began to filter through, and inspired some generous minds—with which France abounds—to indignant protest, numerous causes combined to defeat these efforts and to perpetuate the evil. This will be made clear to the reader as the narrative proceeds.

Let us not lose sight of the following point, which is of capital importance in considering the Congo "System." The barbarities which disgrace the culmination of impolicy and wrong, and which are familiar to us in the story of German South-West Africa, of Southern Rhodesia, of Tripoli, and so many others—these are episodical, temporary. They do not represent a permanent state of affairs. Once the recalcitrant African community has been defeated and "punished," there is no longer any intelligent reason for continuing the killing process. On the contrary, the utilitarian motive of preservation steps in. The interest of the conqueror is to conserve—for no African land is of use to the white man without black labour. Injustice, cruelty—these may persist. But self-interest stops short at destruction. The purpose in hand has the character of permanence—whether the object be white settlement or political control.

But the motives and circumstances operating in the Congo differed absolutely in those vital respects. The beneficiaries aimed at no work of permanence, no constructive national task. They had no enduring interest in the Congo. Their one and only object was to get as much indiarubber out of it as they could in the shortest possible time, and to inflate their rubber shares on the stock exchange. And a *perennial* state of warfare all over the Congo was necessary to the accomplishment of that object, because there was no finality in the demand. It was incessant. An act of political submission after the usual massacre of unarmed—in the modern sense—men by armed men did not suffice. The community, clan or tribe, must produce indiarubber and *continue* to produce it, and must be fought and fought and fought again, tortured through its women, deprived of homesteads and foodstuffs; until broken, hunted, starving, fugitive, despairing, every capacity to resist demands, however outrageous, every shred of self-respect, had vanished. For *twenty years* in the Congo Free State, for *ten years* (at least) in the French Congo this process continued, its victims being numbered by *millions*.

What I desire to emphasise in these introductory lines is the importance of the System itself, and of the claims upon which it is based, being thoroughly grasped by the public. In the latter years of the Congo Reform movement they had become well understood, and

FOREWORD

people had seized hold of the essential fact that the real issue was not the saturnalia of atrocity raging in the Congo forests, but the reason of it, viz : The avowed principles upon which King Leopold's administration in the Congo Free State, and the French Government's administration in the French Congo were based, and officially defended by the Belgian and French Governments and by a cohort of international lawyers. It had become clear that in those principles, which differentiated radically and completely from the principles governing the exercise of political power by European Governments in every part of tropical Africa, including the French dependencies themselves, was involved the future of the black man and the future character of European policy in Africa; that if they prevailed, if the contagion spread, the future of Africa was a future of slavery imposed in the interests of European capitalism, degrading by its accompanying and resultant effects the whole political life of Europe, and owing to its nature, calculated rapidly to destroy the African race, thereby sterilising the natural resources of the Dark Continent.

There is need for this appeal. The vividness of the conviction that an issue of transcendental potency, a something elemental, going right down to the roots of human morality, was at stake in the Congo controversy, faded with the eventual success which attended the Reform movement so far as the Congo Free State was concerned. But although that final success was registered no further back in point of time than the spring of 1913, humanity has gone through such convulsions since then, the thinking mind has been so wholly turned from its normal functional methods, that pre-war events have a tendency to appear vague and shadowy, dim ghosts of some ancient epoch. Things are forgotten, or but half remembered. And, too, the peoples of Europe have for the past four and a half years been so fed with lies; history has been so cynically falsified to serve the momentary interest of Governments; changes so revolutionary in the structure of European policy and sociology have occurred; misery so profound and loss of life on so huge a scale have eventuated—that the collective reasoning power has got out of focus. It is at such times of cataclysmic upheaval that the dark forces in the nations see their opportunity, and if public opinion be not vigilant, make haste to use it.

There is a movement on foot to apply to British tropical Africa the self-same policy, based upon the self-same principles, which decimated and ruined the Congo. The motive behind it is identical. It is being astutely engineered, sophistically urged, presented in a new garb. It is a real danger, for it is supported by great wealth and also by democratic influences, either suborned, or, as one would prefer to believe, misled by ignorance.

CHAPTER IX.

THE STORY OF THE CONGO FREE STATE.

Botofi bo le iwa—"Rubber is death" (a native proverb current in the Upper Congo when the atrocities were at their height).

I do not propose to narrate here the European history of the Congo Free State. There is an abundant literature on that subject. I shall confine myself as far as practicable to describing the system of exploitation set up in the Congo basin and maintained therein from 1891 to 1911; and its effects upon native life. I am conscious of the difficulty of the task. It is no easy matter to compress in a few pages in such a way as to leave an indelible impression upon the reader's mind, the record of twenty years' continuous warfare upon native peoples. Nor is it easy to convey a sense of the *immensity* of the drama of which the Congo has been the scene.

The Congo Free State—known since August, 1908, as the Belgian Congo—is roughly one million square miles in extent. When Stanley discovered the course of the Congo and observed its densely-populated river banks, he formed the, doubtless very much exaggerated, estimate that the total population amounted to forty millions. In the years that followed, when the country had been explored in every direction by travellers of divers nationalities, estimates varied between twenty and thirty millions. No estimate fell below twenty millions. In 1911 an official census was taken. It was not published in Belgium, but was reported in one of the British Consular dispatches. *It revealed that only eight and a half million people were left.* The Congo system lasted for the best part of twenty years. The loss of life can never be known with even approximate exactitude. But data, extending over successive periods, are procurable in respect of a number of regions, and a careful study of these suggests that a figure of ten million victims would be a very conservative estimate.

In considering the story which follows, it should be borne in mind that the facts concerning the Congo methods of administration took many years to establish, and still longer to become known and appreciated. The truth was cleverly concealed, and much laborious effort was required to tear aside one by one the wrappings which veiled it from the gaze of men. It must also be remembered that direct evidence from the Congo—in an accessible form—was rare and spasmodic for a considerable time. It only became abundant after 1903.

In 1884 the "International African Association," founded by Leopold II., King of the Belgians, "for the purpose of promoting the civilisation and commerce of Africa and for other human and benevolent purposes," was recognised as a friendly Government by the Powers assembled at the Great West African Conference held at Berlin. Its claim to recognition, as such, was based upon treaties of amity and friendship which its agents had contracted with native rulers in the Congo. Foreigners would be guaranteed the free exercise of their religion, and freedom of commerce, industry and navigation. Everything possible would be done to prevent the Slave trade and slavery. Formal and collective recognition was granted on these assurances, and the Congo "Act" of the Conference laid down that the trade of all nations should enjoy "complete freedom"; that no Power exercising sovereign rights in the Congo basin should grant therein "a monopoly or favour of any kind in matters of trade," and that Powers exercising such rights should "bind themselves to watch over the preservation of the native tribes." The International African Association blossomed out into the "Congo Free State." King Leopold declared himself its Sovereign, having obtained the consent of the Belgian Chamber to the "fusion of the two crowns." He thus fulfilled in his person two distinct functions, viz.: that of constitutional Monarch of Belgium, and that of Sovereign of the Congo Free State, unfettered in his latter capacity save by the limitations of the Congo "Act" and the separate agreements concluded between the International African Association and the signatory Powers, among them Great Britain.

. . . .

Realisation of a great human tragedy is vivid and historically enduring in the measure in which we are able to conjure up a mental vision of its victims, their circumstances and surroundings. This is especially required when the victims belong to a race whose skin is not white. We Europeans do not find it easy to understand that despite differences of colour, climate, and environment, the main channels along which travel the twin emotions of suffering and joy, are much the same in all races and peoples. Emotions are deeper, more sensitised with civilised man than is the case with uncivilised man: but the difference is only one of degree.

Roughly speaking, the region drained by the Congo and its affluents is, except in the extreme south-east, one huge forest bisected by innumerable waterways, and broken here and there with open spaces. Before the main river flings itself into the sea after traversing half Africa, its course is interrupted by a long series of cataracts, rendering navigation impossible. This natural obstacle had always hindered communication between the lower Congo and the vast regions of the interior, until Belgian enterprise turned it by constructing a railway round them. Nevertheless, a brisk commercial intercourse between the upper Congo and the outer world had grown up since the disappearance of the oversea slave trade. There were three principal intermediary agents to this trade: the European merchant settled in the lower river; the Ba-Congo (i.e., lower Congo) people, who acted as go-betweens, and the Batekes, settled about Stanley Pool at the head of the cataracts, who acted as middlemen for all the up-river tribes. The Ba-Congo carried goods up the line of cataracts from the lower river to Stanley Pool, and brought down the produce from the Batekes. The ramifications of this commercial intercourse penetrated to great distances, and native tribes as far inland as the Aruwimi—over 2,000 miles from the sea—were eager purchasers of the white man's goods before they had ever seen a white man's face. The chief article of import was cloth, which was ardently coveted; after cloth came satin strips, kettles, red baize, umbrellas, brass rods, iron cooking pots, pipes, looking glasses, rough knives, beads, snuff boxes, muskets, and powder. In exchange for these articles the natives bartered red-wood, camwood powder (a crimson cosmetic), wax, ivory, tin, copper, lead, and palm oil—to which, in latter years, was added india-rubber, when the demand for that article developed in

Europe, and when, in an evil hour, it was discovered that the Congo was a great natural rubber preserve. I have emphasised this early commercial intercourse between the peoples of the Congo and their European clients because it is, in a measure, the keynote of the story. M. A. J. Wauters, the foremost Belgian historian of the Congo, wrote about that time:

> Trade is the dominant characteristic of all these peoples. They are warriors only for defence, agriculturists only for their own needs. They are not pastoral. They are one and all *traders*, and it is trade that will redeem them. They welcome and invite those who promise them protection in order to trade freely and in safety.

It is very difficult for anyone who has not experienced in his person the sensations of the tropical African forest to realise the tremendous handicaps which man has to contend against whose lot is cast beneath its sombre shades; the extent to which nature, there seen in her most titanic and ruthless moods, presses upon man; the intellectual disabilities against which man must needs constantly struggle not to sink to the level of the brute; the incessant combat to preserve life and secure nourishment. Communities living in this environment who prove themselves capable of systematic agriculture and of industry; who are found to be possessed of keen commercial instincts; who are quick at learning, deft at working iron and copper, able to weave cloths of real artistic design; these are communities full of promise in which the divine spark burns brightly. To destroy these activities; to reduce all the varied, and picturesque, and stimulating episodes in savage life to a dull routine of endless toil for uncomprehended ends; to dislocate social ties and disrupt social institutions; to stifle nascent desires and crush mental development; to graft upon primitive passions the annihilating evils of scientific slavery, and the bestial imaginings of civilised man, unrestrained by convention or law; in fine, to kill the soul in a people— this is a crime which transcends physical murder. And this crime it was, which, for twenty dreadful years, white men perpetrated upon the Congo natives.

The Congo man, whom Stanley and the explorers of his epoch revealed to Europe, was "natural man," with natural man's vices and virtues. Europe heard much of the latter and comparatively little of the former until Leopold II., forced to defend the character of his

THE STORY OF THE CONGO FREE STATE 113

administration before the bar of public opinion, found a convenient weapon in the shortcomings, real and alleged, of the peoples he was oppressing. Cannibalism and human sacrifice were endemic in some parts of the Congo basin, as in other parts of Africa. They were made much of by the defenders of the Leopoldian System. Probably no branch of the human family has not indulged at some time or another in these practices, and, not infrequently, after attaining a degree of culture to which the terribly handicapped dwellers in the forest belt of equatorial Africa never attained. The policy of the Congo Free State Government, at any rate in the earlier years, tended rather to encourage cannibalism than otherwise. A comparison of the literature which preceded the creation of the " Congo Free State " and which followed it until its Sovereign patented his " red-rubber " slavery, with the literature which from that time onwards professed to give a veracious picture of the inhabitants of the country, forms instructive matter for reflection. When there was no object in painting a false picture, we find travellers and residents of all nationalities laying stress upon the physical vigour, the commercial aptitude, and the numerical importance of the aboriginal peoples. Undesirable traits were not ignored, but they retained their proper perspective in the general presentation.

Particular emphasis was laid upon the keen commercial proclivities of the Congo peoples, which were rightly regarded as indicating a high standard of intelligence. Stanley was particularly eloquent on this theme. Here is one of the many striking passages in which he describes their acuteness of perception in handling European merchandise:

> This was the populous district of Irebu, the home of the champion traders on the Upper Congo, rivalled only in enterprise by Ubanghi on the right bank. . . It was, in fact, a Venice of the Congo, seated in the pride of its great numbers between the dark waters of the Lukangu and the deep, brown channels of the parent stream. . . These people were really acquainted with many lands and tribes on the Upper Congo. From Stanley Pool to Upoto, a distance of 6,000 miles, they knew every landing place on the river banks. All the ups and downs of savage life, all the profits and losses derived from barter, all the diplomatic arts used by tactful savages, were as well-known to them as the Roman alphabet to us. They knew the varied length of "sina" ("long" of cloth), the number of "matakos" (brass rods) they were worth, whether of Savelish, Florentine, unbleached domestic, twill, stripe, ticking, blue and white baft; the value of beads

per 1,000 strings, as compared with the uncut pieces of sheeting, or kegs of gunpowder, or flint-lock muskets, short and long. They could tell, by poising on the arm, what profit on an ivory tusk purchased at Langa-Langa, would be derived by sale at Stanley Pool. No wonder that all this commercial knowledge had left its traces on their faces; indeed it is the same as in your own cities in Europe. . . . It is the same in Africa, more especially on the Congo, where the people are so devoted to trade.

The "Venice of the Congo" has long since disappeared, and the "champion traders of the Congo" have perished miserably.

But this European trade was, after all, but a very small affair in the lives of the Congo peoples as a whole. Their own internal trade, industries, and avocations filled up most of their time. Their external trade intercourse, through a whole series of intermediaries, with the working classes of Europe, only affected a microscopic portion of the vast territory in which they dwelt. There is a copious literature enabling us to form an accurate estimate of the daily life of these promising races. We read of innumerable centres of population varying from 5,000 to 40,000; of settlements extending for hundreds of miles along the river banks; of communities of professional fishermen; others making a speciality of canoe building and fashioning brass-bound paddles; others proficient in pottery, basket-making, net-weaving, cane-splitting, carving wooden handles for hoes. We are shown a busy people manufacturing salt from the ashes of certain river reeds, and beer made from malted maize; making rat-traps and twine; digging and smelting iron; repairing thatch-roofed dwellings; turning out weapons for hunting and for war, often of singularly beautiful shape, the handles of battle-axes and knives tastefully and richly ornamented; weaving the fibres of various plants into mats and handsome clothes of raised pile, dyed and designed with remarkable artistic instinct. The village forge is everywhere to be seen; sometimes the tannery. We are shown towns and villages, surrounded with plantations—on land hardly won from the forest—of sugar-cane, maize, ground nuts, bananas, plantains, and manioca in variety; tobacco, many species of vegetables such as sweet potatoes tomatoes, vegetable marrows, "as finely kept as in Flanders," writes one enthusiastic Belgian explorer. "If civilisation," exclaims a French expert observer, "were measured by the number of vegetable conquests, these

THE STORY OF THE CONGO FREE STATE 115

people would rank amongst the most advanced in Africa." Agriculturists, artisans, fishermen, merchants, all plying their various trades, interchanging their products, travelling long distances. " The natives must be imbued with great enterprise," writes another Belgian traveller, " to explain their lengthy business travels and their opening of relations with distant tribes. The inhabitants of the Upper Congo have never seen the Coast. The trading tribes travel 120 to 150 miles north and south of their homes and exchange their produce with other tribes, who, in turn, sell it to others."

The prevalence of well defined customs in the tenure of land, of established institutions and forms of government among the Congo peoples was not only never questioned, it was repeatedly and emphatically affirmed. Indeed, the existence of an indigenous polity all over the Congo formed the basis of justification on which King Leopold relied in claiming recognition for his Congo enterprise from the great Powers. The " 450 Treaties " which were flourished in the face of the world were treaties with " legitimate " rulers, holding land in trust for their respective communities, by undisturbed occupation, by " long ages of succession." Early explorers of the Congo : Catholic and Protestant missionaries with long years of experience in different parts of the territory; British consuls, indeed, a whole host of witnesses could be cited in support of the jealous regard of the native population for their rights in land.

It was only after the royal decrees had swept away these rights that the Congo natives were presented to the world by the official defenders of the Congo Free State and by the Belgian Ministers who made themselves its accomplices, as little better than animals, with no conception of land tenure or tribal government, no commercial instincts, no industrial pursuits, " entitled," as a Belgian Premier felt no shame in declaring, "to nothing."

Such in brief was the country in which, such the people among whom, modern capitalistic finance in the hands of a European King and his bodyguard of satellites attained the climax of its destructive potency.

. . . . . .

From 1891 until 1912, the paramount object of European rule in the Congo was the pillaging of its natural wealth to enrich private interests in Belgium. To achieve this end a specific, well-defined System was thought out in Brussels and applied on the Congo. Its essential features were known to the Belgian Government from 1898 onwards. They were defended in principle, and their effects denied, by successive Belgian Ministries, some of whose members were actively concerned in the working of the System, and even personal beneficiaries from it, for twelve years; although the Belgian Government did not govern the Congo, and, while apologising for and acclaiming the methods of administration there pursued, washed its hands of responsibility for the actions of what it termed "a foreign State." The System had its European side and its African side. In Europe—the formulation of a Policy which should base itself upon the claim of sovereign right and be expounded in decrees, promulgations, and *pièces justificatives*; in whose support should be enlisted the constitutional machinery of Belgium, including the diplomatic and consular representatives of Belgium in foreign countries, buttressed by a body of international legal authorities well remunerated for the purpose. In Africa—the execution of that Policy.

The Policy was quite simple. Native rights in land were deemed to be confined to the actual sites of the town or village, and the areas under food cultivation around them. Beyond those areas no such rights would be admitted. The land was "vacant," *i.e.*, without owners. Consequently the "State" was owner. The "State" was Leopold II., not in his capacity of constitutional Monarch of Belgium, but as Sovereign of the "Congo Free State." Native rights in nine-tenths of the Congo territory being thus declared non-existent, it followed that the native population had no proprietary right in the plants and trees growing upon that territory, and which yielded rubber, resins, oils, dyes, etc.: no right, in short, to anything animal, vegetable, or mineral which the land contained. In making use of the produce of the land, either for internal or external trade or internal industry and social requirements, the native population would thus obviously be making use of that which did not belong to it, but which belonged to the "State," *i.e.*, Leopold II. It followed logically that any third person— European or other—acquiring, or attempting to acquire, such produce from the native population by purchase, in exchange for corresponding goods or services, would

THE STORY OF THE CONGO FREE STATE 117

be guilty of robbery, or attempted robbery, of "State property." A "State" required revenue. Revenue implied taxation. The only articles in the Congo territory capable of producing revenue were the ivory, the rubber, the resinous gums and oils; which had become the property of the "State." The only medium through which these articles could be gathered, prepared and exported to Europe—where they would be sold and converted into revenue—was native labour. Native labour would be called upon to furnish those articles in the name of "taxation." Richard Harding Davis, the American traveller, has given colloquial expression to this Policy, whose effects on the spot he had the opportunity of studying in 1908:

> To me the fact of greatest interest about the Congo is that it is owned, and the twenty millions of people who inhabit it are owned, by one man. The land and its people are his private property. I am not trying to say that he governs the Congo. He does govern it, but that in itself would not be of interest. His claim is that he owns it. . . . It does not sound like anything we have heard since the days and the ways of Pharoah. . . . That in the Congo he has killed trade and made the produce of the land his own; that of the natives he did not kill he has made slaves is what to-day gives the Congo its chief interest.

In the nature of the case, the execution of this Policy took some years before it could become really effective and systematic. The process called for some ingenuity and a certain breadth of vision, for a good many issues were involved. In the first place, the notion that an economic relationship existed between the European and the Congo native, *that the native had anything to sell*, must be thoroughly stamped out. Regulations were issued forbidding the natives to sell rubber or ivory to European merchants, and threatening the latter with prosecution if they bought these articles from the natives. In the second place, every official in the country had to be made a partner in the business of getting rubber and ivory out of the natives in the guise of "taxation." Circulars, which remained secret for many years, were sent out, to the effect that the paramount duty of Officials was to make their districts yield the greatest possible quantity of these articles; promotion would be reckoned on that basis. As a further stimulus to "energetic action" a system of sliding-scale bonuses was elaborated, whereby the less the native was "paid" for his *labour* in producing these articles of "taxation," *i.e.*, the lower the outlay in obtaining them, the higher was the Official's commission. Thus if the outlay amounted to 70 *centimes* per *kilo* (2 lbs.) of rubber, the Official got 4 *centimes* commission *per kilo*; but he got 15 *centimes per kilo* if the outlay was only 30 *centimes*. In the third place, outside financiers had to be called in to share in the loot, otherwise the new Policy would be unable to weather the storm. "Concessionaire" Companies were created to which the King farmed out a large proportion of the total territory, retaining half the shares in each venture. These privileges were granted to business men, bankers, and others with whom the King thought it necessary to compound. They floated their companies on the stock exchange. The shares rose rapidly, so rapidly that they became negotiable in tenths of a share, and were largely taken up by the Belgian public. The " tip " was passed round among influential Belgian public men and journalists. By these means a public vested interest of a somewhat extensive character was created throughout Belgium which could be relied upon to support the King's " System " should it ever be challenged by " pestilent philanthropists." The more lucrative the profits and dividends—and both attained in due course to fabulous dimensions—the louder, it might be assumed, would an outraged patriotism protest against any agitation directed to reducing them. The network of corruption thus spread over Belgium was not confined to that country. Financiers, journalists, politicians, even Ministers in some other countries were placed from time to time in the position of benefiting by inside knowledge of the Congo share-markets. Their favour was thus purchased, and was not negligible as a diplomatic asset.

These various measures at the European end were comparatively easy. The problem of dealing with the natives themselves was more complex. A native army was the pre-requisite. The five years which preceded the Edicts of 1891-2 were employed in raising the nucleus of a force of 5,000. It was successively increased to nearly 20,000 apart from the many thousands of " irregulars " employed by the Concessionaire Companies. This force was amply sufficient for the purpose, for a single native soldier armed with a rifle and with a plentiful supply of

THE STORY OF THE CONGO FREE STATE 119

ball cartridge can terrorise a whole village. The same system of promotion and reward would apply to the native soldier as to the Official—the more rubber from the village, the greater the prospect of having a completely free hand to loot and rape. A systematic warfare upon the women and children would prove an excellent means of pressure. They would be converted into "hostages" for the good behaviour, in rubber collecting, of the men. "Hostage houses" would become an institution in the Congo. But in certain parts of the Congo the rubber-vine did not grow. This peculiarity of nature was, in one way, all to the good. For the army of Officials and native soldiers, with their wives, and concubines, and camp-followers generally, required feeding. The non-rubber producing districts should feed them. Fishing tribes would be "taxed" in fish; agricultural tribes in foodstuffs. In this case, too, the women and children would answer for the men. Frequent military expeditions would probably be an unfortunate necessity. Such expeditions would demand in every case hundreds of carriers for the transport of loads, ammunition, and general impedimenta. Here, again, was an excellent school in which this idle people could learn the dignity of labour. The whole territory would thus become a busy hive of human activities, continuously and usefully engaged for the benefit of the "owners" of the soil thousands of miles away, and their crowned Head, whose intention, proclaimed on repeated occasions to an admiring world, was the "moral and material regeneration" of the natives of the Congo.

Such was the Leopoldian "System," briefly epitomised. It was conceived by a master brain.

. . . . . .

Fighting began with the riverain tribes on the main river, which the merchants abandoned after a struggle with the King, not without placing on record a weighty protest, supported by several leading Belgian statesmen, including the Belgian representative at the Berlin Conference of 1884, and by the Governor-General, who resigned:

> To deny to the natives the right to sell ivory and rubber produced by the forests and plains belonging to their tribes, which forests and plains form part of their hereditary natal soil, and in which they have traded from time immemorial, is a veritable violation of natural rights.

The natives naturally refused to yield up their ivory stocks; to indulge in the perils of hunting the elephant:

to carry out the arduous task of tapping the rubber vines, gathering the flowing *latex* in calabashes, drying it, preparing it, reducing it generally to a marketable condition, and transporting it either by land or water, often for long distances; unless they received, as before, the value of their produce at current market rates. To be suddenly told that this labour must no longer be regarded as a voluntary act on their part, but was required of them, and would be periodically required of them; to be further told that its yield must be handed over as a " tax " or tribute; that they would get no value for the produce itself because their property in it was not recognised, and only such " payment " for their labour as the recipients of the " tax " might arbitrarily determine: this was tantamount to informing the native population inhabiting the part of the Congo which had been in trade relationship with Europeans, either directly or indirectly, from time immemorial, that it was in future to be robbed and enslaved. It refused to submit to the process. Nor could similar demands fail to meet with a similar resistance, where European trade had not penetrated. In *every* part of the Congo, the natives were perfectly well aware that ivory had an intrinsic value. In such parts of the Congo where the natives had not become acquainted with the fact that rubber was a marketable commodity, the people appear to have acquiesced, unwillingly enough, with the requisitions when first imposed, hoping that the white man would presently go away and leave them in peace. But when they saw that the white man was insatiable, that they could only carry out his orders by neglecting their farms and dislocating their whole social life, when they found men of strange tribes armed with guns permanently stationed in their villages, interfering with their women and usurping the position and functions of their own chiefs and elders—they, too, rose.

Evidence of the atrocious incidents which characterised the enforcement of the " system " would fill many volumes. The earliest in date, but not in time of publication, are in reports of the Belgian and other merchants from the main river, describing the period immediately following the edicts inaugurating the new " System." In less than twelve months the whole country was transformed. It was as though a tornado had torn across it and destroyed everything in its passage. But the effects

THE STORY OF THE CONGO FREE STATE

were much more lasting than any natural phenomenon. Thriving communities had been transformed into scattered groups of panic-stricken folk: precipitated from active commercial prosperity and industrial life into utter barbarism.

> There is not an inhabited village left in four days' steaming through a country formerly so rich: to-day entirely ruined. . . . The villages are compelled to furnish so many kilos of rubber every week. . . . The soldiers sent out to get rubber and ivory are depopulating the country. They find that the quickest and cheapest method is to raid villages, seize prisoners, and have them redeemed afterwards for ivory.

The system thus inaugurated on the river banks was methodically pursued inland. *For twenty years* fighting became endemic all over the Congo.

. . . . . .

The judicial murder of an English trader by one of King Leopold's officials, the revelations in Captain Hinde's book of the feeding of King Leopold's armed auxiliaries with human flesh, and Glave's diary published in the *Century Magazine*, first called attention to what was going on. Sir Charles Dilke raised the matter in the House of Commons (1897). The appalling revelations of the Swedish missionary Sjoblöm followed shortly afterwards. He was the first to disclose the practice (which seemed incredible at the time, but was later confirmed from many sources, and conclusively established) started by certain officials, requiring the native soldiers whom they sent out to "punish" recalcitrant villages, to bring in trophies of hands and the sexual organs of males to prove that they had duly performed their work. This mutilation of the dead as a system of check and tally rapidly spread through the rubber districts and developed, as it naturally would do, into the mutilation of the living.

Here are short extracts on this particular theme from a series of letters by the American missionary Mr. Clark, referring to the district in which he laboured:

> It is blood-curdling to see them (the soldiers) returning with hands of the slain, and to find the hands of young children amongst the bigger ones evidencing their bravery. . . . The rubber from this district has cost hundreds of lives, and the scenes I have witnessed, while unable to help the oppressed, have been almost enough to make me wish I were dead. . . .

This rubber traffic is steeped in blood, and if the natives were to rise and sweep every white person on the Upper Congo into eternity, there would still be left a fearful balance to their credit.

Some of the wretched Europeans employed by the Concessionaire Companies wrote home boasting of their exploits. Their letters found their way into the papers. One such " agent " confessed to have " killed " 150 men, cut off 60 hands, crucified women and children," and hung the remains of mutilated men on the village fence. A simulachre of judicial repression followed these embarrassing disclosures, and the Congo courts condemned the culprits to long terms of imprisonment which, of course they never served. In each case the defence was the same. They had acted under instructions from their superiors to get rubber by any and every means. Needless to say their " superiors " were not proceeded against.

While these abominations were taking place in the Congo, some of us were engaged in unravelling the mysteries of the Congo " System " at the European end. Investigation revealed such depths of infamy that it was difficult sometimes to believe that one was living in the opening years of the 20th Century. Finally, after three years sustained public effort, the whole question was brought before the House of Commons (May 1, 1903). All political parties united in demanding that the British Government should invite the signatory Powers of the Berlin Act to another International Conference. This the Government did. The chief cause of its failure to secure such a conference is given in the next chapter.

From that date onwards evidence from the Congo accumulated in ever-increasing volume. The era of the publication of the British consular reports (the earlier ones had been suppressed) began with Sir Roger Casement's detailed narrative, bracketed in the same White Book with Lord Cromer's scathing comments confined, however, to the centres of Congo Free State influence on the Nile. Sir Roger Casement, whose inquiries had not extended beyond the vicinity of the banks of a part of the main river, did not return to the Congo. His work of exposure was carried on over a long term of years, and prosecuted into almost every part of the Congo by his successors, Consuls Thesiger, Beak, Mitchell, Armstrong, etc.; by the Consular staff appointed

THE STORY OF THE CONGO FREE STATE 123

by the American Government; by the Commission which King Leopold was himself forced by public opinion to send out and whose evidence, but not whose report, damning even its whitewashing attenuations, he suppressed[1]; by the King of Italy's envoy, Dr. Baccari, who was dispatched on a special mission to the Congo owing to the bitter complaints and protests of Italian officers who had been induced to take up commissions in the King's African armies; by Protestant and Catholic missionaries. and by one or two Belgian officials like the courageous magistrate Lefranc.

The "Crown domain," the portion of the territory whose revenue (*i.e.*, whose ivory and rubber) the King kept for his own private uses, produced in the ten years 1896-1905, 11,354 tons of india-rubber, the profit upon which, at the comparatively low prices prevailing over that period of years and after deducting expenses, yielded £3,179,120. This leaves out of account the ivory, the particulars of which remained inaccessible. In this region fighting was incessant for years and the loss of life was immense. It was reckoned that in one district alone 6,000 natives were killed and mutilated every six months. The rubber was eventually worked out and the wretched remnants of the population were constrained to gather *copal* (gum exuding from certain trees) the whole year round. In the early nineties the territories of the "Crown domain" included some of the most densely-populated regions of the Congo, with many large and flourishing towns. The early travellers—Belgian, British and others—along the rivers which bisect it, spoke of the "dense masses" of natives who crowded its river banks, the prosperous, well-cared villages, the abundance of live-stock. In fifteen years it was reduced to a desert. Scrivener, who travelled through a considerable portion of it in 1903, and Murdoch four years later by another route, pursued their way for weeks on end without encountering a single human being, passing on every hand vestiges of a once abundant population, long miles of ruined, mouldering villages thickly strewn with skeletons, plantations merging again into "bush," bananas rotting in erstwhile groves that supplied the wants of these vanished communities, the silence of the tropical

[1] The evidence tendered before the Commission by the British and American missionaries was published in English and French by the Congo Reform Association.

forest broken only by the occasional trampling of the elephant and buffalo, the chatter of the white-maned monkeys, the scream of the grey parrot.

The *Abir* Concessionaire Company, whose managing council included the " Grand Master " of King Leopold's Belgian Court, made a net profit in six years of £720,000 on a paid-up capital of £9,280; and each share of a paid-up value of £4 6s. 6d. received in that period £335 in dividends. This company's shares were at one time freely speculated in at £900 to £1,000 per share. In this area the atrocities, incidental to the " system," attained proportions of Dantesque horror. The company enrolled thousands of natives, armed with rifles and cap-guns, to force the rubber output upon the general population. It kept some 10,000 natives *continually at work* all the year round collecting rubber, and some 10,000 men, women and children passed every year through its "hostage-houses." All the chiefs were gradually killed off, either outright or by the slower processes of confinement and starvation in the ' houses of detention," or by tortures which rival those inflicted upon the plantation slaves in the West Indies. When certain areas became denuded of rubber, the remaining male population was carried oft wholesale under escort and flung into another area not yet exhausted, their women handed over to the soldiers. This is but the bald framework of the picture.

The Concessionaire Company working the Kasai region, whose native peoples, once renowned above any other in the Congo for their "moral and physical beauty " (to quote a Belgian explorer) made a profit of £736,680 in four years on a paid-up capital of £40,200. The value of a single £10 share stood at one time as high as £640. At the time of the annexation (1908) the Kasai was producing 50 per cent. of the rubber from the Congo. Apart altogether from the " atrocities "—murder, mutilation, starvation in hostage houses, floggings to death, and all the horrible concomitants of the " System "—the general condition of the natives in that year, may be estimated from the following extracts from Consul Thesiger's report:

> The rubber tax was so heavy that the villages had no time to attend even to the necessities of life . . . the *capitas* (the Company's armed soldiers stationed in the villages) told me they had orders not to allow the natives to clear the ground for cultivation, to hunt, or to fish, as it took up time which should be spent in making rubber. Even so, in many cases the natives can

only comply with the demands made on them for rubber by utilising the labour of the women and children. In consequence, their huts are falling to ruin, their fields are uncultivated, and the people are short of food . . . and dying off . . . This district was formerly rich in corn, millet, and other foodstuffs. . . . now it is almost a desert.

This passage—and hundreds of others of a similar kind could be quoted from every part of the Congo—illustrates what has been, perhaps, the most fertile cause of depopulation, both in the Congo Free State, and in the French Congo (see next chapter): *i.e.*, depopulation by starvation. That, and the colossal infant mortality induced by the well-nigh inconceivable conditions to which native life was reduced in the Congo, far exceeded the actual massacres as determining factors in the disappearance of these people.

The above are but a few examples selected, more or less haphazard, of the Leopoldian " System " in its actual working. A similar system must yield similar results wherever it is enforced. If, for instance, the desires openly expressed by certain influential persons in this country were acceded to, viz.: that the oil-palm forests of Nigeria, which are of infinitely greater value than were the rubber forests of the Congo, should be declared the property of the British State; that the native population should be dispossessed of its ownership in those forests and of the oil and kernels which its labour produces from them, should be forbidden to sell their products to the European at their market value as it does at present and has for generations, and should be required to gather and prepare them as a " tax " demanded by the usurping and expropriating alien Government; precisely the same results would ensue. Nigeria would become another Congo. You cannot steal the land of the natives of tropical Africa, degrade them from the position of agriculturists and arboriculturists in their own right, lay claim to possession of their actual and potential wealth, destroy their purchasing power, deny them the right to buy and sell by denying their ownership in the natural or cultivated products of their own country, which their labour alone can make accessible to the outer world, and impose upon them the duty of harvesting their products for you as a " tax." You cannot do this, and thereby convert them into slaves of European capitalism, without the use of armed force, pitilessly, relentlessly and, above all, continuously applied. And the circumstances under which that force must be exercised in tropical Africa are such that its application *must* involve the destruction of the population, if only because it must be pursued in utter disregard of the natural needs and requirements of the native population, and at the cost of the complete annihilation of African society.

It is impossible to believe that any British Government will be wicked enough and stupid enough to lend ear to these appeals of an insensate egotism. But it is just as well to state with the utmost frankness what the policy that is urged would necessitate, if only that we may take the measure of the men who insult the nation by recommending it.

BIBLIOGRAPHY.

"White Books" (in particular Nos. 4 and 5, 1885; No. 5, 1894; No. 8, 1896; No. 1 and 7, 1904; No. 1, 1905; No. 1, 1906; No. 1, 1907; Nos. 1, 2, 3, 4, and 5, 1908; No. 2, 1909; No. 2, 1911; Nos. 1 and 2, 1912; Nos. 1 and 3, 1913).
"Belgian Parliamentary Debates."
"Congo Free State Bulletins and Budgets."
"Publications of the Congo Reform Association."
"Publications of the American Congo Reform Association."
"Publications of the French League for the Defence of the Congo Natives."
"Publications of the Swiss League"—for the same.
"Droit et Administration de l'etat Independant du Congo. Cattier."
"Etude sur la Situation de l'etat Independant du Congo. Cattier."
"L'etat Indépendant du Congo." Wauters.
"Le Mouvement Geographique."
"La Belgique et le Congo." Vandervelde.
"L'Annexion du Congo." Brunet.
"The Fall of the Congo Arabs." Hinde.
"Affairs of West Africa." E. D. Morel. (Heineman).
"King Leopold's Rule in Africa." *Idem*. (Heineman).
"Great Britain and the Congo." *Idem*. (Smith Elder).
"Red Rubber." *Idem*. (Fisher Unwin; Revised edition : National Labour Press, 1919).
"The Life of Sir Charles Dilke." Gwynne and Tuckwell. (Murray).

CHAPTER X.

THE STORY OF THE FRENCH CONGO.

Ruin and death . . . terrifying depopulation . . . . universal exodus . . . the continuous destruction of the population—purely and simply.—De Brazza.

In 1899 King Leopold planned what, after his initial triumph in hoodwinking public opinion fifteen years before, was the master-stroke of his African career. And he succeeded in carrying it out. He induced the French Government of the day by "scandalous, financial and political intrigues, bribery, corruption and cowardice," as a French author of repute remarks, to adopt and apply in the coterminous territory of the French Congo, the principles and the policy that he had inaugurated in the Congo Free State. Thenceforth the French Congo was ringed round by a fence of Franco-Belgian financial interests. His object in doing so was obvious. The Congo Reform movement in England was still weak and had aroused little or no echo abroad. But it was gathering in volume, and the Sovereign of the Congo State was uneasy. By persuading one of the great Powers to imitate his methods, he established a community of interest with its Government, thus enormously strengthening his position should it be severely assailed. He sought, indeed, to contaminate not only the French Congo, but the whole of the French West African dependencies and the German Kamerun also. His success in Kamerun was shortlived. The German Government granted two concessions to Belgo-German financial groups, but after about twelve months' experience, drastically restricted their privileges and refused to grant any more. The attempt to introduce the System into French West Africa, though supported from Paris, was defeated by the combined opposition of the high officials and of the powerful trading firms established there. M. Ballay, the Governor-General, bluntly described it as requiring for its enforcement "a soldier behind every producer," and set his face against it absolutely.

So far as the French Congo was concerned, circumstances played into the hands of King Leopold and his financial bodyguard. As in the Congo Free State, the bulk of the French Congo forests are full of rubber vines and trees. Emulation and envy were aroused in French colonial circles by the prodigious development in rubber exports from the Congo Free State. French finance was excited by the wild wave of speculation in Congo rubber shares which swept over Belgium, and by the prodigious profits of the great Belgian Concessionaire Companies. These results were contrasted with the conditions prevailing in the French Congo, which had long been the Cinderella of the French African dependencies, and where French commercial enterprise had been almost wholly lacking. What trade existed, and it was by no means inconsiderable, was confined to the maritime region and to the Ogowe basin. It had been largely built up by British firms, and was almost wholly in their hands, although there was plenty of room, even within that area, for dozens of French firms had they chosen to embark on the venture. The whole of the middle and upper French Congo was commercially untouched. King Leopold played his cards skilfully. The French press was flooded with articles contrasting the "prosperity" of the Congo Free State with the "stagnation" of the French Congo. Much pressure was brought to bear upon the French Government of the day. The King's personal friendship with a prominent politician conspicuously identified with the French "Colonial Party" was a useful asset. In due course the plunge was taken. Before the close of 1900 the whole territory of the French Congo had been parcelled out among forty financial corporations on a thirty years' charter. Belgian capital figured in most of them, and the men at the head of the Congo Free State corporations reappeared on the boards of many of them. With Belgian capital, Belgian methods, and Belgian agents to execute them, the "Belgianising" or, more justly, the Leopoldianising of the French Congo was, indeed, carried out in thoroughgoing fashion.

Other methods, other men. When these revolutionary changes were in their preliminary stage the necessity of getting rid of the then Governor of the dependency, De Brazza, was recognised and acted upon. De Brazza played so prominent a part in subsequent developments that his personality is woven into the story and demands brief reference. This naval officer of Brazilian descent and French naturalisation is an unique figure in modern African annals. For a quarter of a century, from 1874 to 1899, he toiled continuously and almost uninterruptedly for the political interests of his adopted country in this tropical region so deadly to white men. It was entirely owing to his labours that France was able to claim this vast territory as coming within her sphere of influence in the African Settlement of 1884. He possessed an extra- ordinary influence over the native mind. The type of political agent and administrator who carved bloody tracks through the " bush " he held in abhorrence. He travelled with no military retinue and, with few personal attendants. He never fired a shot against the natives, whose internal quarrels he healed, and by whom he was venerated as the " great white father " over an enormous area. For these simple and primitive forest dwellers, whose many qualities he discerned and appreciated, he possessed a real affection, and the sight of their agony and ruin after six years of frantic exploitation broke his heart.

The System imported into the French Congo being fundamentally identical with the Congo Free State original upon which it modelled itself, the inevitable consequences followed as a matter of course. French officialdom shrank at first from avowing the logical interpretation of its decrees. It was, however, soon compelled to do so owing to the legal resistance offered by the British firms in the Lower Congo to the proceed- ings of the representatives of the Concessionaire Companies. Having committed the initial and fatal error, the French Government and the local Administration in the French Congo found themselves involved deeper and deeper in the mire, until the French Congo became an almost exact replica of its neighbour.

The Concessionaire Companies acquired by their charters the sole right of *possession* of the negotiable products of the country. They became *de facto owners* of the rubber trees and vines within their respective concessions. This implied, of course, dispossession of the native. Dispossession of the native implied, in its turn, the immediate cessation of the act of purchase and sale—

otherwise trade—between the native population and
white men. Where such trade was non-existent no vocal
objection by third parties to the cardinal feature of the
system would arise, since there were no third parties to
raise it. It was otherwise where such trade had long
existed, *i.e.*, in the lower Congo, the portion of the
territory nearest the Coast-line. Some of the Europeans
engaged in it compounded with the Concessionaires and
cleared out of the country. To their infinite credit, the
British firms declined to do so. Their respective heads
were prominent men in the civic and commercial life of
Liverpool. One of them, Mr. John Holt, was one of the
foremost living authorities on West Africa, and a man of
very great personality and force of character. If he had
followed the dictates of his business interests he would
have allowed his firm to be bought out. But he realised
that something over and above material interests was
concerned; that a vital principle affecting his country's
Treaty rights, the interests of a helpless population, and
the sanctity of international law was in question. Thanks
to his influence, the British firms made a firm stand.
The moral strength of their position was unassailable.
They had been in the country for a quarter of a century.
Their enterprise furnished the local Administration with
a substantial portion of its revenue—in the seven years
preceding the introduction of the system they had paid
£112,000 in custom dues, patents, and licences. They
had always been on excellent terms with the French
officials, with whom they had co-operated in exploring
and opening up the country. They had received no
communication of any kind from the French Government suggesting that their presence in the dependency
was no longer desired. They took their stand upon the
rights of law-abiding Englishmen to equitable treatment,
and upon the clauses of an international Act—to which
their Government was a signatory. The struggle they
sustained for several years in the local Courts of the
dependency, and, subsequently, by public action in
which they were supported by all the important Chambers
of Commerce in the country, was of immeasurable value
in helping the wider public to understand the basic
iniquities of the Congo System. The wrong inflicted
upon them was ultimately acknowledged, and substantial
compensation was paid them by the French Government.
But the British Foreign Office could not be induced to

THE STORY OF THE FRENCH CONGO 131

take the wide view of the case which they themselves continuously urged: to treat it, *i.e.*, not as a matter of personal injustice, but primarily as an international issue involving consequences of profound international importance.

. . . . . .

"One idea dominates the system. All the products of the conceded territory, whatever they may be, are the property of the Concessionaire Company," thus ran the Decree which a Colonial Minister saw fit to promulgate as the result of the continuous litigation in the lower Congo Courts between British merchants and the Concessionaires. Thus officially guided, the Courts, which in several instances had rendered temporising or conflicting judgments, hastened to bring themselves into line with ministerial decisions. The Loango Court held that the Concessionaire Companies had "the exclusive right of collecting and exploiting the natural products of the soil." The Libreville Court proclaimed that "the rubber belongs to the Concessionaires, and not to the natives who gather it." This Decree and these judgments produced a painful effect among the few Frenchmen who knew what they portended. De Brazza came out of his retirement and wrote a letter to *Le Temps*:

> France—he said—has assumed a duty towards the native tribes. . . . We must not sacrifice them to the vain hope of immediate results by thoughtless measures of coercion. We should be committing a great mistake by enforcing . . . taxes upon the products of the soil. . . It would constitute a great blow to our dignity if such labour and such taxes were converted into a sort of draft-to-order in favour of the Concessionaires.

M. Cousin, a well-known authority on colonial questions, who had been a warm defender of the Concessionaire experiment, published a pamphlet, in which he declared that he had been mistaken. M. Fondère, another authority of repute, wrote an open letter to the Colonial Minister, in the course of which he said:

> The right to sell his products to whomsoever he may please cannot be denied to the native, because he has always possessed it. Moreover, it would be quite illusory to think of taking this right away from him. That could only be done by force of arms.

No consideration of the latter kind was likely to stand in his way. The years which followed were to witness the attempt to compel "by force of arms" some nine million African natives, or as many of that total who could be reached, to submit not only to be robbed, but to spend their *lives* in the extremely arduous and dangerous task of gathering and preparing india-rubber in the virgin forests, on behalf of a few wealthy financiers in Brussels, Paris and Antwerp.

The Concessionaires settled down to their work, and the local Administration, which under the concession decrees received a royalty of 15 per cent. upon the Companies' output, associated itself still more closely with the latter by establishing a direct tax payable in rubber, the proceeds of which were turned over to the Companies. The local Administration and the Concessionaires thus became partners in a common object, that of forcing as much rubber as possible out of the natives. In the lower part of the French Congo the effect was immediate. Here, as already explained, the native population had been traders with white men, directly and indirectly, for decades. To their bewilderment they found themselves suddenly faced with a demand for rubber as a "tax" from the Administration, and with a demand for rubber as by right divine from strange white men who claimed to OWN it, and claimed power to compel the real owners to collect it for whatever the former chose to pay. The trading stations where the natives had been wont to carry their produce and barter it—and haggle over the price, as the native knows so well how to do—they were forbidden to approach. The natives of the French Congo did what any other people would have done. They declined to be despoiled of their property and robbed of the fruits of their labours. The chiefs appealed to the authorities and asked what they had done to be so "punished." Appeals were in vain. Refusal to "work rubber" was met with attempted compulsion. The natives rose, with that absence of combination and with that virtual powerlessness in the face of modern weapons of offence which characterises the unhappy inhabitant of the equatorial forest. The first year of the new "System" closed amid scenes of chaos and destruction, with raiding bands armed by the Concessionaires, and punitive expeditions conducted by the Administration carrying fire and sword from one end of the country to the other. The work of twenty years had been undone in twelve months.

THE STORY OF THE FRENCH CONGO 133

In the upper French Congo, where European trade had not yet penetrated, the demand for rubber came with equal suddenness and was accompanied by the same results, but it was not until long afterwards that these results came to light. In Paris every effort was made to conceal the true state of affairs, and for three years the rubber saraband went on, a large quantity of that article finding its way to Bordeaux and Antwerp. As the new " System " took root, the *morale* of the Europeans involved in enforcing it followed the inevitable downward grade. Gradually the local Administration became demoralised from top to bottom. Reports from experienced officials of the old *régime* who, appalled at what was going on, communicated direct with the Colonial Office in Paris, were suppressed. The increasing vigour of the British agitation against the Congo Free State was an additional reason for keeping the truth from the French public. King Leopold's policy was bearing its fruits. The French Administration was committed to the hilt in a system of exploitation, which was being denounced in the Parliament and the Press of France's ally.

Up to this time specific information was lacking, although the air was full of unpleasant rumours. A bombshell had been dropped into the Concessionaire camp by the remarks of the reporter of the Colonial Budget for 1904. The Colonial Budget in France is presented every year to the Chamber in an elaborate report drawn up by a deputy who is appointed for the purpose. M. Dubief, the reporter for that year, vigorously condemned the new " System," declaring that " slavery " was its " indispensable corollary." He was smothered in an avalanche of abuse in the French and Belgian Press, and his indictment was not discussed in the Chamber.

But murder will out. In this case the murders were numbered by tens of thousands.

Early in 1905 an " indiscretion " was committed, and a whole batch of suppressed official reports were precipitated into the light of day. The French public was edified to learn that crimes and atrocities similar to those with which the world was becoming familiar in the Congo Free State were of every-day occurrence in the French Congo, and apparently, although as yet the connection was only vaguely understood, from the same causes.

They learned of floggings and burning of villages, of rape and mutilation, of natives being used as targets for revolver practice, and as human experiments to test the efficacy of dynamite cartridges; of " hostage-houses " in which men, women and children perished—and all this in connection with the procuring of india-rubber. The sensation was considerable. " Interpellations " in the Chamber were threatened. The Government of the day was struck with panic. In its extremity, it turned to the man who had been neglected and put on one side, and whose warnings had been disregarded—De Brazza. He was asked to take charge of a Commission of investigation which should proceed at once to the French Congo. He accepted. The decision struck the Boards of the Concessionaire companies with consternation. Immense pressure was at once brought to bear upon the Government, and, repenting of their action almost ere the ink was dry on the letters of appointment, Ministers strove by every means to thwart their own nominee. Only by natural pertinacity and the considerable influence he wielded in certain quarters did De Brazza succeed in securing an official staff and in defeating an attempt to send out another Commission, independent of his own, to spy upon his movements. As it was, he was forced to leave without having been furnished by the Colonial Office with a single one of the dozens of reports from its officials in the French Congo, which had been accumulating in its bureaux for the past four years!

For four months De Brazza and his staff pursued their investigations. De Brazza did not spare himself. His activity was prodigious: his increasing grief pitiful to behold. " Ruin and terror," he wrote home, " have been imported into this unfortunate colony." The river banks were deserted where formerly a numerous population fished and traded. From the Ogowe and its affluents whole tribes had disappeared. Floggings, armed raids, " hostage-houses," had everywhere replaced the peaceful relationship of commercial intercourse. All over the country the wretched natives, goaded into rebellion, were struggling against their oppressors: fleeing to the forests, they subsisted—or starved—on roots and berries. Great numbers had perished. The following specific instances are selected from the mass of evidence. In the Upper Ubanghi the agent of a Concessionaire company had summoned the Chiefs of a number of neighbouring villages, which had been slow in gathering rubber, to " talk over matters." They were then seized, tied to trees, and flogged until the blood ran down their backs. Correspondence found in the offices of another company included letters from the Board in Paris containing such sentiments as these: " Do not forget that our agents must play the part of miniature pirates " *(pirates au petit pied);* and, in connection with troubles that had arisen with a particular Chief, stress was laid upon the utility of " that plaything which is called a Maxim." In the Lobaye region, the scene of repeated uprisings and bloody reprisals, the agent of the local Concessionaire company was an ex-agent of the infamous and notorious Abir company of the Congo State. In the N'Gunié region no fewer than five military expeditions had been sent against the natives in as many months at the request of the local Concessionaire company. In the Shari, the Chief of an important tribe had been arrested because his people did not bring in enough rubber, and had died in prison. In the neighbourhood of Bangui an official had caused fifty-eight women and ten children to be taken as hostages to compel their male relatives to bring in rubber: in three weeks forty-five of these women and two of the children had died of starvation and want of air, packed tightly in a small dwelling place. At Fort Sibut one hundred and nineteen women and little girls had been similarly arrested, and many had died. An official circular had prescribed that these " hostages-houses " should be erected *in the bush and out of sight of possible travellers.* In one of the concessions of the Lower Congo the natives had been forbidden to make salt in order to compel them to buy it from the company, which would only sell it against large quantities of rubber; widespread sickness ensuing, salt being an indispensable article of native diet in tropical Africa. The judicial machinery had become hopelessly corrupted, and the gravest abominations were left unpunished. This was hardly surprising in view of a circular from the Governor-General of the dependency to his officials complaining of the small yield from the rubber taxes and stating : " I do not conceal from you that I shall base myself, in recommending your promotion, especially upon the yield of the native taxes, which should be the object of your constant attention." In the interior "terrifying depopulation," a "universal exodus." "In the Ubanghi-Shari," wrote De Brazza, "I have found an impossible situation, the continuous destruction of the population—purely and simply."

Another Frenchman of note, Auguste Chevalier, whose reputation as an expert in tropical forestry is world-wide, has since recorded in a bulky volume the state of the French Congo, whither he was sent on an official scientific expedition. His descriptions are pen pictures not of the more revolting atrocities, but of the daily, deadly, permanent effects of the "System" upon native life. They help, too, to bring home to us, all that there was of promise in these primitive peoples, before they were handed over body and soul to the cynical vileness of modern capitalistic finance. Commenting upon the ruined and abandoned villages on the river banks, as he proceeds on his northward journey, he writes:

> It is impossible to describe the lamentable impression made upon one in the contemplation of these huts torn asunder by the storms. The neglected fruit trees and fields of manioc,* where monkeys and hippopotami now find nourishment. And yet how considerable was the effort involved on the part of these so-called lazy people. They had to conquer the forest and carve out of it their few acres of cultivated lands, fight the forest continuously to prevent it from winning back its ascendancy. And now, once again, the forest invades the site. The seeds of forest trees have germinated in the fields, and the high grasses grow upon the desolate pathways.

He goes on:

> The majority of the inhabitants, terrified by the military oppressions, have fled. . . One gathers a very favourable impression from those that remain. . . Their thatch-roofed houses are spacious and clean. . . They have goats, hens, cats and dogs. Their plantations are most excellently kept. (He enumerates seven different cultivated vegetables, besides bananas and plantains.)
> No doubt remains in my mind as to the cause of all these disturbances. . . The Concessionaires and the Senegalese soldiers treat the natives in the cruellest fashion, impose all kinds of forced labour upon them, often pillage without restraint. The agents of the Companies call the native a brute who will not gather rubber for them, talk of suppressing them and importing labour from other countries. It is odious and absurd. But some of the officers who are travelling on this steamer, especially the higher grade officers, agree with these views. The natives fly at the approach of the steamer. (He

---

* The tropical plant, "Janipha-maniot" from which tapioca, and cassava —one of the staple food supplies of the Congo peoples—are prepared.

then narrates several specific cases of burning of villages and slaughter of natives, and continues) : It is this sort of policy which explains why the native is abandoning these rich and admirable valleys. . .

These are typical observations selected from a great number, and common to all the regions Chevalier traversed. Every phase of the system in the Congo Free State, reported by innumerable witnesses, is seen by Chevalier's narrative to be reproduced in the French Congo. Thus Chevalier notes everywhere famine resulting from requisitions in rubber and in foodstuffs, which leaves the inhabitants no time to attend to the cultivation of foodstuffs for their own sustenance; utter exhaustion among the men leading to sexual incapacity; tribal women forced to feed great numbers of idle female camp followers attached to the administrative centres, themselves dying of hunger, seeing their children perishing for lack of nourishment, compelled to thrust water into their babies' mouths through narrow-necked gourds to stop their cries as they suck vainly at withered teats; children so reduced that they appear like walking skeletons; one or two powerful so-called Arab chiefs in the far interior raiding right and left for slaves, whom they sell to cattle-raising communities further north in order to procure bullocks demanded of them by the Administration as tribute, or employed as agents to collect rubber and ivory for Concessionaires, who give them guns in exchange, which facilitate their raiding operations. He sums up the whole position as he then found it thus:

> Soon, if this policy is persisted in, if the incendiarism and devastation of villages does not stop . . . if the concessionaires are always to enjoy the right of imposing such and such a "corvée" upon the inhabitants, and to place an embargo upon all the latter possess, the banks of the Congo, the Ubanghi, and the Sangha will be completely deserted. . . If this policy be not changed, in half a century from now these hardworking races will have completely disappeared, and the desert will enter into possession of French Central Africa.

One may compare that passage with another from one of the most terrible books which have ever illustrated the systematic prostitution of civilisation in the Congo Basin, by a junior French Congo official, himself a participator in this welter of abomination, unable to alter it and presently sinking to its level:

> The dead, we no longer count them. The villages, horrible charnel-houses, disappear in this yawning gulf. A thousand diseases follow in our footsteps. . . And this martyrdom continues. . . We white men must shut our eyes not to see the hideous dead, the dying who curse us, and the wounded who implore, the weeping women and the starving children. We must stop our ears not to hear the lamentations, the cries, the maledictions which rise from every foot of land, from every tuft of grass.

. . . . . .

De Brazza had been furnished upon his departure with secret instructions from the French Government, in which he had been urged to make it clear in his report that the system established in the French Congo since 1899 was not identical with that of the Congo Free State. These instructions, which were subsequently published with the authority of the Comtesse de Brazza, are extraordinarily interesting. They show on the one hand, that French governing circles were fully aware as far back as 1905 of the character of the Belgian " System " (described in the " instructions " as " proceedings of methodical tyranny ") which had been so calamitously imitated in the French Congo and of its necessary consequences; and their anxiety, on the other hand, to be able to dissociate their country from the charge of pursuing an identical policy in the French Congo. They ran, in part, as follows:

> 1. That the system of land concessions which she (France) has created (*mis en vigueur*) reposes upon principles differing from those inaugurated in the Congo State; that she has never instituted a "domain" analogous to that of the "domaine privé" of the King, thus identifying in the direct interest of a commercial exploitation conducted by herself, the principles of sovereignty, demesniality (Crown lands), and private property.
> 2. That she maintains an army (*force publique*) solely for the purpose of upholding general security, without ever compelling the natives, by various measures of coercion, to enter the service of a commercial, agricultural, or industrial concern.
> 3. That she has taken all necessary precautions to allow of third parties being able to trade freely in the French portion of the conventional basin of the Congo, even in conceded territory.
> 4. That she has scrupulously reserved all the customary rights and all the food crops of the natives (*cultures vivrières*), even in conceded territory.
> 5. That she has always been careful to punish acts of violence committed upon the natives when brought to the knowledge of the authorities; that these acts have, moreover, always been limited to individuals, without it being possible to attribute

them to an organised system; that the French Congo has never witnessed a whole public or private enterprise having recourse as a principle, in order to maintain itself in being (*pour subsister*) or to hasten its success, to proceedings of methodical tyranny, analogous to those employed in the portion of the Congo State actually forming the object of investigation.

The policy which dictated these instructions and the investigating mission confided to De Brazza, was clear enough. In the first place the revelations of what was taking place in the French Congo had caused so great a stir that there was no option but to order an inquiry, and to appoint a man to carry it out, whose integrity was universally acknowledged and whose reputation was international. In the second place the French Government had reason to believe that the Balfour-Lansdowne Government would not be able to resist the growing national demand for an international Conference into the affairs of the Congo Free State, and intended to press for such a conference which Lord Lansdowne had suggested in his circular Note to the signatory Powers. French Ministers were prepared to fall in with the British request, the more so as French diplomacy had been quietly working for several years for an international partition of the Congo Free State. But, if such a conference were held, it was indispensable that the French Government should be in a position to go into it with clean hands, vouched for as clean by a man of De Brazza's international standing. The French politicians then in office calculated, perhaps, that De Brazza would play the politico-diplomatic game they desired him to play. But De Brazza was determined to get at the truth, the whole truth, and nothing but the truth. His principal biographer on that memorable inquiry, M. Felicien Challaye, has recorded that "De Brazza felt a great personal responsibility weighing upon him." It was due to his influence that these millions of African natives had accepted French "protection." It was his manifest duty to secure justice and redress for them, if injustice had been inflicted.

In his very first reports from the French Congo, De Brazza made the Government understand that he could not do what was demanded of him in the secret instructions. He was driven to the painful necessity of telling his Government that the conditions he found in the French Congo could not be explained by individual actions of an atrocious character, but were due to the " System " itself. He felt impelled to inform his Government that France was permitting piracy and murder as an institution under the tri-colour; and that " liberty, equality and fraternity " in the French Congo, spelt liberty to rob and massacre, equality with the systematised scoundrelism reigning on the other side of the great African river, fraternity in crime with Leopold's slave-drivers.

. . . . . .

From that moment French diplomacy placed every obstacle in the way of an International Conference into the affairs of the Congo Free State, and Franco-Belgian diplomacy worked all over the world against the efforts of the reformers, while the increasing tension between London and Berlin over the Morocco affair gave the Foreign Office a further excuse for doing nothing. Diplomatic intrigue, capitalist finance, the general anarchy of European relationships, combined to perpetuate for many years the agony and the extermination, in a literal sense, of millions of human beings in both Congos. From that moment, too, French Ministers, vigorously pressed by the Boards of the Concessionaire companies and by Belgian diplomacy, determined to hush up the scandal.

What prodigious happenings hang upon apparently slender issues. Had De Brazza lived to return to France the whole history of the ensuing seven years might well have been wholly different. French national policy is unutterably selfish and finance-ridden to a supreme degree. But no country in the world contains more individuals capable of casting aside every personal consideration in the pursuit of abstract justice. As it was, a few courageous men did arise who strove manfully to clear their country from the stain inflicted upon it. But De Brazza would have made an appeal direct to the hearts of the French people, which it is difficult to believe would not have proved irresistible. And who knows but that the coming together of the great Powers in a cause of human justice and mercy would not have proved a solvent to the bitter suspicions which divided them, and saved humanity the terrible experiences of the past five years. That was the thought which inspired some of us in the sustained efforts we made before and after De Brazza's untimely end, to bring such a conference about. The ways of

Providence are, indeed, inscrutable. De Brazza died on his way home. M. Felicien Challaye, who was with him to the end, describes the last days of this distinguished man in terms of poignant emotion:

> The fate of the Congo troubles him more than his own. When he has the strength to talk it is of the Congo that he speaks. . . . He was bowed down by an immense sorrow. M. de Brazza passionately loved the Congo, which he had explored and acquired for France, then governed and organised. He suffered to find it in a truly lamentable condition. . . From these sinister discoveries M. De Brazza suffered in the deepest recesses of his soul. They hastened his end.

. . . . . .

The members of De Brazza's staff returned with all the necessary documents to elaborate a report. They were forbidden to do so. A bitter personal campaign was at once started against them in the French Colonial Press, wholly subject to the Concessionaire Boards. They were instructed to hand over their documents to a Committee appointed by the Colonial Minister. The Committee as appointed was not free from bias in favour of the "System" which De Brazza condemned. But the evidence was so overwhelming that it could not but substantiate his findings. The Ministry suppressed the Committee's Report on two grounds. First, that its effect internationally would be prejudicial to France—a further tribute to the anarchy of international relationships. Secondly, that its publication would lead to actions at law by the Concessionaire companies which had threatened to take proceedings against the Government. This admission momentarily staggered the French Chamber before which it was made by the Colonial Minister. "But that is blackmail," remarked one Deputy. "And you have capitulated at its threat!" shouted another.

The three days' Debate (February 19—21, 1906) in the Chamber to which the suppression of the evidence collected by De Brazza and his staff and the suppression of the Committee's report gave rise, was notable for further appalling revelations, greeted with cries of " monstrous," " scandalous," "unbelievable," from all over the Chamber. The most perfunctory accounts were given of those debates in the British Press. Indeed, acting no doubt under direct official inspiration from Downing Street, the tragedy of the French Congo has, from first to last, been withheld as far as possible from the British people. In the course of the debates in the Chamber, the Socialists and the Radicals joined forces. The gravamen of the charge against the Government was that it was upholding a system shameful for the honour of France, and that it was guilty of concealing atrocities "less to be imputed to men than to the ' System ' itself, of which they constitute the expression." A large number of official documents were cited. It was conclusively shown that the practice of seizing women and children as hostages from villages and towns short in the rubber tribute had become "general in the Congo for the past five years," and that this organised warfare upon the helpless section of the population had become, as in the Congo Free State, one of the recognised *media* of coercion, "regarded as the natural complement of all disciplinary measures." These wretched women, thus torn from their homes, served other ends. They were used to attract, or to retain, the services of carriers to carry the foodstuffs and general equipment of the numerous "disciplinary expeditions" traversing the country in every direction, and to satisfy the lusts of the native soldiers. " I am sending you," ran one of the official documents quoted, a communication from one official to another, "to-day, by canoe, 54 women and children for Fort Possel. No doubt the presence of a considerable number of women will soon attract the men. . ." Grafted upon the demand for rubber came the demand for carriers to convey the stuff from long distances to the river banks, and also for the purposes mentioned above. Districts which did not produce rubber were taxed in carriers, i.e., in human labour, and became exhausted and drained of their population. An official report stated :

> In order to find carriers we have to organise regular man-hunts amongst empty villages and abandoned plantations; everywhere thrust back, north, east, south and west by military posts, which are instructed to prevent the mass-exodus of the population, the natives hide in the remoter parts of the forest or seek refuge in inaccessible caves, living the life of animals, and subsisting wretchedly off roots and berries.

Another official report spoke of the "awful mad terror of this race, which a few years ago was rich, numerous and prosperous, grouped in immense villages, to-day dispersed." Of 40,000 natives living in *one* particular region, 20,000 had been "destroyed" in two years. Many quotations were given of typical extracts from officials in the course of punishing native villages which had not furnished a sufficient quantity of rubber to the Concessionaires, or which refused to pay the rubber tax. Here are some of them:

> Action against Kolewan village. The Fans of the Upper Cuno river had declined to pay the tribute. The village was burned and the plantations destroyed. . . Expedition against the Bekanis: The village was again burned and 3,000 banana trees (staple food supply) destroyed. The village of Kua was also burnt, and the plantations razed to the ground. . . Action against Abiemafal village: All the houses were set fire to and the plantations razed to the ground. . . Action against Alcun: The villages were bombarded, and afterwards destroyed, with the plantations. . . Action against the Essamfami: Villages destroyed. The country on the Bome river has been put to fire and sword.

The following passage was quoted from the report of one of the inspectors appointed by De Brazza:

> What villages burned down, what plantations destroyed, what hatreds engendered against us in order to get in a few thousands of francs! Are not such deeds unworthy of France?

With terrible force the accusers in the Chamber drove home again and again the official circulars of the Governor-General to his officials, notifying them that their promotion would depend upon the measure of their success in increasing the yield of the rubber taxes. They commented upon the close connection between the Concessionaire Companies of the French Congo and the Belgian Congo Free State Companies. They emphasised the sinister influence of the Concessionaire Companies upon successive French Colonial Ministers, illustrating it with such facts as, for instance, that the *chef de cabinet* of one such Minister had subsequently become the director of six Concessionaire Companies. They asked what conceivable advantage could accrue to France from the prosecution of so atrocious a policy; what was the mysterious influence which permitted a number of financial corporations to impose their will upon a French Colony, making the Administration of it their active accomplices, massacring its inhabitants, ruining the country? They cited more official documents, in which specific

agents of the Concessionaire Companies were charged with
"torturing natives to death," or "raiding villages, carrying off their inhabitants and demanding ransom," or
"inflicting acts of such bestiality upon the natives that
it is difficult to narrate them "; or, again, importing large
quantities of guns, raising levies, arming them and letting
them loose upon the native villages. They showed the
declension in the morality of the whole official hierarchy
in the Congo, from the Governor-General, who had at
first resisted the pressure brought to bear upon him by
the Concessionaire Companies, and had even written to
the Colonial Minister of the day: " They are relying upon
me to organise the production of ' red ' rubber in the
French Congo. I have no intention of justifying such
hopes ": to officials of the lowest rank who could not be
punished for their crimes without involving the whole
Administration.

They brought forward an " Order of the Day " (Resolution) stating that the honour of France demanded the
production of the whole of the De Brazza evidence, the
whole of the official reports, and the report of the Committee of Inquiry. The chief sensation of the debates
occurred when the President of that Committee, M. de
Lanessan, formerly Governor of Indo-China, rose in his
seat and urged the Government to accede to the request.
The Minister persisted in his refusal, and the Chamber
divided, 167 voting for the resolution, and 345 against.

. . . . . .

This was the one serious effort made by the French
Parliament to drag the full truth into light. Its defeat
ensured immunity for the Concessionaire Companies and
the prolongation of the " System." Everything went on
as before. Not a single Concessionaire Company's charter
was annulled. All that was done was to appoint a number
of Government inspectors to travel about the French
Congo. All their reports were suppressed as they were
received, and it is only through the brave handful of
French reformers that the contents of some of them have
become known. In 1910 the French Government, finding that despite its efforts the nature of these reports
was leaking out, and urged thereto by the Concessionaire
Boards, suppressed the inspectors. All these things were

kept from the knowledge of the British public. In 1908 an American traveller passed through the maritime regions of the French Congo and thus recorded her impressions:

> Who is to blame for the annihilating conditions existing to-day in French Congo? Commerce is dead, towns once prosperous and plentiful are deserted and falling into decay, and whole tribes are being needlessly and ignominiously crushed for the aggrandisement of the few. . . . Towns are sacked and plundered; fathers, brothers, husbands, are put in foul-smelling prisons until those at home can get together the taxes necessary to secure their relief. France has granted exclusive rights to *concessionaires* who claim everything upon, above, in or about any *hectare* of land described in their grant. . . . To be hurled from active, prosperous freedom into inactive and enforced poverty would demoralise even a civilised country; how farther reaching, then, is it with the savage? . . . As the French say, the entire country is *bouleversé*, *i.e.*, overthrown, in confusion, subverted, agitated, unsettled. And the French are right in so naming the result of their own misdeeds. All is desolation, demoralisation, annihilation. Native customs are violated; native rights ignored. . . . Great plains which not long since swarmed with the life and bustle of passing trade caravans are now silent and deserted. Ant-hills and arid grass and wind-swept paths are the only signs of life upon them.

The following are typical illustrations of the character of the reports received by the French Colonial Ministry from its inspectors between 1906 and 1909, and which successive French Ministers suppressed. They were published in full from time to time by the French League for the Defence of the Congo natives, but were suppressed by the entire French Press, with the exception of the *Courrier Européen*, the *Humanité*, and one or two other papers. An agent of the N'Kemi Keni Company is denounced for having allowed a native named Oio to be tied up by one of the armed ruffians in the Company's employ, so tightly that his hands sloughed away at the wrists. A judicial investigation ensued (one of the very few judicial decisions in the French Congo which have ever seen the light since 1899, for, like all other reports, they have been officially suppressed). The examining magistrate absolved the incriminated agent of direct responsibility, but fined him fifteen francs! The mental condition of the French Congo magistracy may be estimated by the following extract from this magistrate's report: " Oio presented himself in good health, *minus*

his hands, and in cheerful fashion, deposed," etc. A
dossier against the Lobaye Company deposited with the
Court at Brazzaville contains one hundred and fifty-three
counts of " crimes and delinquencies " against the Company's agents. The inspector reporting to the Ministry
as to this Company and others, urges that " prosecution
should no longer be directed against individual agents,
but against the Companies themselves who have counselled, or even tolerated, practices against which
humanity protests." Fraud to the detriment of the
natives on the part of the *Sette Cama* Company is
reported, and its suppression suggested. Of the *Fernan
Vaz* Company, it is reported that the Company has caused
" the exodus and revolt of the natives by the proceedings
of its agents "; that it does not trade, but practises
" coercion and slavery " and has violated " the most
elementary rules of honesty." The Colonial Minister is
urged to cancel its charter, as also that of the *Brettonne*
Company. The *Lefini* Company is reported as treating
its labour " with brutality and dishonesty " the Company's monopoly " becomes in its hands an odious
weapon." The *Mobaye* Company is similarly denounced
and its suppression recommended. The *Haute N'Gunie*
Company is charged with having " by its exactions and
brutalities caused uprisings in regions where merchants
were formerly welcomed." The withdrawal of its charter
is urged. A formidable indictment is drawn up and forwarded to the Colonial Minister in connection with the
Company *du Congo occidental*. It includes the burning
of 20 villages, and the capture of hostages—visited by a
fine of £8 in the local court! There is a whole list of
murders and acts of violence : the Company's proceedings
have brought about " the gravest disorders " and its
charter should be withdrawn. Of the *Lobaye* Company,
a later report says that its recent profits " have been
made in blood." Our silence would make us the accomplices of all its crimes and all its thefts. The Administration has the remedy—suppression. " The methods of
the *Bavili* Company are described in yet another report
as " methods of ruin, and a perpetual menace to public
safety . . . methods especially resented by the natives
after two hundred years' experience of freedom of commerce." The *M'Poko* Company is accused of having
caused the murder of 1,500 natives in its concession.

THE STORY OF THE FRENCH CONGO 147

Not only did successive French Governments suppress these reports of their own inspectors, but *not a single Concessionaire company was proceeded against, or ever has been.*

In 1910, M. Violette, the reporter for the French Colonial Budget of that year, concluded that:

> The Dependency is absolutely exhausted. . . . The rights of the natives continue to be violated with the connivance of the Administration. . . The Concessionaire Companies are the most formidable enemies of the Dependency; it is time that they were spoken to in the only way which they are capable of understanding. . . . In this unfortunate dependency the Governor-General, the Governor, the Commissioners exist, and do not govern. There is no law, no authority, other than that of the Boards of the Concessionaire Companies.

If the Concessionaires ruled the French Congo on the spot, they also ruled the Colonial Ministry in all that pertained to Congo affairs. In 1909, the Colonial Minister was an honourable and amiable politician, who would have taken a strong line had he dared. He confessed, in his own cabinet, to the writer of this volume, that he was powerless. The financial interests had become too strong to be assailed; the financial ring too strong to be broken. Two years later these same interests played a predominant but hidden rôle in bringing about the Franco-German Morocco crisis. They laboured strenuously to prevent the agreement of November of that year, which momentarily allayed it, and after the agreement was signed they did their best to precipitate another crisis.

The suppression of the travelling Inspectors dried up the sources of information from the French Congo, and since 1911 the veil has not been raised except as regards the coast region. There the long training which the native population had had in genuine commerce, the resolute character of most of the tribes, and the continued presence in the country of English merchants—who clung doggedly to their ground—have combined, more or less, to break down the " System " which has virtually perished after making a holocaust of victims.

An impenetrable mist still lies upon the forests of the middle and upper Congo, shutting them out from the observation of men.

BIBLIOGRAPHY.

"French Parliamentary Papers, and Colonial Budgets."
"Affairs of West Africa." E. D. Morel. (Heinemann.)
"The British Case in French Congo." E. D. Morel. (Heinemann.)
"Great Britain and the Congo." E. D. Morel. (Smith, Elder and Co.)
"Le Congo français." Challaye. (Paris : Cahiers de la Quinzaine.)
"Les deux Congo." Challaye and Mille. (Paris : Cahiers de la Quinzaine.)
"La dernière mission de Brazza." (Paris : L. de Saye et fils.)
"L'Afrique centrale française." Chevalier. (Paris : Challamel.)
"Les illegalités et les crimes du Congo." Anatole France, Mille, etc. (Paris : Jeulin.)

CHAPTER XI.

THE STORY OF ANGOLA AND THE " COCOA ISLANDS."

The Portuguese Dependencies in West Africa comprise Angola, the islands of San Thomé and Principe, and the enclave of Kabinda north of the Congo. They cover some 480,000 square miles. They represent the crumbling relics of an ancient splendour identified with an inhuman traffic. The cancer of the slave trade gnawed at the vitals of this territory so long that it has never recovered. Indeed, until a few years ago, the slave trade persisted although appropriately garbed in the raiments of modern hypocrisy. The earliest Portuguese settlement in Angola dates back to the close of the 15th Century. In 1600 the Governor of Angola secured the " Assiento " contract (see Chapter III.) for the supply of slaves to the Spanish West Indies. About the middle of that century the Portuguese authorities began raiding for slaves in the interests of the sugar planters of Brazil. A more intensive demand for slaves arose in Brazil early in the 18th Century with the discovery of gold and diamonds. Slave hunts in Angola kept pace with this demand and led to great depopulation, the area of operations steadily increasing with the years. Although Portugal officially abolished the slave trade south of the Equator in 1830, enormous numbers of slaves continued to be transported to the Brazils by Portuguese slavers up to 1850-60, these " illegal " activities being connived at by the Portuguese officials in Angola and Brazil respectively. From that date onward the increasing energy of British and French cruiser squadrons put an end to the cross-Atlantic traffic. But it was fated that Angola should continue to be drained of its life-blood for many years to come. Slavery of the old-fashioned kind, the raiding, kidnapping and purchase of human beings for plantations under white overseers, did not die out with the legal abolition of the trade. It is very doubtful if it is wholly dead in Angola to-day. A few years before the Great War it would have been accurate to state of Angola that its native peoples were in the same hapless condition as they used to be in other parts of the western tropical Continent when the slave trade was looked upon by all nations as a legitimate form of human activity. Every man's hand was against his neighbour's. No individual was safe. The whole place was mined with slavery. No less a person than the Governor of Mossamedes (southern Angola) who, like several of his compatriots, deplored and denounced the situation obtaining, declared as recently as March, 1912, that he found it impossible to discover a free man in that town even to serve in his own household. National inertia, political troubles and powerful vested interests were jointly responsible for this state of affairs.

During the quarter of a century preceding the Great War, slavery in Angola received a fresh external incentive. Some two hundred miles from the coast-line, a couple of volcanic islands thrust themselves out of the ocean. They are called San Thomé and Principe, and their total area is about 4,000 square miles. They enjoy a heavy rainfall and are admirably suited for tropical cultivation. Originally discovered by the Portuguese, they attained great prosperity during the "golden age " of the slave trade, the slaves on the sugar plantations being, of course, transported from the mainland. Their prosperity declined with the abolition of the Slave trade. It revived somewhat in the middle of last century, coffee taking the place of the sugar cane. But the profits derived from the cultivation of coffee gradually sank, while the demand for another and more valuable crop increased. This was cocoa, first introduced into San Thomé from Brazil in 1822. San Thomé and Principe were destined to become for a time the most important cocoa-producing centres in the world, until the natives of the Gold Coast built up a free industry on their own land, which eclipsed the Portuguese slave industry despite the great care lavished upon it and large sums of money invested in it. But at what a price in human lives and in human misery did San Thomé and Principe acquire their importance! And what a price is still paid in adult mortality, although the conditions of "recruiting" have wholly changed!

The discovery that a slave traffic was still in full swing between Angola and the "Cocoa Islands" came about in this wise. In the opening years of the present century about one-third of the cocoa produced in San Thomé

ANGOLA AND THE COCOA ISLANDS 151

found its way to England. The bulk of the crop went to the United States, Germany and France. The cocoa was then, and continues to be, grown upon estates owned by Portuguese planters. The chocolate manufacturers of the world bought the raw material on the open market. They had no more to do with the methods of its production than the manufacturers of rubber tyres or toys, who bought Congo rubber on the open market had to do with the system under which rubber was produced in the Congo. In 1901 and 1902 sinister rumours reached Cadbury Brothers in regard to the manner in which labour was procured for these estates, and they took it upon themselves to make inquiries in Lisbon as to the truth of the allegations. Mr. William Cadbury saw the Portuguese Colonial Minister and Sir Martin Gosselin, then British Minister at Lisbon. The former admitted the existence of evils connected with the "recruiting," but undertook that a pending "Labour decree" would do away with them. Sir Martin Gosselin, who was keenly interested in native questions and a man of real human sympathies, advised that the Portuguese Government should be given twelve months within which to set its colonial house in order. At the end of that period—the end of 1903—Cadbury Brothers, continuing to receive similar reports to those which had inspired their original complaint, Mr. William Cadbury again visited Lisbon, interviewed the Government, the planters and Sir Martin Gosselin. The planters denied the charge, and challenged open investigation. The British Minister approved the idea. Cadbury Brothers were no more concerned in righting such wrongs as inquiry might prove to exist in the production of the raw material they turned into the finished article than were other firms in the same line of business. They rightly felt that collective action by the largest British, Continental and American manufacturers would have more weight than isolated steps of their own. They thereupon approached their colleagues and competitors in the industry, placing the facts as they then appeared before them, detailing what they themselves had already done, and what was proposed. Fry's of Bristol, Rowntree's of York, and Stollwerck's of Cologne, agreed to participate in a commission of inquiry: the Americans refused. The difficulty was to find an independent and wholly unbiased person, who possessed a knowledge of Portuguese, the latter qualification being a very vital necessity in the case. Failing in this they selected Mr. Joseph Burtt, who spent several months in Portugal studying the language and fitting himself for the task, a delicate one, rendered even more difficult than it would otherwise have been by the close diplomatic relations existing between the British and Portuguese Governments. Mr. Burtt set out on his mission in June, 1905. As the result of his disclosures the firms mentioned boycotted San Thomé cocoa and ceased entirely to purchase it.

I have placed these facts on record here in some detail because they appear to me to have a direct bearing upon one aspect of the whole comprehensive problem with which this volume is concerned: the problem of white responsibility towards the African races. The attitude adopted by Cadbury Brothers, and, subsequently, in co-operation with other firms engaged in the cocoa and chocolate manufacturing industry, typifies what *ought* to be the attitude of public opinion generally on these questions. Although merely purchasers of raw material on the open market, when they found reason to believe that a portion of that raw material represented the output of forced or slave labour, these firms felt their moral responsibility involved. The firms who did not join them took the view that it was not the business of the manufacturer to worry himself about the origin of the stuff he handled. Now the moral responsibility of all these firms *was* involved. But no more and no less than in the case of rubber manufacturers, soap or margarine manufacturers, or cotton spinners under like circumstances—*in short, manufacturers of any article whatsoever of which the raw material is produced by coloured labour.* But this is the only case I have ever heard of in which manufacturers in Europe have recognised that it would be wrong of them not to investigate reports as to the ill-treatment of the distant coloured peoples producing the raw material which they turned into the finished article; and not only to spend considerable sums in investigation, but to take action and refuse to buy the raw material so long as the conditions under which it was produced remained substantially unaltered. No such action was taken by rubber manufacturers in regard to Congo rubber, although the whole world rang with the iniquity of the methods by which that rubber was put on the market.

Nor is such moral responsibility confined to manufacturers. It is shared by Trade Unions, by Industrial Councils. It is shared to a lesser degree, but distinctly, by the consumer. We hear a great deal about "missionaries of Empire." A much-needed missionary work is that of interesting the labouring classes of Europe in the human associations connected with the raw material they handle. Those who might be disposed to deride the idea do not, in my humble opinion, know the working man—the British working man at any rate. The fact that the conditions he suffers from himself are often atrocious, would not deter him from becoming politically conscious, or politically active in the defence of the defenceless. I believe it is perfectly possible to arouse the interest and the sympathy of the British working man in the producers of the material he turns into candles, soap, rubber tyres, furniture, or clothing; or for that matter of what he eats and drinks in the guise of margarine, nut butter, tea, coffee, or cocoa— but *there* he is merely a consumer, not a unit in an organisation which can make itself politically felt. But as a fashioner of the raw material into the finished article, his profes sional intelligence should be easy to awaken, his sympathy would be certain to follow and, with its dawning, would come a great democratic drive for the honest, just, and humane treatment of the coloured races. Had I known then what I know now, I should not have limited myself during the decade of the Congo agitation to approaching the statesman, the administrator, the heads of the churches, and the man in the street. I should have gone direct to the leaders of the Labour movement. I received much unsolicited support from some of the latter, and from many an individual working man. But, unhappily, I was not in touch with the Labour movement in those days and neglected a powerful weapon in consequence.

· · · · ·

While the cocoa firms were thus engaged, that *preux chevalier* of modern journalism, Henry W. Nevinson, was travelling in Angola, and visiting San Thomé and Principe on behalf of *Harper's Monthly Magazine*. His terrible book, "A Modern Slavery," appeared in the spring of

1906, and revealed the slave-trade masquerading as contract labour, in full swing in Angola, and between Angola and the Cocoa Islands. His disclosures were subsequently confirmed by Mr. Joseph Burtt and Dr. Claude Horton, who accompanied the latter in his prolonged journey into the interior of Angola. Later on further revelations completed the picture, the most important being a series of British Consular reports, the Foreign Office having been induced by the growing agitation to increase its Consular staff and to set it at work on the business of investigation.

The circumstances under which San Thomé labour was "recruited" were briefly these: The interior of Angola was covered with a network of "agents"—Europeans, half-breeds, and natives in European pay—employed by, or connected with, the estate managers on the plantations on the mainland and in the islands, who bribed such officials as they could and intrigued against the others at Lisbon. The purpose of these "agents" was to secure labour by any means: upon that labour they received handsome commissions. The traffic was lucrative. Open raiding, bribery of native chiefs, encouraging litigation among the natives, stirring up inter-tribal warfare, and using as intermediaries the rebellious Congo Free State soldiery which held the frontier country for more than a decade—these were the chief methods employed. The slaves were convoyed along the old slave roads leading from the far interior to the coast, upon which millions of Africans had tramped, and stumbled, and died through the centuries on their way to the Brazils. Once the neighbourhood of "civilisation" was reached and escape became impossible, the shackles were knocked off, the "agent" handed on his captures to his employer, the employer proceeded with them to the nearest magistrate. In the presence of this high official the forms prescribed by "law" were duly enacted. The miserable crowd of broken, half-starved wretches were duly inscribed as having entered for five years upon a "voluntary contract." They bound themselves under this precious deed " to work nine hours on all days that are not sanctified by religion " [sic]. Legality having been thus complied with, the slaves departed with their masters to plantations on the mainland, or, furnished with a new cloth and a metal disc, to the steamer waiting to convey them to the

Islands, whence they never returned. An additional cloak of respectability was given to the system after 1903 by the creation of a "Central Committee of Labour and Emigration," with a supervising Board in Africa. The Committee and its Board consisted of officials and planters, that is to say, of the two classes directly affected. Of course, the system went on as before. The truth was known to everyone concerned. Protests by individual Portuguese were never lacking, and were marked in certain instances by rare courage. It is true also that successive Portuguese Cabinets contained individuals who would have stopped the traffic if they could. But after a steady agitation had effected some reforms, nine years after the creation of the "Central Committee," the Minister for Foreign Affairs in the young Portuguese Republic was fain to confess to the British Minister at Lisbon that "the governors whom he had sent out to give effect to its (the Government's) instructions had been to a great extent paralysed by the power of the vested interests" arrayed against them.

The procuring of the slaves was marked by all the features of the old slave-trade. In their march into the interior, Nevinson and Burtt found the sides of the roads littered with wooden shackles and bleaching bones. At that time the traffic was just recovering from a desperate and ineffectual attempt to throw off the Portuguese yoke on the part of a number of interior tribes.

It seems strange at first sight that public attention in Europe was not directed earlier to the scandal. But it is only within the last twenty years or so that the searchlight of modern inquiry has been able to penetrate the vastness of the African interior, and the individuals who, either by their direct discovery or by an accidental combination of circumstances have learned the truth and ventured to expose the more hideous of the tragedies perpetrated in these remote regions, have invariably found themselves opposed by powerful and unscrupulous vested interests, and by the blocking effects of European diplomacy. With the exception of the Amazonian forests, whose indigenous population—which Roger Casement tried to save as he helped to save the natives of the Congo—is now reduced to vanishing point, *tropical Africa is the last stronghold of unfettered capitalism, the last resort of the man-hunter and slave-driver on a large scale.* And the latter covers up his tracks and disguises his practices with a cunning which increases as the means of investigation become perfected. Even the methods of a Leopold II. are beginning to be out of date. More subtle means are now required. But the end in view has suffered no alteration. Carefully planned legislation, combining land expropriation with taxation, can bring about the desired results—a cheap and plentiful supply of black labour—if a little more slowly, as surely and far more scientifically than the old system.

The procuring of the Angolan slaves for the "Cocoa Islands" was one thing. Their treatment in the plantations was a distinct problem of its own. Owing to the circumstances already narrated, public opinion became concentrated almost entirely upon conditions in the Islands. Conditions in the mainland plantations have really never been investigated at all. These produce no cocoa.

It would be tedious to narrate the peripatetics of a long campaign to secure fundamental reforms in the recruiting of labour on the mainland, and the improvement in the treatment of the labourers on the Islands, which appears to vary a good deal according to whether the plantations are well or ill managed.

The position at present appears to be this. The labour which finds its way to the Islands is no longer slave labour. There can, I think, be no longer any real doubt on that point. One thing at least is certain: Repatriation, which never occurred before, is now regular, although whether efficient agencies exist on the mainland for seeing the repatriated labourers back to their homes is another matter. Anyway, the Angolan who goes to San Thomé returns to the mainland at the expiration of his contract, unless he dies on the Islands in the interval. Men from Angola are now returning as fast as they are going in. In the two years, 1914-15, 5,732 Angolans entered San Thomé, and 6,842 left it. In the first half of 1916, 2,703 entered, and 1,994 left. This implies, of course, a revolutionary change. Previously some 4,000 Angolans were drafted into San Thomé annually. They never left it. It swallowed them up. As M. Auguste Chevalier put it a few years ago: "There is a door by which to enter San Thomé; there is none by which to leave." Mr. Joseph Burtt now feels moved to write: "A great human drama has been acted, and it has ended happily." I do not altogether agree, for the reasons given further on. The Portuguese planters on the Islands are now directing their efforts to secure labour from Mozambique —Portuguese East Africa. I have never heard it alleged that the Mozambique labour is not free, as free as any contracted labour is. But in view of the particulars which follow, I am beginning to doubt whether it can be. The blunt truth about the Islands to-day is that they are a palpable death-trap. There is nothing peculiar in the climatic conditions which should make them so. Sleeping sickness which used to prevail in Principe, but not in San Thomé, has been extirpated through the devoted labours of Portuguese medical men. There is nothing in the character of the cultivation itself which can account for the fact. It is, indeed, a healthy, out-of-door, not particularly strenuous occupation, which compares, in many, if not in most respects, very favourably with the growing of other tropical crops. Ill-treatment on the plantations is not the cause, although ill-treatment may, and probably does, occur on some plantations. But the individual Portuguese is not habitually inhuman in his treatment of coloured labour. He is probably in some ways less heavy-handed than the Anglo-Saxon. Nevertheless these Islands are a death-trap, and nothing else. The admitted mortality among the labourers remains what it was before the system of procuring labour on the mainland of Angola was changed. But to-day it is the Mozambique natives who suffer most. A mortality of 10 per cent. among adults in the prime of life is monstrous. Yet that is the admitted death-rate which continues to obtain, according to the official figures supplied by the British Consular staff. The total number of contracted labourers on the Islands, exclusive of the children, varies between 35,000 and 40,000. It is acknowledged that 4,000 deaths occurred among contracted labourers on the Islands in 1915, and even then there is a balance of 4,246 unaccounted for, on the basis of the Portuguese statistics of imported and exported labour for the year. Nor is the tale even then complete. The Portuguese statisticians make separate returns for the children born to contracted labourers. From these returns it appears that between August, 1915, and July, 1916, 519 children were born while the death rate mounted to 643. In other words, the mortality among the children of contracted labourers is 100 per cent., a staggering figure, exceeding the worst records of the estates in the old slavery days. The death rate of 10 per cent. among the Mozambique labourers is the *minimum*. The close analysis of the official figures which has been made by Mr. William Cadbury and by Mr. Joseph Burtt would seem to indicate an even higher proportion, the deaths being one in seven on the basis of a total of 40,000 contracted labourers. Labour drawn from precisely the same source for the South African mines, shows a mortality of one in twenty, and even that figure is officially regarded "with grave concern." The figures of 1919 are not yet available in a British consular report.

. . . . . .

What is the reason of this appalling mortality? A high death rate was to be expected in the case of the Angolan labourer under the circumstances narrated in this chapter, for the African dies from unhappiness more readily, perhaps, than any other human being. But those circumstances have now disappeared and, as has been pointed out, it is the free, or alleged free, Mozambique man who is stricken in such numbers.

I believe the cause to reside in unnatural conditions of life, operating in two main directions. The big estates house thousands of labourers in small walled-in compounds made of permanent buildings; the sanitary arrangements are bad; in a few years the whole area becomes contaminated with disease germs; the streams which flow down from the mountains are poisoned by the over-populated estates built along the water courses The normal conditions of African life in the damp forest regions of the tropics are small villages of separate and often scattered huts which are frequently destroyed and rebuilt; sometimes the site of the villages is shifted; purging fires are started at regular intervals, usually for agricultural purposes. That is one point. The other is this: The tropical African cannot stand, in tropical Africa, the European labour system with its prolonged hours of work under constant supervision, its monotony, the absence of freedom, joy and sociability in life, the perpetual discipline. These things in conjunction depress the African. He loses hold on existence. His capacity to resist disease, weakens. His procreating powers decline. He becomes spiritless, unhappy, collapsible.

It is a question primarily of psychology. The tropical African is essentially a creature of moods; a child of joy and a child of sorrow; a being of strong emotions which must find an outlet. He likes to dance, to linger chatting over camp fires, to vary his life according to the seasons. In his natural state the twin emotions of joy and sorrow merge into one another. The African woman will cry bitterly over her dead child, exclaim that the sorrow is sweet because it is not hopeless, mingle with her lamentations many loving messages of appeal to the dead. The African is an intensely sociable being. He droops under perpetual restraint. Solitary confinement kills him. European industrialism saps his vitality. Every race and every people has its peculiar psychology. That is why alien rulers, however just according to their own lights, never reach the hearts of the subject race. With some notable exceptions, the European knows little and cares probably less about the psychology of the African he governs as an administrator or as an employer of labour. But, put a Russian to rule over Englishmen, a German to rule over Spaniards, an Italian to rule over Swedes—what an unholy muddle they would make of the job. Yet the difference is trifling by comparison. Climate also steps in with its inexorable laws. As man's *habitat* advances nearer to the equator, his power for sustained and continuous labour decreases: his need for relaxation increases. The southern European is incapable of the prolonged labour, month in month out, which the northern European is able to endure: nor can the latter when transplanted to these warmer climes keep up the pace he was accustomed to. The tropical African has flourished exceedingly in North America and the West Indies, despite the abominable treatment to which he was so long subjected. But he passed from a tropical zone to a temperate or semi-tropical one. He has multiplied in the tropical parts of the southern American continent where men work less prolonged hours and at less high pressure. The climate of tropical Africa makes immense demands upon the human constitution, white and black. Europeans who can spend several years at a stretch in Burma, which is hotter than tropical Africa, can rarely stand more than eighteen months or two years continuous residence in tropical Africa. Few African women can bear more than three or four children, and they age rapidly, although, notwithstanding all that is said by casual observers who have no sense of analogies, they work no harder than the wives of the ordinary European working man. Wherever in tropical Africa the people are driven into the European system, both political and economic, they wilter. The Baganda of Uganda are one of the most intelligent of African peoples. Yet they are dying out under the influence of the European system, or nominal system, of monogamous unions. The Europeanised African of the West Coast towns who wears European clothes, and whose women don corsets, stockings and fashionable footgear, is far less long lived than his ancestors, and has far fewer children. As a class the educated West African is a perishing one: a class which, at heart, is profoundly unhappy. The whole notion and policy of Europeanising the inhabitant of the tropical belt of Africa is a profound error of psychology, totally unscientific. The tropical African is a bad labourer when he is working for the white man; an excellent labourer when he is working for himself, a free man. In the former case, although capable of great attachment, he will, if that attachment is lacking, which is usually the case *et pour cause*, desert at the first opportunity. And the lash, which is freely used all over tropical Africa where the system of European-managed plantations has been introduced, is a brutalising medium, alike for those who suffer from it and for those who have recourse to it: it is also the invariable precursor of bloodshed. Tropical Africa can produce, and does produce, abundantly as we shall see in the next chapter, under its own system of land tenure, co-operative labour and corporate social life.

A last reflection would seem to be called for in connection with the Portuguese Cocoa Islands. The reasons of the excessive death rate among the contracted labourers may have been accurately diagnosed in these pages, or it may not. But there it is. If it cannot be overcome, what right has an industry to continue, however great the trouble lavished upon it, however obvious the utilitarian argument militating against habitual and deliberate ill-treatment; which destroys one hundred out of every thousand men in the prime of life every year, so that in ten years the thousand men have vanished from the face of the earth?

PART III
Reparation and Reform

CHAPTER XII.

The Land and its Fruits.

With the exception of Abyssinia and "Liberia," the whole of Africa is now parcelled out among five European Powers and one State ruled by white South Africans. Of those five European Powers, France is politically responsible for the government of African territories one-third as large again as Europe; the Belgians, who number 7½ millions, are politically responsible for African territories 95 times larger than their own country, the Portuguese who number 5½ millions, are politically responsible for African territories 21 times larger than Portugal. No particular knowledge or prescience are required to predict that this represents an artificial state of affairs which cannot last. A far more important issue, however, than the future distribution of political control in Africa is the policy which the governing elements in the white races intend to apply to Africa in the years and generations to come. The white peoples of the earth have just experienced the severest convulsion in their history. Vast numbers of them are embarked upon uncharted seas. Their mental and spiritual outlook has been profoundly affected. What consequences will these events have upon the peoples of Africa, henceforth associated more closely than ever with Europe and America?

The previous chapters convey, inadequately enough, some notion of the debt of reparation which the white peoples owe to the blacks; some idea of the wrongs which have been inflicted by the former upon the latter. The quarter of a century which preceded the war, witnessed sincere and successful efforts in a number of parts of Africa to establish a different record. I shall have occasion to refer to these efforts in the present chapter. But it will not escape observation that precisely the same period is also noted, not merely for the revival of the old slave trade spirit "swinging back to power," but for the actual perpetration in other and, unhappily, vaster sections of the Continent, of infamies on a scale exceeding anything the world has seen since the old-fashioned slave trade was abolished. True, that the uprising of the public conscience against the worst of these infamies was evidential of the continued prevalence among the British people of the countervailing spirit which destroyed the old slave trade; and that it also testified to the existence of similar sentiments in individual citizens of other lands. The comfort to be derived from this is real. On the other hand it must not be overlooked that this countervailing spirit which, considered as a national force, is peculiar to Britain, was able to make itself felt effectively as an international influence, only because its manifestations had a basis of historical justification in formal conventions. Where that historical basis was lacking, the national influence could not be exercised; and the anarchy reigning in international relationships precluded reform. Moreover, these events proved to demonstration that even among so naturally generous a people as the French, national protests inspired alike by considerations of humanity and national honour were unable to prevail against the power of sectional interests, although those sectional interests were not wholly French and although the manner in which they were exercised was admittedly disastrous to French national interests.

Such was the general state of the African question when the Great War shattered all the hopes which some of us entertained that the very wrongs of Africa, and the incessant friction resulting among the European Powers politically concerned with Africa through the pursuance of selfish and short-sighted aims, might give rise to another International Conference, which would furnish the occasion for elaborating a native policy towards Africa worthy of civilisation. If such a conference, whose propelling motive would have been a desire to redress wrongs, to guard against their repetition and to avoid causes of international irritation directly or indirectly imputable to their perpetration, could have been held, some of us thought that Europe would have been ministering to the peaceful future of her own peoples as well as to that of the peoples of Africa. It fell to the lot of the author, three years before the Great War, to place this view, which was received with approval, directly before a some-

THE LAND AND ITS FRUITS

what unique audience including distinguished men from several European countries, and Englishmen who had been, or were actually then responsible, for the government of tens of millions of Africans. I recall the incident only because of its relevancy to the plea I am desirous of putting forward in the ensuing pages.

For on the morrow of the Great War the peoples of Africa are threatened with the gravest dangers. There is but too much reason to fear that amid the welter of chaos into which Europe as a whole, and every State in Europe, is plunged, opportunity may be taken to enforce policies and practices in Africa which must prove fatal to its inhabitants and, in the ultimate resort, disastrous to Europe. Europe, even that section of it which has been triumphant in arms, is impoverished to a degree which its peoples do not yet fully appreciate because the bill of costs has not yet been presented, and because their Governments are still making lavish promises which they cannot by any possibility fulfil. The triumphant peoples are not yet convinced that it is impracticable for them to live as parasites upon the beaten peoples, without inviting consequences even more detrimental to their interests than the future already holds for them. They still believe that vast sums will be presently available for social improvements without revolutionising the whole economic fabric of society. They have as yet no clear notion of the proportions of the financial millstone around their necks. They have not yet grasped the fact that the purchasing and producing population of Europe has been reduced by something like twenty-five millions. When the ruthless logic of facts comes home, the possessing and ruling classes will be driven to every conceivable expedient to lessen the burden of direct and indirect taxation, in order to retain their privileged position in the State. Africa is a vast reservoir of labour, and preserve of natural riches. The temptation to force that labour into the service of the European Governments, to resuscitate 16th Century colonial conceptions—will be very great. Again, European industries depend for their resurrection and extension upon abundant supplies of raw material—both vegetable and mineral. Africa, especially tropical Africa, is the natural home of products in the highest degree essential to modern industry. The desire to speed-up the supply of these products and largely to increase the output will, again, be very great.

Industrial capitalism and the political interests of the ruling classes will here find common ground. The drive towards some comprehensive form of forced or slave labour to hasten output will be considerable. These perils are not imaginary. Certain prospectuses and public speeches issued and delivered in this country during the past two years cannot be overlooked: a literature is already growing up on the subject. The "idleness" and "indolence" of the African native are being insidiously taught to a section, at least, of working-class opinion at home, with a view to securing Labour support for policies and practices alike immoral and anti-social. The impression that the Empire "owns" vast estates in Africa, which are lying fallow owing to the incurable sloth of the aboriginal inhabitants is being sedulously propagated. The immunity enjoyed by the Chartered Company of South Africa in its treatment of the native peoples of Rhodesia and the almost complete subordination of the Administration of British East Africa to the capitalist theory of tropical African development, are profoundly disquieting. Nor, in considering these dangers, must we blind ourselves to two facts, which the Great War of 1914-18 has brought out with special prominence. One is that no Government need be deterred in future from imposing an unjust policy upon African peoples through fear of the military risks attendant thereon. The latest inventions in the science of human destruction have removed that brake. Not even a homogeneous people fairly well armed and good shots like the Basutos could offer an effective resistance to modern engines of slaughter. The other fact is the employment of many African troops in the war. The European governing classes have now ocular demonstration that their capacity to bend the peoples of Africa to their will through the conscripted African, is limited only by considerations of prudence in thus staking the future of their domination in Africa upon an African militarism. Of this more anon.

Against these dangers may be set the creation of a new international mechanism—the League of Nations—which may succeed in evolving an international conscience in the affairs of Africa. This is not the place to discuss

THE LAND AND ITS FRUITS 167

whether the League, as at present constituted, contains within itself the promise of a fuller growth, or the germs of dissolution. It is sufficient for the purpose of the case which is here being set out that the League has proclaimed as the guiding policy which should determine the future relations between the white races and the black a recognition on the part of the former of an obligation of trusteeship for the latter. As the African peoples were prefigured in 1884 so are they described to-day—the wards of civilisation. Once more the profession is announced, the determination proclaimed. Will its upshot but re-echo the bitter mockery of the past?

The answer to this question will be largely determined by the measure in which the fundamental problems of relationship between Europe and Africa are really understood by the present and rising generation. If they are understood, the lessons derivable from the recent history of Africa will at least have been learned, and ignorance, the parent of error, will be eliminated.

It is, therefore, imperative that in considering the future relationship of the white and black peoples, we should distinguish between the fundamental and the accessory. The first question is not one of method. It is one of principle. The relative merits of "direct" and of "indirect" rule in the administration of African communities, in the form of representation of African communities and of individual Africans in the mechanism of white government; the processes of education; labour regulations; segregation—these problems and many others, weighty as they severally are, are still of secondary importance, because they do not go to the root of the matter.

The root is the land. Are the peoples of Africa to be regarded and treated as *land-owning communities?* Or is native tenure in land to be swept away? That is the fundamental issue, because in that issue is involved the destinies of the African peoples, and the whole character of the future relations of Africa with the outer-world. As it is resolved, so will the African peoples develop along lines of freedom, or along lines of serfdom. As it is resolved, so will the white peoples be acting as trustees for their black wards, or as exploiters of black labour. The issue underlies the problems of trade, labour, government. It can be approached from different directions, but upon examination these are seen to lead to the same common centre. Divorce the African communities from the land, and you reduce the units composing them to the level of wage slaves. You thereby reproduce in Africa all the vices which lie at the base of social unrest in civilised States. But you reproduce them in infinitely aggravated form. The white proletariat in the mass can never attain to true economic independence until it has won back the rights of the common people to the soil. But it can live, and even prosper, because owing to the improvements in transport, labour-saving appliances and a network of trade relations, it can be fed through external sources. But the prosperity of African communities wholly depends upon the use of their soil, and by robbing them of the soil you deprive them of the means of life.

Again, the existing land system of a large part of Europe is a system which has evolved internally by gradual processes, and which internal action can modify, or abrogate altogether. The matter can be solved by the citizens of the State: it is a question for the latter of the conquest of political power, either by revolutionary or evolutionary means. But for an alien race to deprive African peoples of the land, is to strike at the foundations of human liberties, to disrupt the whole conditions of life, and to impose from outside a servitude only maintainable by the constant exercise of brute force. The revolutionary movement sweeping through Europe has various precipitating causes, and responds to mixed and, apparently conflicting motives. Fundamentally it is, consciously and unconsciously, an impulse of the mass of the people to win back the land, the pivot of their economic and human liberties, the nursing-mother of man. Is it precisely at this stage in the evolution of the white races, that the European ruling classes are to be allowed to reproduce in Africa the confiscatory and monopolistic policy, which for centuries has maintained the peoples of Europe in a condition of economic servitude?

This, then, is the first pre-requisite to the performance of the duties of trusteeship towards the African peoples, that the latter must be guaranteed in the possession of the soil and the enjoyment of its fruits.

. . . . . .

A general conviction that the freedom and progress of the African peoples were dependent upon the possession of the land, inspired the deliberations of the first great African Congress held in 1884-5. The problem was there approached from the standpoint, not of the land itself, but from that of the utilisation and enjoyment of such of the land's fruits as were suitable for external trade. It is useful to recall this first and only attempt to interpret that spirit of trusteeship, which the League of Nations now invokes.

Thirty-five years ago the Powers of Europe, with which were associated the United States, laid down the broad principles which should govern the relations of Europe with an enormous section of tropical Africa, then for the first time in history, brought into direct contact with the political lfe of Europe. Their spokesmen recalled the fatal political error which had vitiated the discovery and the development of the tropical regions of the American Continent, whose natural wealth had been regarded as the natural property of the pioneering European nations, and the labour of whose inhabitants had been ruthlessly exploited to enrich the national treasuries. They perceived that the antidote to a repetition of that error lay in stressing a principle which constituted its antithesis— the principle of *trade*. The conception which underlay the colonising efforts of the 16th Century visualised aboriginal populations as a mass of human material with no rights in its soil or in the products of its country, through whose labour those products should be transmuted into revenues for the invading and occupying nation. The framers of the provisions of the Act of Berlin, standing on the threshold of a new experiment in tropical colonisation on a huge scale, visualised the aboriginal populations as sentient human beings, and in proclaiming that the principle of *trade* should be the basis of the relationship between them and the outer world, they implicitly recognised that those populations were possessed of rights in the soil and its products— the operations of *trade* involving the proprietorship on both sides of exchangeable articles; of buyers and sellers.

Trade, regarded as a principle in human relationships, is one thing. The intrinsic properties of trade, and the methods under which trade is carried on—this is an altogether different thing. The failure to distinguish between the two has tended to obscure issues which are perfectly simple and defined. People who feel strongly in regard to certan forms which trade has assumed in some parts of Africa—the trade in liquor for instance—or who are impressed with the injustice which an African population may suffer in the lowering of the purchase price of African produce by rings and combines on the part of European firms buying that produce; are apt to confuse these and similar evils with the *principle* itself. The operations of trade need constant regulation and supervision; it is the business of the administrator and the legislator to provide them. But the maintenance of trade itself as the economic factor in the relationship between civilised and primitive communities, producers respectively of commodities desired by both, is synonymous with the recognition that the latter are possessed of elementary human rights. If that *principle* be set aside, slavery, which is a denial of human rights, must in some form or another necessarily take its place.

That is why the framers of the provisions of the Act of Berlin were profoundly wise in putting in the forepart of their program the right of the native peoples of Central Africa to *trade*, to sell the produce of their soil against imported European merchandise. Recognition that this natural right was inherent in African communities necessarily implied, as has been already pointed out, recognition that African communities have proprietary rights in the land. But the instrument forged at Berlin in 1885 did not *explicitly* provide for this. It contained no safeguards against expropriation. It made no attempt to define native tenure. This was, perhaps, natural enough. No one could have supposed that a few years later some thirty millions of Africans would be dispossessed by simple decree, of their proprietary rights in a territory almost as large as Europe. Nevertheless the fact that this danger was not foreseen and provided against, proved of great assistance to King Leopold in defending his African policy, on the ground that the right of a " State " to appropriate " vacant " lands was an established principle of jurisprudence; that the natural fruits of the land thus appropriated became *de facto* the property of the " State," and that no violation of the Act of Berlin had, therefore, occurred.

THE LAND AND ITS FRUITS 171

The case of the Congo Free State and of the French Congo reveal in the most conclusive fashion how indissolubly connected in African economy are the problems of Afro-European trade and of African labour required for the purposes of that trade, with the ownership of land. In destroying Afro-European trade in the Congo regions on the plea that the African peoples possessed no proprietary rights in the raw material of Africa—i.e., in the fruits of the soil, King Leopold and the French Government implicitly denied to the native communities of the Congo any proprietary rights in the land itself. But as all these denials, both explicit and implicit, of African rights, and the corresponding assertion of alien rights, meant nothing unless African labour could be utilised on behalf of the alien claimant to the soil's products, so the claim to those products was seen to involve a claim alike to the land and to the labour of the African. With the land and its products went the man.

. . . . . .

Where trade, expressed in a large export of produce which has been paid for in goods and cash, is not present as a factor in the relationship between white man and black, the possession of land is just as essential to the native population, although the problem takes on a different complexion. Conditions in colonisable South Africa, in tropical West-Central Africa, in tropical East Africa, and in Mediterranean North Africa, vary enormously. Nevertheless in every section of the Continent the same truth holds good—possession of land is for the African community as for the individual African, the criterion of human liberties, protection against poverty and serfdom, the sheet-anchor of material, mental and spiritual development.

It would be absurd to pretend, of course, that the problem of the land as it presents itself to-day in imperial South Africa, can be envisaged from the same standpoint as in British West Africa. Imperial South Africa comprises an area of 1,204,827 square miles, containing an indigenous population of 6,872,164; the average density being a fraction over 5. British West Africa covers 445,234 square miles with an indigenous population of over 20 millions; the average density being a fraction over 45. The line of demarcation between trusteeship and exploitation in imperial South Africa is the line which divides a policy designed to provide a sufficiency of fertile land for the requirements of the native population—allowing an ample margin for natural growth—for agricultural and ranching purposes; and a policy which aims by successive encroachments, under one pretext or another, upon the native "reserves," or by shifting native communities from good, arable land to arid or swampy locations, to prevent the increase of a native farming, planting and ranching class working as its own master under the native system of tenure, and thereby gradually to reduce the native population to a landless proletariat working as hired labourers for the white men on the land, or in the mines. There can be no doubt on which side of the line lie duty, justice and (if the average white South African could bring himself to a mental contemplation of the not-far-distant future when South Africa will be mineralogically exhausted) commonsense. Neither unhappily, is there any doubt upon which side of the line average South African opinion is ranged, nor towards which side of the line South African official policy has usually inclined. The Chartered Company's land claim in Southern Rhodesia is the latest and the most striking object lesson open to study in this regard: but it is not an unique phenomenon by any means. Abundant and cheap supplies of African labour—that is the avowed purpose of the controlling spirits of industrial South Africa, as of the financial magnates at home, and their gramophones in the Press, who talk at large about the Empire, but whose conception of imperial responsibilities begins and ends with dividends. Nor, it would seem, is a section of white labour in South Africa above supporting that policy, although it is actuated in so doing by different, but not by worthier motives.

This demand for cheap and plentiful black labour in colonisable Africa is quite intelligible, and within limits is justifiable. But those limits are exceeded when, in order to realise it, policy is deliberately directed to lowering the human quality and undermining the economic independence of the aboriginal population by uprooting it from the soil, thereby converting land-owning communities, kept self-respecting under their own institutions, into a disrupted mass of shiftable labour. A certain proportion of an aboriginal population, even when settled on the land, is always procurable for external labour

THE LAND AND ITS FRUITS

except (where it is agricultural) in the sowing, planting or harvest seasons (which will vary according to the crop) if the wages are sufficiently attractive, the treatment fair, and the period of contract of reasonable length. Given those conditions, a smaller section, dissatisfied with agricultural life under the tribal system, is permanently available. It is the business of government to adjust the demand for labour to the requirements of its wards—the native population, whose lasting interests ought never to be sacrificed to the exigencies of an alien interest. After all, there is plenty of time! One of the worst curses of the European industrial system is the absurd degree to which custom and competition combine to press upon the lives of the people. It is really due to nothing more respectable than the hurry of the employing class to get rich—the mad rush for large profits rapidly secured, which flows like a destructive virus through the veins of European capitalist society. There is absolutely no need to transplant this disease into colonisable Africa. It is fatal to all the legitimate and stable utilitarian interests of the country. To allow the native population to suffer from its ravages is for the trustee to violate his trust.

Study the work and the utterances of men like Sir Godfrey Langdon and Lord Selborne (when High Commissioner for South Africa). You will find in them the conception of trusteeship in *esse*. The test of trusteeship, which is merely good government, *i.e.*, government in the interests of the governed, *all* the governed, in those parts of Africa which are colonisable, or partly colonisable by white peoples, is the determination of the trustees to provide for the free expansion not only of the white population and their descendants, but of the aboriginal population and their descendants, whose numbers and whose ratio of increase are immeasurably greater. There can be no free expansion for the latter without land: but only helotry. Many hold that where in Africa the white man can permanently reside and perpetuate his race, helotry is the pre-destined and necessary lot of the native. The argument is immoral, and like all immoralities it is unsound, because it looks only to the moment and excludes the future from its purview. In this particular case the error lies in the fact that while it is possible to reduce the native population in these parts of the Continent to helotry by expropriating it from the land, it is impossible to maintain it perpetually in that position. And for this reason, that if civilisation brings with it the power to impose helotry, it also automatically generates forces which in course of time acquire a sufficient strength to destroy helotry. The helots of to-day become the rebels of to-morrow, but rebels of a very different calibre to the primitives whose opposition to the original injustice was so easily overcome. The truth is so obvious that it requires no labouring. The human mind cannot be permanently chained, least of all in Africa, where it functions in a vigorous physical tenement, is highly adaptable and imitative; where man is altogether a very *vital* being. And the subject has another side to it, of which colonisable or semi-colonisable Africa provides many illustrations. I select one: its moral is generally applicable. Within a few hours steaming from Marseilles, you set foot in France's oldest African colony, upon which, owing to its proximity to the homeland, a great nation has been able to bring to bear a continuous and irresistible influence for nearly a century. The results are superficially brilliant. Beneath this surface glitter achieved at enormous financial outlay, a canker gnaws. A proud race has gradually become dispossessed of its land, largely, it is fair to state, through initial mistakes committed with the best of intentions: helotry has replaced economic independence. And after nearly a century of French occupation, this is how one of the deepest students—a distinguished Frenchman—of this subject people, describes their sentiments towards their alien rulers: ' Without having lived for a long time among them and having observed them constantly and critically, it would not only be difficult, it would, I think, be impossible, to form even a faint idea of the profound hatred, of the contemptuous aversion which their manners and their speech conceal. . . . '[1]

·" The land question," states the famous report of the South African Native Affairs Committee, " dominates and pervades every other question; it is the bedrock of the native's present economic position and largely affects his social system." If that can be said as to the importance of ownership in land for African peoples in a region where a white people is growing up side by side with the

[1] "Recherches sur la constitution de la propriété térritoriale dans les pays musulmans, et subsidairement, en Algérie." Worms (Paris: Franck).

THE LAND AND ITS FRUITS

indigenous inhabitants, where the export industries are wholly in the hands of the white population, and where white men are able to undertake at least some forms and some measure of manual labour, and a great deal of immediate supervision; how much more can be said of its importance in the tropical regions of the Continent where the white man is but a bird of passage, and where he is utterly incapable of manual labour? In the former regions, expropriation of the natives leads to an economic servitude, which for reasons already explained, will be accompanied by deeper social wrongs than in Europe: it may develop into actual slavery. In the latter regions it can at best be but veiled slavery: at its worst it involves a Slave system more ferocious and destructive than any in the history of the world.

Let us examine the question of the land as it affects the inhabitants of the tropical regions of Africa—*i.e.*, roughly, three-fifths of that huge Continent.

. . . . . .

Circumstances have combined to create marked divergencies in the conditions generally prevailing in the eastern and in the western portion of tropical Africa respectively. We must look for the explanation in past history. Slavery and the slave trade imposed from outside ravaged both sections of the Continent for centuries. On the west the European was the scourge: on the east, mainly the Arab. The objects pursued differed radically, with corresponding results. On the west, except in Angola, the European system threw no roots into the soil: it did not maintain itself in the mainland *as an institution*. That was not its purpose. The slavers, and the Governments that employed or encouraged them, had no interests *in* Africa. Their interests lay outside Africa. They were traders in African flesh and blood, not slave owners in Africa, using their slaves on African estates. Neither they, nor their clients, sought the economic development of Africa; but that of America, for which African labour was required. They looked upon Africa as a reservoir of human material to exploit the soil, not of Africa, but of the New World. The result was, that while the slave trade decimated the population of Western Africa, it did not crush the spirit of its peoples. It did not destroy their independence. In some measure it served to intensify the passion for freedom among them

By giving a prodigious extension to internecine warfare and investing it with a distinct economic motive, the slave trade strengthened all the instincts of self-preservation among the native communities. Just because every community lived under the perpetual menace of aggression from its neighbour, it became more wary, more intent upon preserving its liberties, more devoted to its land and homesteads, more sturdy in its defence. And the Western Slave trade had another consequence. It increased the strong commercial trend of mind, the love of barter and bargaining, inherent in the West African peoples. For, examined from the standpoint of its rôle among the West African peoples whom it affected, the Slave trade was not merely a stimulus to war: it was a stimulus to gain, to profit. Innumerable intermediaries participated in the purchase price which the European slaver, installed on his hulk moored beyond the surf-line, or encamped on shore, haggled over with his African agents and their armed followers when they reached the coast dragging with them their shackled captives. Those captives had passed from hand to hand along many hundreds of miles in the interior, and contractors and sub-contractors had each claimed their share of commission on the human live-stock. The double effect of centuries of this traffic in West Africa tended thus to accentuate the spirit of independence and the commercial spirit of the native peoples.

The purpose of the Arab slaver and *conquisitador* in Eastern Africa was wholly different. A certain number of captives were, of course, deported to Arabia and the Levant. But the interests of the Oman Arab of Southern Arabia, who founded the Zanzibar Sultanate and extended domination as far inland as the Great Lakes, were primarily in the soil. True, he was a great trader, and the loss of native life involved in his activities was chiefly caused through the terrible mortality among the carriers who transported the ivory he secured from the interior to the coast. He was ruthless in his warfare. But having achieved his intention in subduing the aboriginal population by force of arms, he settled down in the country, founded rich and prosperous settlements, and laid immense tracts under cultivation, through the labour of his defeated enemies. With this end in view, he maintained the peoples he had conquered under his per-

THE LAND AND ITS FRUITS

manent yoke. It was a despotic but not ordinarily a heavy yoke; for once installed as a conqueror it was his obvious policy that the land he had conquered should be prosperous and peaceable. He became an institution in the country, assembled round him large retinues of slaves and concubines. His rule was patriarchal, but it was permanent. The people remained a beaten people. They became servants. He remained the master and concentrated in his own hands the external trade and the industry of the country. The stigma of serfdom was never lifted from the people he had subjugated in arms. Their power of initiative was undermined.

Portuguese rule, which alternated with Arab rule for three centuries in Eastern Africa, was in many respects similar to the latter in its effects upon the native population, except that it was more destructive. The first period of its activity was marked by all the characteristics which distinguished contemporary Spanish and Portuguese policy in South America—the enslavement of the population and the pillage of the country on behalf of the national treasury. The second period of its activity was cursed by the Slave trade in order to supply the increasing demand of the Brazilian markets. And here, as in Angola, but unlike the rest of Western Africa, the Slave-trading Power was its own purveyor: actually established in and occupying the country: breaking the people. When the Slave trade disappeared, the Portuguese grip upon the East Coast relaxed, and the edifice of Portuguese rule became like the pillars of a building invaded by the white ant—without substance. Thus the combined effect of centuries of Arab and Portuguese domination in the major portion of the eastern part of the African Continent, went to crush the spirit of independence and initiative in the native peoples and to make of them slaves and domestics rather than traders and producers in their own right.

This difference in the history of their contact with the outer world is, in the main, explanatory of the divergence in the economic *status* of the peoples of East and West Africa to-day. Native export industries may hardly be said to exist in the eastern part of the Continent except in Uganda, and the sytem of European plantations worked by hired, or forced, native labour is the rule. An inherited tendency has inclined the various European

Administrations to favour the European planter rather than to promote the far more healthy and potentially promising system of encouraging the native communities to develop their own land. This has been the marked characteristic both of German and of British policy in East Africa. It continues to be that of British policy with consequences which are making for disaster. One visible result can be seen in the economic situation of the European dependencies in West Africa and in East Africa respectively. The export of natural produce from the whole of East Africa—British, German and Portuguese—does not exceed the output of the small West African Protectorates of the Gold Coast and Sierra Leone combined. It would fall below it but for the export of cotton from Uganda, and this, the most considerable of the articles of export from Eastern Africa is a native and not a European industry—i.e., the cotton is grown by the Baganda themselves on their own land, and for their own profit. For in Uganda proper the British Administration has, up to the present, wisely assisted the native population to grow economic products for sale for its own account, although it is constantly pressed to adopt the European plantation system existing in British East Africa proper.

In this connection it is advisable to touch upon a subject on which there is much popular misconception. The idea that tropical Africa can be developed more rapidly by creating a population of thriftless labourers in European employ, instead of keen farmers benefiting from the fruits of their enterprise is altogether unsound.* It is unsound, apart from the very doubtful proposition which assumes " rapidity " of development to be synonymous with lasting prosperity. Those who favour the development of tropical Africa by white overseers commanding native labour, can never in the nature of the case be impartial. Unhappily they have the ear of the Government and access to the Press. A far larger material output under the system of native industries is certain, and that policy does undoubtedly coincide with the permanent interest of

* It is even beginning to be seen to be unsound in certain Southern States of the American Union among a negro population, over whom the taint of slavery still lingers. In those States where the better class labour is beginning to acquire land, the plantation system is going downhill fast. Experience is showing that where the negro works his own land better results are being obtained, even from poor soil, than from plantation labour on good soil.

the dependency viewed even from the strictly utilitarian standpoint. And for these reasons. An African resembles other human beings. If he is working and producing for himself, he will work better and produce more than if he is working for someone else. That is elemental.

Again, the purchasing capacity of an African or arboricultural community growing or gathering and preparing crops for export, is necessarily far greater than the purchasing capacity of an agglomeration of African wage earners. In the former case the equivalent earned represents the value of the crop *plus* the labour devoted to its production. In the latter case the equivalent merely represents labour, the intrinsic value of the product remaining the property of the white employer. Now the white employer of African labour in a tropical African dependency does not spend his profits in that dependency, but outside it. The native agriculturist, on the other hand, spends his profits in a way which cannot but benefit the revenues of the dependency, because he spends them on the purchase of European merchandise, and that European merchandise pays customs' dues upon entering the dependency. The desire to acquire the products of the outer world is the stimulus which induces the African to grow crops *for export*. He is not driven to do so from economic necessity.

I fully realise, of course, that neither the argument adduced above, nor any other arguments of a like kind, meet the objections of those who contend that a tropical African dependency should be regarded as a milch cow for the direct enrichment of the protecting European State, or for that of a few individual capitalists within that State. I quite recognise the force and logic of that point of view, but I maintain that it ought not to be allowed to exercise a determining influence upon European Governments responsible for the administration of tropical African territory. I oppose these views to the utmost of my power, and have done so consistently for a quarter of a century. I oppose them because I look upon those who entertain them as representing an element which makes for degradation in human affairs. The just, equitable, understanding government of the primitive, but highly intelligent, adaptable, kindly and politically helpless races of tropical Africa, is one of the finest and most unselfish tasks which remain for white men to fulfil in the world: a task requiring in its performance the utmost patience, much self-repression, all the high moral qualities indeed. *These races cannot escape being sucked into the vortex of white economic expansion.* Steam, electricity, aviation, industrial development combine to make it impossible. If to-morrow the Governments washed their hands of them and retired from the country, these races would become the prey of international freebooters far more numerous and infinitely more powerful than the adventurers who fought for supremacy in the Slave trade up and down the West Coast of Africa, ravaged the Carnatic and pillaged the Americas. *Such a withdrawal would deprive these races of their only present safeguard—public opinion.* But the government of these races can be transformed from the noble human mission it ought always to be, into an agency of oppression and injustice. This transformation cannot take place without degrading all parties directly affected by it, whether as victims or beneficiaries, and the public opinion which tolerates it.

I oppose, then, the persons and the interests that make themselves responsible for the promulgation of these views and practices for the reason stated, and for the kindred reason that I hold these African races to have as great a right to happiness, peace and security as our own people at home. It is, to my way of thinking, utterly intolerable that they should be exploited, made miserable, dragged down, ill-used, their home and social life broken up, themselves enslaved or destroyed. That is a purely instinctive sentiment for which I am no more responsible than the man who instinctively approaches all questions connected with coloured peoples from the standpoint that the coloured man—the black man especially—is little better than an animal. It is not, I admit, capable of rationalistic defence, whereas the other reason I have advanced is. But such as it is, I hold it and minister to it.

I quite understand, however, that the humanistic appeal is not sufficient to defeat the purposes of those whom I oppose. This became clear to me in the course of the twelve years' agitation against the misgovernment of the Congo. That is why I invariably

THE LAND AND ITS FRUITS

seek to demonstrate to public opinion, which in the ultimate resort dictates and governs policy, that what is morally wrong, is also foolish and unsound when tested by severely "practical" standards. If I fail in this, it is not because the "practical" case is incapable of convincing demonstration, but because of my own incapacity to establish it. But if it be to the advantage of the European manufacturer and working man that tropical Africa should produce an increasing quantity of raw material, conveyed to Europe to be there turned into the finished article, and should consume an increasing quantity of goods manufactured in Europe to pay for that raw material; then it is to their advantage that the administrative policy applied in tropical Africa should be such as will ensure that result. And if it be to the advantage of the European manufacturer and working man, and the general body of tax-payers that the native communities of tropical Africa should increase in numbers, in prosperity and in intelligence; then it is contrary to their interests that an administrative policy should be applied in those regions calculated to impoverish these communities, to give rise to unrest and to foment wars, thereby decreasing both the numbers and the productivity of the people, and involving the home or local Government in military expenditure.

The long-view and the common-sense view is to regard African communities producing raw material for export as partners with the working classes of Europe in a joint undertaking. The aptness of the description will not diminish, but will gather fresh emphasis in the measure in which the working classes of Europe receive a larger share in the profits derived from industry. The more considerable the output of raw material by these African communities, the greater their purchasing power expressed in terms of European merchandise. Thus the producers of Africa and the producing classes of Europe *are* partners, and one of the chief hopes which those who wish to preserve the African races from the cruelties, injustices, and stupidities of the European capitalist system, centres in the increasing recognition of that partnership by the organised forces of Labour in Europe.

. . . .

In no part of Africa does the land and its beneficial usage bulk so largely in the economy of the people as in the tropical western part of the Continent, the most populous as it is intrinsically the richest. When the slave-trade received its death blow, an export trade in natural produce, which had preceded the slave-trade in many parts of the west coast and had never been wholly extirpated, revived and extended inland. Thanks to the improved transport facilities of the last thirty years it has attained very large dimensions, much larger than most people suspect. In the territories drained by the Congo and its affluents, the Congo Free State and the French Congo, Leopoldianism, sweeping like a pestilence over the land, has flung back this natural growth for generations, perhaps for centuries; perhaps the damage done is irreparable. But north of the Congo, in the British, French, and German dependencies, European administration has in the main proceeded on rational lines, with corresponding economic results. Although, with the notable exception of Northern Nigeria, little or no legislation directed specifically to safeguarding native rights in land has yet been evolved, the native population has, generally speaking, been left in undisturbed possession of the soil, and has been encouraged to develop its fruits for export purposes in freedom, on its own indigenous land-holding and labour system, and on its own account. The Germans in the Kamerun did, it is true, import East African practices by introducing the plantation system for the cultivation of cocoa, and pursued it for some years with commendable enterprise and scientific care The economic results, however, were anything but brilliant, and the remarkable achievements of the Fanti and Ashanti farmer in the Gold Coast with the same crop—which I shall refer to later on —had made a profound impression upon German experts who had studied both systems *de visu*. In their other West African dependency of Togoland the Germans, imitating the policy of the British Administration in Nigeria and the methods of the British Cotton Growing Association in that dependency and in Uganda, had succeeded in getting cotton growing for export started as a native industry by native farmers in their own right.

Western Africa offers a remarkable, indeed, a unique, field for profitable study in the capacity of aboriginal peoples to develop the natural or cultivable riches of their land as free men and landowners, to the advantage of themselves and of the rest of the world. West Africa is the country of great native export industries, created and maintained by the native communities themselves on their own land, under their own native systems of land tenure and co-operative effort. The most important of these native export industries are the palm-oil and kernel industries, and the cocoa industry. As both of them have attained their highest development in British Protectorates—the former in Southern Nigeria, the latter in the Gold Coast and Ashanti —it is doubly suitable that they should be selected for comment in a volume not free from criticisms of maladministration in other parts of British protected Africa.

West Africa is the natural home of the oil-palm, of which there are many varieties. From time immemorial this tree has played a daily and vital part in the domestic economy of West African communities. Its fruit is a staple article of food. Variously treated in accordance with the special purpose in view, it is used medicinally for cleansing the body, as a disinfectant, an insecticide, a rust remover, and as a substitute for yeast in the making of bread. When fresh, its leaves are employed to dress wounds; when dry, as tinder; pounded with other substances, prophylactically; with the mid-ribs, as roofing material, for the manufacture of rope, baskets, nets, mats. and brooms. The male flower is burnt into charcoal and used as a dressing for burns. The stalks of the fruit-branches are beaten out to make sponges. The shell of the kernel is an admirable fuel. The "cabbage" or growing plant is a succulent vegetable. Mixed with the juice of other palms it provides a sustaining beverage known as palm wine.

Apart from its being an article of consumption, the fruit is an article of extensive *internal* trade between village and village, market and market. One community will be specially trained in preparing the oil for consumption; another for different purposes. Some communities are deficient in the tree, and eagerly exchange other commodities for the fruit. As one travels along the roads and by-ways of this populous region,* the commonest

* The average density of the population in Southern Nigeria is 98 to the square mile—a considerable proportion of the surface area is uninhabitable—but in many districts the density is very much greater, reaching to nearly 400 per square mile in some places.

sight to be observed is that of men and women carrying palm-oil in pots or pans on their heads. The thick, orange-coloured strong-smelling stuff is on sale at every little village market. Guilds exist, not in Southern Nigeria only, but probably in every part of West Africa where the oil-palm grows, to protect the tree from being "tapped" for the wine at the wrong time. There are professional oil-palm climbers—climbing the tree is a hazardous experiment for all but the expert, for it rises a sheer 40 to 60 feet without a branch, and the fruit is at the top. There are also professional palm-wine preparers. "It is impossible to exaggerate," writes an experienced District Commissioner, "the important part this sovereign tree fills in the life of the country . . . it provides the people among whom it flourishes with meat and drink, and with nearly all the simple necessaries of daily life." It is these oil-palm forests which the gentlemen of the Empire Resources Development Committee desire the British State to lay claim to and exploit, with armies of native labourers—the proprietors of the trees converted into British Government employees—for the dual benefit of British company promoters and British tax-payers! So much for the domestic rôle of the oil-palm.

About the middle of last century some British trading firms began the experiment of purchasing the oil from the native and putting it on the home market. A demand then arose for the oil obtained from the kernels, which is of a different quality and put to different uses.

From these small beginnings the export trade in palm-oil and kernels arose. To-day it gives employment directly and indirectly to many tens of thousands of European and American working men, and is the principal freight-feeder of hundreds of steamers employed in the West African carrying trade. The native population eagerly availed itself of the opening offered to it for trade, as it has invariably done all over Western Africa in similar circumstances. In the seven years preceding the war the native communities of Southern Nigeria alone, gathered, prepared and conveyed to the European trading stations on the rivers, palm-oil and kernels to the value of twenty-four millions sterling. In the same period the Gold Coast produced these articles to the value of nearly two million sterling, and Sierra Leone to the value of just over four million sterling. How immense is the aggregate of labour

THE LAND AND ITS FRUITS 185

involved in providing for the demands of this export trade, in addition to the necessities of production for internal trade and consumption, may be estimated from a series of careful official calculations made by the Forestry Department of Southern Nigeria, based upon the output for 1910. These show that the output for that year involved the exploiting of no fewer than 25,227,285 trees! To this work, in itself prodigious, must, of course, be added transport in canoes along the rivers and creeks with which the region is bisected; preparation, and marketing. The processes of preparation of the oil for export vary according to districts and traditional customs. They call for no little skill, patience, and a great variety of forms of activity, while the operations of bartering and purchase among competing local producers and "middlemen" for the markets, involve a constant appeal to enterprise and resourcefulness. The entire population of Southern Nigeria in the oil-palm zone—men, women, and children, for the industry, like all native industries, is a social and family affair, in which each member plays his allotted part—*i.e.*, literally several millions of peoples spend months at a time in various branches of the industry. Thus—the "idle native"!

Let us briefly note how the voluntary labour, the national industry, of these Nigerian peoples affects the interests of the working classes of Europe. European merchants established in Southern Nigeria purchase the raw material from the native communities. They purchase it with European merchandise of all kinds, chiefly cotton goods, of which the Nigerian is a great consumer. Until recently spirits also loomed large in the annual turnover: a highly undesirable trade which is now abolished. A number of other European and American interests are linked up with this native industry. There is the treatment of the raw material in industrial establishments; its transmutation into soap and candles, for instance. There are millions of casks in which the palm-oil is conveyed to Europe. These, taken to pieces, are shipped out in bundles of what are called "staves." The casks need iron hoops, which must also be sent out. They need caulking to be made oil-tight when put together, and there is—or used to be—a considerable trade between Liverpool and Ireland for this purpose in the stems of the common sedge (*scirpus lacustris*). The kernels are sent home in canvas bags, and millions of such bags must be manufactured in Europe and dispatched to Nigeria. There is the handling, haulage, cartage, and distribution of this bulky produce at the European end; its conveyance to the railway depôt and the store; its re-shipment to other parts of the world. There are the mills erected to crush the kernels. These details are merely illustrative of the argument already advanced as to the community of interest between the African producers of raw material and the working classes of Europe. The industry of the one feeds the industry of the other.

Reduce the Southern Nigerian communities from the position of producers in their own right of the fruits of the soil and of free traders in that produce, and you make them, in the words of Mr. Thompson, the chief conservator of the Nigerian forests, "slaves on their own land." If the precepts of elementary morality forbid such a policy, so do the principles of elementary common-sense. In these days the latter consideration requires, perhaps, exceptional accentuation.

. . . . . .

The rise and growth of the cocoa industry in the Gold Coast and Ashanti is one of the most romantic episodes in the history of tropical cultivation. If such results had been achieved under the *ægis* of Europeans, the financial and commercial Press would have taken care to familiarise all of us with the result. But as the enterprise is wholly due to the African farmer, the world, specialists apart, knows little or nothing of it. The "man in the street" continues to accept the interested falsities about the invincible indolence of the "nigger." The real sin of the African native, let it be emphasised once again, is not his indolence, but the fact that he is capable of putting his land to fruitful use, *for his own profit, working as his own master*. It is this which gravels, as Mark Twain used to say, your exploiting capitalist and your grasping syndicates in Europe. As one of his kind is recently reported to have exclaimed at a public meeting: "It is time the natives were made to understand that they have got to work, not for themselves, but for the white man." Precisely. The entire philosophy of your modern slaver is epitomised in that single sentence.

In the early eighties of last century, a native of Accra, a town on the Gold Coast, returned from a term of employment on the European-managed cocoa plantations on the Spanish Island of Fernando Po. He brought back some cocoa pods with him and sowed the seeds on his own family land. The first consignment of native-grown cocoa was exported from the Gold Coast to Europe in 1885. It weighed 121lbs. and was valued at £6 1s. In 1895 the export had risen to 28,906lbs., valued at £471. In 1905 the export was 11½ million pounds, valued at £186,809. In 1913 the export amounted to 113¼ million pounds, valued at £2,484,218! The quality of the article produced in the last few years has well-nigh kept pace with the quantity. In 1908 only 5 per cent. of the Gold Coast cocoa was "good quality," 15 per cent. was "fair," and 80 per cent. "common." In 1912 the proportions were 35 per cent. "good," 50 per cent. "fair," and 15 per cent. "common." In 1913 the crop showed a further considerable improvement, the situation then being that "90 per cent. of Gold Coast is marketable anywhere, and only 10 per cent. thoroughly common and unfit for manufacture of a better class." In thirty years the Gold Coast and Ashanti farmers have placed this small British dependency of under 50,000 square miles, much of it unsuitable to cocoa cultivation, at the head of the cocoa-producing countries of the world. The Gold Coast now grows over 30 per cent. of the total world supply, its output being twice as great as that of Brazil, which is the next largest producer. In twenty-five years the small Gold Coast farmer—the despised West African native who sits in the sun all day, opening his mouth for a ripe banana to fall into it when moved to hunger—has outpaced Brazil, the West Indies, Ecuador, and San Thome as a tropical cultivator. He has shown what he can do under an honest administration, *as a landowner, and working for himself*. Every yard of land put under cocoa cultivation has been won from the hungry forest. The jungle has had to be cut down, cleared, planted and kept cleared—and with the most primitive of tools. Anyone who has had personal experience of the tropical African forest will appreciate what this means. Indeed, the native farmer in his enthusiasm is endangering the rainfall by a too wholesale destruction of the forests, and has to be checked in his own interest. In the early years of the industry every barrel of beans had to be rolled along hundreds of miles of tracks, which only by courtesy were called roads, to the port of shipment. The only assistance the native farmer has had is the technical assistance afforded by an under-staffed, hard-working Agricultural Department, which has done admirable work in distributing masses of leaflets in the native languages, containing cultural directions, in supplying sprays, issuing recommendations for dealing with insect pests, making such judicious representations as have encouraged careful farmers and stimulated careless ones, and so on; and the help of Cadbury Bros., who have established buying centres in the country, created one or two model farms, and given a practical incentive to careful cultivation by paying higher prices for the better prepared article.

These facts speak for themselves on what may be termed the moral issue. But, once again, the utilitarian aspect may be stressed with advantage. I will not repeat the arguments already advanced in this respect. There is, however, one point which may be usefully noted Compare this system of native industries with the attempt at the *direct* employment of European capital in the agricultural and arboricultural development of the African tropics. A company is formed in Europe; land is leased or sold to it in Africa; large sums are invested, a European staff at necessarily high wages is appointed, and further expense entailed in housing it; native labour is engaged at great cost, relatively speaking, is generally unsatisfactory in quality, perhaps unprocurable without official pressure, or in other words, it is more or less forced, with resultant internal economic dislocation, the immediate effect of which is seen in a shortage of food supplies. The Government is forced to import food into a natural granary. This means expense. Revenue, instead of being devoted to increase the general productivity and prosperity of the country, is used to bolster up an artificial economic experiment. The upshot, sooner or later, is political turmoil, risings, bloodshed. And when everything has been done that can be done to make this artificial venture a success, in the interest not of the dependency's revenues, not of the inhabitants of the dependency, but of a small group of Europeans, the venture is more often than not a failure and the capital invested is lost. Who, then, has benefited? All the parties concerned are worse off than they were before the experiment was started. It may be said: "But a native industry can also fail." It can, undoubtedly. A virulent disease may, for example, sweep the native cocoa farms in the Gold Coast to ruin; or production may at a given moment so exceed demand that prices will fall below the figure at which the native finds it worth his while to plant cocoa, or even keep his plantations in existence. A phenomenon of the latter kind occurred some time ago in connection with the Sierra Leone coffee industry, which never, however, attained large proportions. The native population may be temporarily inconvenienced. Its purchasing power, expressed in terms of European merchandise, will rapidly fall. But an event which would cause widespread distress and unemployment, almost amounting to an economic catastrophe necessitating measures of government relief, among a population divorced from its land, leaves no permanent impression upon a population which remains in possession of the land. The land is turned to other uses, that is all. The people grow more remunerative crops. For a time they may even confine themselves to putting an increased area under food cultivation. So long as the people possess the land, they may suffer a diminution of their externally acquired wealth by such an adverse tide of fortune. But their existence and their future are secure. They can live, and they can prosper.

No one wishes to stultify European enterprise in the African tropics. But just as Europe is beginning to perceive that the unequal distribution of communally produced wealth is at the bottom of the preventible social misery identified with what is called "civilisation," so has the time arrived when a concensus of experienced opinion in Europe might be expected to recognise that the *form* which European enterprise assumes in the tropical regions of the earth, must adapt itself to local conditions. Tropical Western Africa needs the assistance which Europe is able to give to its peoples and to its economic development in the shape of railways, good roads, improved waterways, harbours, ocean and river craft, technical instruction, internal security, medical and sanitary services. It needs the European-trained administrator, the merchant, or the buyer for the European manufacturer, the engineer, forestry officer, entomologist. It does *not* require the European company promoter and planter; nor Europe's land laws and social customs. These persons and institutions may be thrust upon tropical Africa and maintained there under duress, but while they will assuredly curse the African, Europe will not in the long run benefit from having insisted on implanting them in his country.

. . . .

I have dwelt in detail upon the native oil-palm and cocoa industries of Southern Nigeria and the Gold Coast. respectively, for the reasons given. But it must not be supposed that this evidence of native enterprise is exceptional, or that the indigenous inhabitants of these particular areas—who are as unlike, racially, as Russians and Portuguese—possess special qualifications which differentiate them from other peoples of tropical Africa. In some parts, particularly in the remote interior of the forest belt, the native communities are backward. But among them all the keen commercial instinct is awake, even if it cannot fully express itself. Nigeria itself is as large as the German Empire before the war, Italy and Holland combined, and a relatively small proportion of it lies within the oil-palm bearing zone. Beyond that zone, in the western and northern provinces, cotton has been cultivated for centuries, in both cases for internal consumption. It is woven into enduring fabrics, beautifully dyed and embroidered. In late years an export trade in cotton lint has grown up through the enterprise of the British Cotton Growing Association. The native farmer, being given an external market for his product, has taken advantage of it to the extent of his capacity, having regard to the requirements of his home market. In certain parts of the central province the native communities, encouraged and helped thereto by the Forestry Department, have planted millions of rubber trees and carefully tend their plantations. They are also planting up their forests with valuable exotic hardwood trees, and the department is training hundreds of intelligent young Africans in the arts of forestry conservation. These rubber plantations are usually communal property, although in some cases individuals have plantations of their own on their family land. The cultivation of cocoa is now taking on a wide extension in the western province, while in the north the advent of the railway has enabled the population to find a profitable return by placing extensive areas under ground or pea-nut cultivation. In Sierra Leone ginger is cultivated by the native communities, and the kola tree is exploited as well as the oil-palm. There is a large timber industry in Southern Nigeria and in the Gold Coast mainly in native hands, although European licencees also have a share in this industry, the native communities receiving a portion of the licence fees, which are spent under administrative supervision and in conjunction with the recognised Native Councils upon improving the sanitation of the native towns, constructing water conduits and so on. The prosperity of the tiny Gambia (4,505 square miles) is wholly dependent upon the cultivation of the ground nut, which involves much hard work.

Throughout British West Africa the authorities have given to the principle of trusteeship its only just and wise interpretation. The consistent policy of the Government has been to assist the growth of native industries, to encourage the native communities to work their land for their own profit. With hardly an exception, every administrator from British West Africa examined before the West African Lands Committee, expressed himself in favour of this policy, and the more experience he had of the country the more emphatic was his testimony. And, observe the economic results! A year before the war, M. Yves Guyot, the French colonial director of agriculture, made an exhaustive personal inquiry into the British West African dependencies. His impression may be gathered from the following passages in his published report:

> There is no more fascinating history than the spread among the dark races—regarded as altogether primitive—of a cultivation hitherto thought to be within the capacity only of white peoples. . . . Everywhere else, cultivation of this kind has come from the initiative of Europeans; such is the case with coffee in Brazil, with tea in Ceylon, rubber in the Malay archipelago, Ceylon, and Brazil, cocoa on the East Coast of Africa. Here in West Africa it is the black man who has done everything; the introduction and the development of these cultivations are the results of his initiative and of his agricultural ability. Government action came later on. . . .

Why? Because the West African native has been left in possession of his land and has been regarded and treated as a trader, cultivator and producer in his own right. It should be added that, with the lamentable exception of the French Congo, the French have pursued much the same policy in their West African dependencies—at least in practice. I make that reservation because, in theory, their land legislation is in many respects incompatible with the preservation of native rights in land. In practice to-day many hundreds of square miles in Senegambia are under ground-nut cultivation by native communities who benefit, as their neighbours in the Gambia, from the fruits of their labour; and the same holds good in the other French dependencies.

. . . . . .

Before proceeding to describe the character of African land tenure, it may be desirable to sum up the conclusions which are warranted by the facts set forth in the preceding pages. Wherever they have received fair play the peoples of tropical Africa have shown themselves to be possessed of the requisite capacity, energy and enterprise to exploit the vegetable resources of their soil which the modern industrial development of Europe demands. They are doing so with no other incentive to labour than is provided by their own marked aptitude for agriculture, arboriculture, and commercial dealing, the volume of whose expression synchronises with transport facilities on land and on the interior waterways. Viewed, then, from the standpoint of strict justice and impartiality, these peoples are fulfilling the obligations which the controlling alien Power has conferred upon them by ensuring internal peace, and by protecting them from the rapacity of an exploiting capitalism. They are doing all that can be legitimately expected of, or claimed from, them. For it is their industry which pays the expenses of the alien administration, the salaries of its officials, the works of public utility, the interest on loans; and it is their industry which provides employment and profit both in Europe and in West Africa for European commercial undertakings, and procures employment for European labour in Europe. It is, therefore, the plain and obvious duty of the alien Power to preserve for these peoples and their descendants liberty of access to, and enjoyment of, the land. Licences to work timber or tap wild rubber can be granted to Europeans, with the consent of the native communities themselves, on payment of licence fees in which those communities shall share, without inflicting injustice upon the latter. But grants of lands to European individuals or syndicates made by the Government, as in British East Africa, or by native chiefs incapable of fully apprehending the result of their actions, as was beginning at one time to threaten the Gold Coast, involving surface rights over large areas of land for prolonged periods, are calculated to prevent or to restrict the growth of native industries, to disorganise and break up the native system of land tenure and co-operative labour. They are thus morally indefensible, politically unwise, economically unsound. The latter policy is sometimes defended at home on the ground of expediency and of justice to the British taxpayer. Neither plea survives investigation. The British dependencies in West Africa, where this vicious policy does not happily obtain, do not cost the British taxpayer a farthing. They would cost him a good many if a policy were adopted within them which would result in the destruction of the native industries, and in fierce conflicts from one end of the country to the other. As for the argument of expediency, what does it mean? At its best, it means that the economic devlopment of the areas of the Empire should be hastened. At its worst it means that, regardless of the major interest of the State and of the interests and rights of the native population, special privileges and monopolies over the soil, its products and the labour of the community, should be conferred upon private, sectional interests in England. A Government which yields to that argument is betraying its trust, primarily towards the African peoples under its protection, secondly towards its European subjects. I have already examined the argument of accelerated development on its moral side. I would add this on its material side. The assertion is occasionally made that, under the system of economic exploitation by the natives on their own account, specific natural products do not give the full yield that they might under the system of European exploitation with hired native labour. It is a pure assumption of more than doubtful accuracy. I have never known a case where the allegation that natural produce was going to waste owing to native "lethargy," substantiated by evidence proving that the fact of such wastage, if fact it were, was not due to local circumstances such as an inadequate local labour supply, social requirements, character of the soil, atmospheric conditions, insect pests, transport difficulties, and so on, of which those who advanced it were ignorant, or had failed to take into account. It is often argued that the agricultural and arboricultural methods of the African are capable of improvement. The statement is undoubtedly true. It applies with equal force to the land of Britain. There is no difference of opinion among British agricultural experts as to the capacities for improvement in the methods of British agriculture. As for British arboriculture it is still an almost entirely neglected field of British home enterprise. We can afford to be patient with the African if he has not yet attained perfection. Why, it is only since the beginning of the 18th century that the rotation of crops has been practised in England! But the Kano farmers in Northern Nigeria have understood rotation of crops and grass manuring for at least five hundred years.

To advance such truisms as an excuse for robbing the native communities of their land, degrading farmers in their own right to the level of hired labourers urged on by the lash, and conferring monopolistic rights over the land and its fruits to private corporations, is to make truth the stalking horse of oppression and injustice. The statement of fact may be accurate. The claim put forward on the strength of it is purely predatory.

Those who urge this and kindred arguments only do so to assist the realisation of their purpose. That purpose is clear. It is to make of Africans all over Africa a servile race; to exploit African labour, and through African labour, the soil of Africa for their own exclusive benefit. They are blind to the cost in human suffering. They are indifferent to the fact that in the long run their policy must defeat its own ends. They care only for the moment, and for the objects of the moment they are prepared to sacrifice the future. But since their purpose is selfish, short-sighted and immoral it must be striven against without pause or relaxation. There can be no honest or safe compromise with these people and their policy. A great moral issue is involved. But although that issue comes first, and must come first, it is not the only issue.

For a time it may be possible for the white man to maintain a white civilisation in the colonisable, or partly colonisable, areas of the African Continent based on servile or semi-servile labour: to build up a servile State. But even there the attempt can be no more than fleeting. The days of Roman imperialism are done with for ever. Education sooner or later breaks all chains, and knowledge cannot be kept from the African. The attempt will be defeated in the north by Islam, which confers power of combination in the political sphere, and a spiritual unity which Europe has long lost in the mounting tides of her materialism. It will fail in the south through the prolificness of the African,[1] through the practical impossibility of arresting his intellectual advance and through race admixture, which is proceeding at a much more rapid rate than most people realise. In the great tropical regions the attempt must fail in the very nature of things; if for no other reason, because it can only be enforced by employing the black man, trained in the art of modern warfare as the medium through which to coerce his unarmed brother. The former will be well content to play that part for a period more or less prolonged, but when he becomes alive to his power the whole fabric of European domination will fall to pieces in shame and ruin. From these failures the people of Europe will suffer moral and material damage of a far-reaching kind.

And the criminal folly of it! The white imperial peoples have it in their power, if their rulers will cultivate vision and statesmanship enough to thrust aside the prompting of narrow, ephemeral interests—anti-national in the truest sense—to make of Africa the home of highly-trained and prosperous peoples enriching the universe as their prosperity waxes, dwelling in plains and valleys, in forests and on plateaux made fruitful by their labours, assisted by science; a country whose inhabitants will be enterprising and intelligent, loving their land, looking to it for inspiration, co-operating faithfully in the work of the world, developing their own culture, independent, free, self-respecting, attaining to higher mental growth as the outcome of internal evolutionary processes. Why cannot the white imperial peoples, acknowledging in some measure the injuries they have inflicted upon the African,

* In 1917 the population of the Union of South Africa amounted to 1,467,457 whites and 6,872,164 blacks and coloured. In 1865 the proportion of white to black and coloured in the Cape Province was 36; in 1911, 23. In 1880 the proportion of white to black and coloured in the Orange Free State was 46; in 1911, 33.

turn a new leaf in their treatment of him? For nearly two thousand years they have professed to be governed by the teachings of Christ. Can they not begin in the closing century of that era, to practise what they profess —and what their missionaries of religion teach the African? Can they not cease to regard the African as a producer of dividends for a selected few among their number, and begin to regard him as a human being with human rights? Have they made such a success of their own civilisation that they can contemplate with equanimity the forcing of all its social failures upon Africa—its hideous and devastating inequalities, its pauperisms, its senseless and destructive egoisms, its vulgar and soulless materialism? It is in their power to work such good to Africa—and such incalculable harm! Can they not make up their minds that their strength shall be used for noble ends? Africa demands at their hands, justice, and understanding sympathy—not ill-informed sentiment. And when these are dealt out to her she repays a thousandfold.

CHAPTER XIII.

Administrative Problems and the Land.

The preservation of the land of Africa for its peoples is thus, broadly speaking, the " acid " test of trusteeship. We have seen that the land question assumes varying aspects in connection with the government of Africans by white men, as the temperate or tropical regions of the Continent are involved. But the main principle holds good in either case. The welfare of the African peoples may be gravely impaired by European policy in a multiplicity of ways. But if they are dispossessed of the land, and prevented thereby from using it for their own account, the injury done to them, and the resulting mischief, are incalculable. From free men, they sink to virtual slaves: the shackles are lacking—that is all. Recognition of this truth should inspire the land legislation of white Governments in the temperate regions of the Continent, and should form the basis of white policy in the tropical regions. How far white policy has turned in the opposite direction in South Africa, in British East Africa, in Algeria, in Morocco, in German South-West Africa and elsewhere, is only too patent. In pursuing that course the white man is raising up for himself the most formidable of future difficulties. So far as South Africa is concerned, an opportunity presents itself for an examination of the whole problem in the demand on the part of the Union Government of South Africa for the incorporation within the Union of the native Protectorates—Basutoland, Swaziland and Bechuanaland—over which the Colonial Office still retains supervision and ultimate control; and also of the Rhodesias. That demand, which can hardly be refused, places the British Government under the moral obligation of securing definite guarantees for the native population in regard to their land rights. The occasion is an excellent one for a joint Commission of investigation into the whole land problem south of the Zambesi.

While a system of native "Reserves" in colonisable South Africa is intelligible, and fairly and justly applied, is perhaps best calculated to ensure the welfare of the native population, its application to the tropical regions of the Continent is thoroughly vicious. Since the white man cannot himself colonise the tropical regions, the only object which such a policy within them can have is that of creating a landless class of natives who can be driven by various measures of direct and indirect coercion into plantation work under white and black overseers—an example of political effort directed to facilitate the *direct* action of capital in a country where such conceptions constitute a political and economic error of the first magnitude. British East Africa is a black spot in the generally sound record of British administration in the African tropics. The native peoples have been dispossessed of their land on an extensive scale, and administrative activities are concentrated upon furthering what is fundamentally an ephemeral enterprise, the exploitation of the soil of tropical Africa by aliens through native labour. The labour problems which are incessantly occurring in East Africa are the direct and necessary result of a wrong conception of policy. From the situation thus produced, the native suffers probably greater hardships than he suffered under the Arab, because the pressure upon him is perpetual. It is "Empire building" of a kind, no doubt, but its foundations are laid in sand.

. . . . . .

Happily, the "Reserve" system has been kept out of British West Africa. So far, however, only one West African Government has given actual legislative endorsement to the right political conception, viz., the British Administration of Northern Nigeria, whose "Land and Native Rights Proclamation" declares that:

"The whole of the lands of the Protectorate of Northern Nigeria, whether occupied or unoccupied . . . are hereby declared to be native lands. . . ."

Among the various reasons given for this wise act of statesmanship in the preamble, is that of the "*preservation of existing native customs with regard to the use and occupation of the land.*"

The importance of this provision is emphasised further on.

In June, 1912, the Colonial Office, under Lord Harcourt, appointed a Committee, of which the author of this volume was a member, to consider the whole question of land legislation in the other West African dependencies. The Committee sat for two years, took an immense amount of oral evidence, and evidence on commission—both European and African—and had nearly completed its draft report when war broke out. A subcommittee, consisting of Sir Walter Napier, Sir Frederick Hodgson and the present writer, which was then engaged upon revising the draft report, continued its labours and completed the work which in the ordinary course of events would have been completed by the full Committee. The Report recommended that the rules and practices of nature tenure should be upheld,[1] and, where necessary, strengthened by administrative action. It condemned the grant of land concessions, and of monopolistic rights over the produce of the soil to European syndicates and individuals.[2]

. . . . . .

It is essential that we should form a clear idea of the dominating characteristics of the African system of land tenure. The African cannot be governed with comprehension, and, therefore, justly and wisely; his sociology cannot be understood, unless the nature of his customary land laws upon which the corporate nature of African social life is based, are thoroughly grasped. The idea is very prevalent that because the majority of the negro and negroid peoples of Africa are in a condition which we call rather loosely "primitive," there is no such thing as a law of tenure, because it is unwritten, and that African governing institutions do not exist. This is an altogether erroneous view. In point of fact, not only is there a real system of African tenure, but it is an infinitely better, sounder and healthier system than that which the British people tolerate and suffer from in their own country. To most English-

[1] Except in certain restricted areas in the neighbourhood of the Coast towns, where European land laws have made inroads upon native custom, and where buying and selling of land has taken root.

[2] The Report has been printed but not presented to Parliament. The printed evidence is accessible in the library of the House of Commons.

men this statement will appear absurd. It is, however, strictly accurate, and it is not too much to say that if the African system of land tenure existed in England, the English people would be a happier people and, in the truest sense of the term, a more prosperous people, *i.e.*, the mass of the people would be more prosperous. "I conceive that land belongs to a vast family, of which many are dead, few are living, and countless numbers are yet unborn." That picturesque phrase, which fell from the lips of a dignified African ruler, examined by the West African Lands Committee, symbolises the entire philosophy of African social life, political, economic and spiritual. The fundamental conception underlying native tenure all over Africa (with a few reputed exceptions) where the white man has not undermined or destroyed it, is that land, like air and water, is God-given; that every individual within the community has a right to share in its bounties provided he carries out his social and political obligations to the community of which he forms part; that in the community as a whole is vested the ownership of the land, and that consequently the individual member of the community cannot permanently alienate the land he occupies and uses. The word "community" may typify the "family," a term which has a much wider significance than it has with us, the standard being a traceable consanguinity; or the clan, sometimes called the "house" and sometimes the "village"; or the tribe, which is a collection of clans, "houses" or "villages"; or, again —the final development—the collection of tribes under a kingship—a kingship which approximates more nearly (with rare exceptions) to a democratic, or rather to a Socialistic republic. But whether the smaller or larger social organisation be regarded as the landowning unit, the same common principle permeates the social structure and lies at the root of all social philosophy.

There is no word in our language which is capable of describing with accuracy this African system under which land is held and used. The terms "communal ownership" and "individual ownership" as employed by us are far too rigid to define a system which partakes of the character of both. In our eyes private property in land signifies freehold in land, and freehold in land implies that the individual is the absolute owner, and can alienate his land for ever. But private property in land conveys no such right, and implies no such power under the African system. Security and perpetuity of tenure the individual possesses: he benefits from his improvements, subject always to the performance of his civic duties. But the land is not his to dispose of, and at his death it reverts to the community. The structural law of tenure for the individual is thus the right of user, not of owner *in our sense of the term*. Land not in actual cultivation by individuals is the common property of the community. When it is allotted, the individual allottee becomes the owner of it, *in the African sense*, i.e., no other individual can interfere with him, trespass upon his ground and expel him from it, or lay hands upon the crops that he has reared upon it.

Under this system no member of an African community is ever in want. If a member of an African family—using the word in its African signification—emigrates for a time, his heritage in the land is waiting for him when he returns. No man starves or can starve. There are no paupers in Africa, except where the white man has created them, either deliberately and for his own purposes, by expropriating the people from their ancestral lands; or, stopping short of that, has allowed European legal ideas and practices with their conception of freehold and mortgage to bring a pauper class into existence. In the latter respect the African system is not free from danger at the hands not only of Europeans, but of a certain class of natives educated in Western notions of law, and of scheming non-educated members within the indigenous community itself. The growth of an aboriginal landlord class is an insidious peril to be guarded against by a vigilant administration. Its extension means social disaster for the majority, and our Indian experiences have taught us how difficult it is to undo that sort of mischief once it has taken firm hold. There are other reasons beyond those already indicated why a European Administration which is inspired by a statesmanlike grasp of the African problem should seek to preserve rather than to shake the foundations of African tenure in land. One of those reasons is the indissoluble connection between the system of African tenure, and the problem of the government of African communities by white men.

. . . . .

Native polity, *i.e.*, native governing institutions—the entire social structure, indeed, of African life, is inseparably bound up with the preservation of the African land system. They stand or fall together. And if native policy falls, social chaos ensues. An African community is ruled by an executive head, sometimes hereditary, sometimes elective, sometimes partly the one and partly the other, assisted by councillors usually composed of the heads, the "fathers" in African symbolism, of the lesser communities composing the larger unit. Save where priestly theocracies have stepped in to the general detriment of native society, the governing mechanism is essentially democratic, and an African "chief," as we term the ruler of an African community, loses all authority if public confidence in him is shaken. The chief, who is deposable for misrule, and is, in fact, not infrequently deposed, is the link between the various units composing the community, and, assisted by his councillors, the judge in all community disputes— his court being the supreme court of appeal. He and his council become the guardians and trustees of all unoccupied lands between the boundaries of the units composing the community. That position invests him additionally with spiritual functions and authority as incarnating the original ancestor of the community. The chosen heads of the different units within the community are the arbiters in all land disputes between their members. They allocate the unoccupied lands according to the increasing needs of the unit. They enjoy the privileges pertaining to that position—personal service at stated intervals, contributions from crops or from the sale of forest produce, the proceeds of which are partly spent in various ceremonials and festivities, and hospitality of diverse kinds. Their subjects, or strangers who have been admitted within the community, possess and enjoy the land subject to the fulfilment of the obligations recognised by the community as binding upon its members. Their power, exercised with the sanction of the community, to expel an occupant guilty of serious misdemeanours is the community's ultimate safeguard against social crime. They are not entitled to interfere in the usage and enjoyment of the land thus allotted: but they are the general guardians of the community's interests. Upon the exercise of these several functions their influence and authority repose.

Now when the European intervenes in regions where the form of native government described above prevails, the European assumes in the eyes of the native population the position of paramount authority over and above all the native authorities of the country. He becomes *de facto* supreme overlord. He has one of two courses to pursue. He must either govern through the existing mechanism of native government, contenting himself with exercising supervisory control without actually interfering in the ordinary functions of native government—this policy is known as indirect rule—or he must subvert native customary laws, substituting for them European conceptions of law and justice, either using the heads of the community as puppets to do his bidding (which means that they will lose all authority over the members of the community except as the servants of the white overlord) or he must arbitrarily elevate to positions of power within the community men who have no right to such positions in native custom and who, therefore, possess no local sanction behind them. That policy is known as direct rule. The Germans and, in more recent years, the French have favoured the latter policy in their tropical African possessions, the former partly from lack of experience, partly from the regimentalising tendencies of the home bureaucracy; the French, because the admirable features which distinguished many aspects of their rule in Western Africa proper, between 1880 and 1900, are being gradually obscured by, and their general administrative policy subordinated to, the purpose of militarising their African dependencies—of which more anon. In British West Africa the policy of indirect rule has been mainly followed. In British East Africa, as already stated, policy is so entirely subordinated to the labour exigencies of Europeans that native administration in the proper sense of the term can hardly be said to exist at all.

The school of direct rulers is always influential and is favoured by certain tendencies within the Colonial Office: resisted by others. It is a curious and felicitous circumstance that although Colonial officials are nearly always drawn from classes of the home population, whose training does not make for sympathy and comprehension of native races, Britain continually throws up men who become sincerely attached to the natives and keen students of their institutions. This has been particularly the case in West Africa. Nevertheless, direct rule is a constant temptation. It offers greater opportunities to employment and promotion in some branches of the service. It increases the scope of judicial, secretarial, police and military activities. It assists, too, the educated native barrister trained in English law, and the native educated clerk, which our political system continues to turn out in great numbers, in the exercise of their professions. It helps the European capitalist in a hurry to push on what he calls "development." The missionary is apt to regard an indigenous mechanism of government as a hindrance to Christian propaganda. Finally, there is the type of European who is racially biassed against the retention of any sort of authority by the African in his own country. And, as a matter of fact, as already stated, it is only in Northern Nigeria, which has been blessed with a series of the ablest and most far-seeing British administrators, that the policy of governing the African on African lines has become consecrated in actual legislation, and the pernicious habit of allowing the law of England to encroach upon native customary law in matters affecting the land has been ruled out. In Southern Nigeria, in the Gold Coast and in Sierra Leone, general policy has been directed to preserving the native mechanism of government, but the absence of definite land legislation is permitting encroachments which will work much evil if not soon checked. It was with the intention of exploring the evil and circumscribing it, that the West African Lands Committee, referred to above, was appointed.

There can be no doubt upon which side lies the welfare of the native population. The African system of government, reposing upon a system of land tenure, essentially just and suited to the requirements of the people, is the natural machinery for the administration of the community. It is capable of sustaining the strain of innovation and modification consequent upon the advent of European influences, *provided it is supported by the European executive.* If it enjoys that support it will gradually evolve in such a way as will enable it to cope with changes rendered inevitable by the fusion which is going on, by the growth of permanent cultivation and by the increasing prosperity of the individual. Deprived of that support it will collapse.

ADMINISTRATIVE PROBLEMS, AND LAND

A Europe desiring to deal justly towards its African wards will have increasingly to bear in mind that there can be no common definition of progress, no common standard for all mankind; that the highest human attainments are not necessarily reached on parallel lines; that man's place and part in the universe around him must vary with dissimilarities in race and in environment; that what may spell advance for some races at a particular stage in their evolution, may involve retrogression if not destruction for other races in another stage; that humanity cannot be legislated for as though every section of it were modelled upon the same pattern; that to disregard profound divergences in culture and racial necessities is to court disaster, and that to encourage national growth to develop on natural lines and the unfolding of the mental processes by gradual steps is the only method by which the exercise of the imperial prerogative is morally justified.

. . . . . .

The foregoing remarks apply to regions of Africa where the white man cannot himself occupy and people the soil with his own race. An entirely different set of problems arises where, in the colonisable and semi-colonisable areas, the white man has destroyed, or partially destroyed, native authority and polity and introduced his own economic, political and educational systems. Egypt, Algeria, the Union of South Africa, present as many instances of the latter kind of problem. Widely removed as are its several manifestations in these parts of the Continent, two main issues are in each case involved. The political system introduced from outside must be fairly representative of the governed, and the economic system must provide for the protection and the security of the aboriginal wage-earner. In other words, the European systems implanted in Africa cannot henceforth divest themselves in Africa of the elements which are bound up with their prevalence in Europe. And this, because they must tend to reproduce in Africa broadly the same conditions which they have created in Europe. To imagine that European political and economic systems can be set up in Africa and applied to the government of Africans without giving rise, sooner or later, to the same demands as are made upon the government of Europeans in Europe is to imagine a vain thing. If, for instance, you substitute for indigenous forms of government an alien institution like the franchise, in South Africa, you must make it a reality and not a mockery; and to introduce an honest franchise as a political engine of government without an educational system directed to making the individual worthy of exercising it, is merely to court trouble.

The problem which confronts the British in Egypt is a problem, too, wholly of their own creation. Before the Great War, one would have said that it could only be solved by giving to the Egyptians increased powers to administer the governing machine which has been established in their midst, coupled with the determination to cease paying a hypocritical lip-service to the ideal of self-government, and honestly to define the standards which would justify us, in the light of our own repeated professions and of our international pledges, in surrendering our trusteeship into the hands of the Egyptians themselves. One would have said the same, broadly speaking, of India. But the Great War has created conditions which have infused the problem with greater urgency and invested it with a new character, both in Egypt and in India. India lies outside the scope of this volume. In Egypt, political bungling and military brutality have combined to achieve the seemingly miraculous, in uniting the entire population against us. The British occupation no longer stands as the bulwark between an exploited peasantry and an exploiting ruling-class. Its directors have themselves exploited the peasantry for military and imperialistic purposes, and to the *fellahin* we appear to-day as chastisers with scorpions compared with the whips yielded by their former masters. Matters have reached such a pass that it seems extremely doubtful if we can now maintain ourselves in Egypt with any pretence of moral justification, even by the grant of immediate and extensive powers of self-government; and the position is likely to become completely untenable if the settlement of Asiatic Turkey is such as to outrage the feelings of Mohammedans throughout the British Empire. Egypt is only one of many proofs that the war has been a solvent of Empire, just as a genuine League of Nations must be, where Empire embraces real or nascent civilisations. The French are trying to solve a somewhat similar problem in Algeria by methods for which we do not possess the requisite national faculties. For we are not what the French essentially are, a military people. The attempt to convert the land of the African Arab and of the Berber whether in Algeria, Morocco, or Tunis, into a military annexe of imperialist France can, of course, only have one ultimate ending—a general smash-up of the Frankish dominion in North Africa. But that particular Nemesis may take some time to work out, and if what is called " Bolshevism " invades France, if the French masses realise as some day no doubt they will, that national preservation involves the shedding of a nationalistic imperialism on the part of the governing *bourgeoisie*, the North African problem may settle itself without lighting a general Mohammedan conflagration from one end of North Africa to the other.

European policy in Mediterranean—i.e., Mohammedan —Africa is so closely concerned with Europe's rivalries that unless a League of Nations succeeds in entirely transforming the character of European inter-State intercourse, the notion of white "trusteeship" for the native races is not likely to make much headway in those parts of the Continent. But if one might precipitate oneself into the realms of imagination for the nonce, conjecture a Europe purged of its war system and governed by statesmen imbued with a lofty sense of responsibility towards these African peoples and devoid of sectarian prejudice, one could picture a great revival of letters and arts on the southern shores of the Mediterranean, carrying its message to every part of Mohammedan Africa. Such a policy would involve " support " of Mohammedanism! *Horesco referens!* But there are precedents. Does not the provincial government support by a grant-in-aid the Mohammedan College at Aligarth in the North-West provinces of India, founded by the late Sir Syad Ahmed Khan? It would be more accurate to say that such a policy would give to an African civilisation a chance of political and intellectual expression. True, it would be a civilisation, whose spiritual basis is the Koran. Is the civilisation of Western Europe, whose spiritual basis is alleged to be Christianity, so perfect that any but sectarians need find grounds of objection in such a policy? The great bulk of North-West Africa is Mohammedan, and Mohammedanism is steadily gaining ground over most of the tropical regions of the Continent. In the West it is firmly established. It loses much of its fanaticism on African soil. It has been well said by a great African scholar, that Islam by its social and eugenic laws, "saves Africa alive." It is, in Africa, a social influence before anything else, and an influence which admittedly raises the Pagan to a higher level. It is a cultural force. It is at present the African's strongest bulwark against the de-racialising processes, which come in the wake of European intervention. The African has it in him to become a real Christian which, perhaps, the European under the present social system has not. Meantime, Islam is in Africa a preservative of racial self-respect. To pursue in Mohammedan Africa a truly African policy, reviving ancient centres of learning, binding the African peoples to their land in intensified bonds of reverence, heralding the dawn of an African renascence, raising African universities instead of African levies—here, indeed, would be a work worthy of great international minds. Perhaps when the restless and selfish individualism of Europe has given place to more generous and nobler concepts of human sociology; when much of what has passed for statesmanship in Europe, is seen to have been naught but the petty and vain preoccupations of vulgar minds; when the European peoples, emancipated from the social tyrannies which throttle their freedom and impair their vision are capable of gazing out upon wider horizons then, perhaps, the conditions will be born, out of which a policy of this kind may arise and endure.

· · · · · ·

Meantime, white rule is producing in the colonisable, and even in portions of the non-colonisable Continent a huge, landless, African proletariat under no restraint of tribal law; and with few political and fewer legal rights under the white man's law. So far as the colonisable area of the Continent is concerned, the phenomenon is assuming its greatest magnitude in South Africa. It is raising all kinds of currents and cross-currents of class feeling and race feeling, both of which must become intensified with the natural growth of the native population. In the South African Union the blacks outnumber the whites by over four to one now. The numerical preponderance of the black-man must, short of a general massacre, continue on an increasing scale. And with every year that passes the black population advances in intellect and in ambition, despite the efforts to keep down both, by starving education, restricting political and legal privileges, and punishing openly manifested discontent with a heavy hand. The African demands greater freedom, greater educational facilities, greater opportunities to improve his material well-being and mental development. The white man's rule has been thrust upon him, and with it the white man's political and economic systems. The black man's institutions have been largely broken up and the white man refuses him a share in moulding his own destiny under the new dispensation. Yet the white man cannot help the constructive sides of his civilisation becoming more and more diffused. He cannot arrest learning at its fount. He preaches to the black man a religion whose essence is the equality of all men before God. But his civic laws and political acts are in violent antagonism to the religion he simultaneously inculcates. Christ will not blend with racial domination of the South African type, at any rate. The white man offers the black man Christianity with one hand and helotry with the other. And he works thus contrariwise on the most plastic of human material. I said a while back that the African has it in him to become a real Christian. He has. The white man is teaching him to look upon himself as the latter-day type of the early Christian martyrs. You cannot impregnate the African race with the Christian religion on its own soil, where it outnumbers the white race by four to one even in the most favoured portion of the Continent, and enslave it politically and economically at the same time. You may try: but the two things are incompatible and won't work.

And there is another vital consideration to take into account. The ruling white man in South Africa has recently made use of the black man, and on a considerable scale, to help him in fighting other white men, outside the territory of the Union. Tens of thousands of South and East Africans have perished in the war or in consequence of the war. To the black man this is at once an admission and an incentive. It has intensified his determination not to be treated as a mere hewer of wood and drawer of water. To imagine that he can be for ever so treated, is to imagine a vain thing. Force cannot permanently solve the problem. The South

African black has heard of passive resistance. There are Indians in South Africa. The educated African leaders in South Africa know of the ferment in India. Equally vain is it to suppose that this African proletariat, which the white man has made and is making, can forever be denied the rights of combination and defence against an exploiting capitalism which a proletariat must secure in Europe if it would not sink to the slave level: and if in Europe, how much more in South Africa.

And yet, judging from appearances, white rule in South Africa to-day seems to be directed as though it did really believe these things. And this applies not only to the ruling and exploiting classes, but to the white labouring class. Both appear equally intolerant of the black man's claim; the first, through fear of political and racial consequences; the latter, through fear of being undercut in the labour market, and through jealousy of the black man acquiring proficiency in the higher grades of technical skill. Politically speaking, the policy which is the outcome of these beliefs, assumes the form of an attempt to run a dominant white State in Africa upon the foundations of a servile African labour. Since the federation of the various South African States, liberalising tendencies have become steadily less. The influence of British political liberalism upon South African policy is a dwindling one: nay, it has almost disappeared with the decay of liberalism in British political life, and with the growth of the spirit of independence in South Africa. The political influence of British labour in these difficult and complicated questions of imperial race ascendancy in the self-governing dominions, is as yet a non-existent factor.

South African policy to-day is frankly based upon race discrimination. The Dutch tradition has maintained its ascendancy in the Transvaal and Orange Free State: Natal was always far less liberal than Cape Colony. The Dutch tradition is infinitely harsher than the British home tradition, although not, perhaps, on the whole much more so than the British colonial tradition. There can be little doubt that white policy in South Africa generally is growing steadily more reactionary, as the demands of the black man grow in volume and insistence, and as industrialism lays a greater grip upon the country. One may call attention to a few specific facts in support

ADMINISTRATIVE PROBLEMS, AND LAND

of this. In three out of the four provinces of the Union the native population has virtually no political rights. The tribal mechanism has disappeared so far as a very considerable proportion of the native population is concerned: and *that* population has no real channel through which its grievances can be expressed. It is deprived of the franchise. In three out of the four provinces of the Union the black man is not even entitled to sit on local councils. No black man may become a member of the Citizen Force—for he is not, in fact, a citizen. Every impediment is thrown in the way of a black man obtaining even minor Civil Service posts, although he may have passed the examinations: even in the special post offices for black men, no black man is employed. The average native labourer's wage is 1s. 6d. *per diem:* yet he must pay, in the Transvaal, £2 *per annum* in direct taxes, £1 in the Orange Free State, and 14s. in Natal. For this taxation he receives little or no equivalent in education. But it is in the matter of the Pass Laws, in the Transvaal and the Orange River States, that the servile State is so clearly shown. In the Orange Free State every man and woman; in the Transvaal, every man is compelled to carry a pass, without which he can leave neither his home nor the farm upon which he is engaged, for any purpose whatever. A native travelling in search of work must obtain a special travelling pass. When he arrives at his destination, he must, if he desires to stay there, and search for work, obtain a special pass. This special pass is good for a six-day sojourn at the place where it is issued. If he has not obtained employment at the expiration of that time, the holder of the pass is liable to a fortnight's imprisonment. A great deal more might be said about these Pass Laws, which recall the slavery days in America.

Be it observed that legislation of this kind is imposed upon a population which contributes a substantial portion of the State revenues, which furnished thousands of volunteers for the campaign against the Germans in South West Africa, 17,000 for the campaign in German East Africa, and about 20,000 for manual service in the French docks and behind the trenches in Flanders; which remained absolutely loyal during De Wet's rebellion; which could have paralysed South African economics if it had not kept up a steady supply of labour for the gold mines during the war, and which has been repeatedly lauded and thanked for its services by the Governor-General and by the late Prime Minister of the Union and, in official orders, by Sir Douglas Haig.

No one can be desirous of minimising the tremendous complexities of the racial problem which faces South African statesmen, and which will be intensified when the Union takes over the great native protectorates still administered by the Crown. I once unexpectedly found myself sitting at dinner next to the famous Dr. Jameson, of Matabele and Transvaal raid fame. We talked of the future of South Africa, and I was surprised to hear him express the opinion that the only solution was race admixture. He averred that it had already gone much further than most people would believe or admit. Be that as it may, it is not easy to acquiesce in the view of South African statesmen that the repressive policy they are adopting can in the long run prove racially preservative in the political sense, which is their explanation for it.

Nor is it easy to forecast how the relationship of the Mother Country with the South African Union can preserve its present character if the Union persists in a native policy, which would seem bound sooner or later to involve the whole of the sub-Continent in racial strife. For many reasons the imperial problem in South Africa is the thorniest of the imperial connection. It is not likely to be rendered less so by the incorporation within the Union of German South West Africa, which is bound to strengthen the Nationalist party and increase the " subversive " elements. On the one hand the Union of South Africa is henceforth recognised as a nation, a nation whose representatives signed the Treaty of Versailles on a parity with the representatives of the Mother State. The link of sentiment is not over strong as it is. There will be a natural reluctance on the part of any British Government which desires to retain the imperial connection, to subject that link to undue strain. On the other hand it would seem to be impossible that Labour influence in British internal and external politics, which is the event of to-morrow, could remain quiescent, even if it desired to do so, before the spectacle of a

British dominion, in fact and in law a nation, denying the rights of citizenship to the vast bulk of the population composing it. The educated South African will appeal—is appealing—to British Labour to help him.

No doubt there are men in the Labour movement of Great Britain who are studying the problem, and who are presumably not neglecting yet another of its facets, to wit, that South African capitalism and South African white Labour may be found in the same camp in their opposition to the emancipation of the natives. That white Labour in South Africa is racially inspired as well as class inspired will hardly be denied. The future will show whether it is a racial movement first and a class movement afterwards; whether race will prove a stronger incentive than class.

The native question in South Africa takes precedence from whatever aspect the general problem is examined. It is impossible to believe in the permanence or, in these days, even in the prolonged existence, of a political structure reared upon an economic basis of servile labour.

General Smuts, who desires to retain the imperial connection, is recently reported to have stated that the British Empire had ceased to exist. It is true, in one sense, that the British *Commonwealth* has ceased to exist. The British Empire remains. General Smuts' rival for the leadership of white South Africa, General Hertzog, who desires to sever the imperial connection, has recently declared, in effect, that if he were returned to power on a Republican ' ticket,' King George could not constitutionally oppose the complete severance which General Hertzog's victory at the polls would, according to the General, indicate to be the desire of the majority in the South African Union. This is a polite way of saying that the British Government would have to bow to a white vote in the South African Union favouring a Republic and, therefore, a complete break with the Empire. General Hertzog may with equal politeness be reminded of the fact that his victory would prove nothing more than that a *majority of the white population* in the South African Union favoured a Republic and the cutting of the imperial painter. What of the vast bulk of the inhabitants of the country—the natives? They would not have been consulted. General Hertzog could not justly claim to be possessed of a mandate from them; and there are some very explicit British Government pledges on the duty and the right of the Crown to safeguard the rights of native peoples not represented in local Colonial legislatures. It is as certain as anything can be in this world that, badly as they have been treated by both Dutch and British *in* South Africa, the native peoples look, and will increasingly look, to the forces of Democracy in Britain for support and help in their struggle against the influences of race prejudice, expressed in repressive legislation and in the withholding of social and political rights. The British Democracy cannot with honour, or with safety, turn its back upon them.

CHAPTER XIV.

WHAT A LEAGUE OF NATIONS COULD DO TO PROTECT TROPICAL AFRICA FROM THE EVILS OF CAPITALISTIC EXPLOITATION AND MILITARISM.

Whether a League of Nations can do anything within a measurable distance of time for colonisable and semi-colonisable Africa depends upon a great many considerations closely associated with the European settlement, which it would be out of place to discuss here. But a League of Nations could perform a great work for tropical Africa and perform it, or at least lay the basis for its execution, within a comparatively short period, if it were so minded.

In so far as the problem of the government of Africa by the white race is one which lends itself to international consideration, it is the non-colonisable tropical regions of the Continent which are susceptible of international treatment and decisions. Policy can there proceed, in the main, on simple and predetermined courses, provided that foresight, sagacity, humanity, and some imagination and knowledge are present at the European end. Policy is not there entangled in the ramified complexities of racial relationships. It is comparatively simple.

The task with which the white races are confronted in tropical Africa is that of undertaking for the first time in the history of mankind the *direct government* of the African in an immense region [by far the largest portion of the Continent] where, with a few isolated and restricted exceptions, the European cannot settle and perpetuate his race. Europe has barely crossed the threshold of that endeavour. There has been exploitation by European adventurers of certain parts of this immense area. Wicked systems of pillage and enslavement have been set up within it, and have perished. Others, less odious but nevertheless containing within them the seeds of deadly ills, have been introduced, and persist. But the actual *government* of tropical Africa, in the proper sense of the term, by the white man, is only beginning. There is still time to inaugurate and apply the principles of an enlightened international statesmanship to tropical Africa. And the birth of an international organism, or—if we put it no higher—the birth of a desire for an international organism which may eventuate into a true League of Nations, provides the opportunity.

What are the salient features which tropical Africa presents to our examination?

. . . .

Tropical Africa is about twice the size of Europe. It is, especially in its Western part, the greatest national preserve of tropical raw material in the world. It is more accessible to Europe than any other region of the tropics. It is peopled in some parts densely, in others, sparsely, by a prolific, muscular race in various stages of development, but generally speaking—although the term is open to abuse—primitive, and incapable of offering effective resistance to exploitation and injustice at the hands of Europeans. European intervention in its affairs has given rise during the past thirty-five years to constant international friction in Europe, and has inflicted in some cases monstrous and unpardonable outrages upon its inhabitants.

The dangers which confront this enormous region and its peoples are only too obvious. *They are threatened by European capitalism and by militarism in their worst forms*. Capitalism seeks to exploit their natural wealth and their labour as rapidly as possible, without regard to the interests, liberties, general present and future welfare of the population, and without regard to the major interests of the European State involved. Militarism seeks to make of them a vast reservoir of plastic, human material for military purposes.

. . . .

Capitalism has several ways of encompassing its ends. The crudest was the system applied on the Congo. We have observed its results. The Angola system was a variant. The system in force in parts of East Africa is a variant of the Angola system. Then we have the comprehensive projects of the Empire Resources Development Committee, with which certain members of the present

PROTECTION FROM LEAGUE OF NATIONS 217

Government are coquetting. In the view of the spokesmen of the Empire Resources Development Committee, the population of British tropical Africa is an "undeveloped national asset," and the problem of Empire there consists in converting the African into a "useful human being." The land is not, it seems, the property of the people living upon it and using it; although, throughout the greater part of western tropical Africa, at any rate, the British hold these dependencies by virtue of original treaties of amity and commerce entered into with the native rulers, recognised by us as exercising authority over the land of the country. The land should be regarded as an "estate" of the British Crown, and the Crown should "keep in its own hands the power of producing, trading in and exporting certain special products." It is precisely those products, be it observed, which the native population is now itself producing, trading in and exporting in its own right, and by its own free labour. The mechanism for the production of the natural resources of the country should be in the hands of an "Imperial board composed of not more than 20 live (sic) business men," with a small sprinkling of civil servants. The mechanism itself should take the form of "Joint Stock Companies." The profits derived by the "State" —not the African "State," be it noted, but the British Crown—from this dual enterprise, will help to pay off the interests on the war loans. "The plan is for the State on its own account to develop some of the resources of the Empire, and to secure in this way both a large income with which to pay interest on the debt and also an immense unearned increment, out of which the whole national debt will be ultimately repaid." The profits derived from the corporations thus associated with the British Crown in this patriotic and unselfish enterprise, will naturally be distributed among the stock and bondholders. In short, the proposal is that the natural wealth of British tropical Africa shall be directly exploited by the British Crown, in partnership with particular capitalists seeking substantial profits on capital invested. In other words, African labour is to be regarded and treated as a human force for the furtherance of British national and sectional interests.

In such partnerships all the great colonial tragedies of the past have their origin. A system of this kind necessarily entails (a) the wholesale expropriation of the native population in favour of the British Crown, in defiance of right, and in violation of the plighted word inscribed upon hundreds of treaties between the representatives of the British Crown and the native rulers of the country; and (b) appropriation by the British Crown of the products of economic value which the land yields through the effort of native labour. Both these measures remain totally ineffective, of course, unless the native population can be coerced into working its own lands, no longer for its own benefits, but for the benefit of its despoilers.

In the British East Africa and Nyassaland protectorates, individuals and corporations have already been allowed to do, without the commercial co-operation of the British Crown, what the Empire Resources Development Committee desires the British Crown to besmirch itself by doing in West Africa in direct commercial association with such enterprises. Uprisings and partial famines have resulted, and if the policy is persisted in and extended, these will continue and they will increase, involving the partial massacre of the present European landowners, the usual sanguinary reprisals and the ultimate ruin of the country. But in British West Africa, upon which the committee casts its benevolent eye more particularly, such a policy would entail bloodshed on a large scale from one end of the protectorates to the other, the immediate collapse of the great existing export industries and in the long run complete economic disaster. The West African is not going to be made a slave of the British Crown without a fight, and the struggle would be bitter and prolonged.

Militarism works on different lines and with a different objective. When a few years before the war broke out the author paid a visit to West Africa, he had the opportunity of discussing with the Governor-General of French West Africa, at Dakar, the African Cherbourg, the scheme which was then being put into operation by that distinguished official to impose yearly levies for military purposes upon the male population of French West Africa. The scheme has made great headway since then. It is characteristic of the atmosphere of deceit and dishonesty which war generates that the *potential* militarisation of the inhabitants of the German African Dependencies in tropical Africa has been used as an argument for depriving Germany of them in the good old-fashioned way, while the *actual* militarisation of the inhabitants of the French Dependencies in tropical Africa has been conveniently ignored. The idea of utilising Africa as a military recruiting ground is as old as Hannibal. It had long been favoured, and so far as Algeria was concerned acted upon, by the French general staff. Algerian troops fought in the Franco-Prussian war, and the German literature of the day is full of accounts of alleged atrocities perpetrated by the *Turcos* upon German wounded. By one of those bitter ironies with which war is ever providing us, the fiercest engagement in the struggle between the France of Napoleon III. and the Prussia of Bismarck, was fought between Polish regiments under Prussian command and North African regiments under French command.

During the Great War of 1914-18, the French have used hundreds of thousands of North and West African troops on the Western and Macedonian fronts. They quartered a large number of West African troops in Morocco. They occupied the enemy Consulates in Greece with these black troops. They have employed them in Russia. They actually garrison German towns with them The atrocities perpetualed by these savage auxiliaries on the Western front are known to every soldier. They have been found in possession of eyeballs, fingers, and heads of Germans in their haversacks. Mr. Chesterton's pious hope of seeing "Asiatics and Africans upon the verge of savagery," let loose against the Germans has been more than fulfilled.

Up to October 30, 1918, the French Government employed 695,000 fighting men and 238,000 coloured labourers in the war. Of the former the largest proportion came from Africa, and a large proportion of the latter. The official report of the troops from West Africa describes them as "regular athletes and formidable adversaries for the Germans." M. Diagne's report to the Colonial Minister, published in September of last year, records a total of 60,000 troops recruited under that gentleman's auspices in French West Africa proper, and 15,000 in the French Congo. Documents found upon prisoners attached to the so-called "Senegalese" battalion, No. 70, consisting of 840 men, are of peculiar interest. They have been published in the neutral, as well as in the German

Press. They prove the wide extent of the recruiting area, for the units include representatives of tribes scattered throughout the Western Sudan, comprising, for example, among some thirty other tribes, Fulas, Soninkes, Mossis, Mandingoes, and Guransis. Altogether French West Africa and French Equatorial Africa (French Congo) produced 181,512 fighting men. On the day of the Armistice their numbers on the fronts, in camp in West Africa and in depôts in North Africa, amounted to 136,500 (91 battalions averaging 1,500 to 2,000 rifles), without counting the Madagascar and Somali contingents.

Abominable abuses and bloody and extensive uprisings have attended these forcible recruitings in West Africa. Each district was marked down for a given number of recruits; chiefs were required to furnish the men, and bribed to do so, punished if they did not. Cash *bonuses* per man recruited were offered, and private kidnapping resulted necessarily—the days of the slave trade over again. There was a debate in the Chamber in July, 1917, all knowledge of which was kept from the British public. But the scandals which it brought to light did not lead to any substantial modification of the policy. Indeed, French West Africa produced more black cannon fodder for France in 1918 than in the preceding years, viz.: 63,208 men. The Acting-Governor-General, M. Clozel, an experienced and distinguished official, whose published works on Africa have long been familiar to students, viewed the whole scheme with the greatest aversion. He reported on November 10, 1916:

> My opinion is that the native peoples have no enthusiasm whatever for our cause, that their dislike to military and above all to foreign service cannot be overcome, and that any recruiting that would be really worth while can only be carried out through the operation of fear.

He followed this up by an even more vigorous protest on December 6 of the same year:

> The political condition of the Colony—he wrote—is still a source of perpetual anxiety to us. The drafting of 50,000 men since the close of 1915 has been the pretext, as well as the occasion, for a rising which . . . has assumed considerable dimensions in the Niger region. Energetic and conscientious officials of the Government have strained every nerve to prevent this conflagration from overwhelming the entire Niger country. They have almost wholly succeeded in doing so, but the rising has only been mastered after six months' hard fighting by forces mainly sent up from the coast.

For this outspokenness M. Clozel was sharply rebuked, and broken. His successor, M. Van Hollenhoven, was another conspicuously able and honest official of Dutch extraction. But, invested with supreme control as Governor-General, he declined to countenance what he regarded as a scandalous policy, and resigned rather than carry it out, throwing up a salary of £4,000 a year, one of the highest-paid posts in the French Civil Service, and going back to the front as a simple captain. When recovering from his first wounds he said to a mutual friend, who visited him in hospital: "Not only is the Colony being emptied of its able-bodied men, but the whole population is being led to believe that the slave trade has begun again."

The war is now over. But the present rulers of France show no sign of relinquishing the militarist policy they pursued during the war. Quite the contrary. On July 30, 1919, conscription was decreed for all natives throughout the entire area of French West Africa and French Equatorial Africa—an area over two million square miles in extent and containing a native population estimated at just under twenty million. A decree of December 12, 1919, applies the West African decree to Madagascar, which covers 228,000 miles and has a population of over three millions. The recruiting of a further 28,900 in West Africa is now proceeding in the following proportions: Senegal, 7,000; upper Senegal-Niger region, 5,600; upper Volta, 5,600; Guinea, 4,000; Ivory Coast, 4,200; Dahomey, 2,500. From 1922 onwards it is estimated that this negro army will consist of three classes and will total 100,000. It is anticipated that Madagascar, the French West Indian islands, the French Somali coast and the group of islands in the Pacific will furnish between them a further 100,000 men. This, of course, does not take into account the Arab and Berber contingents from Algeria, Tunis and Morocco, which may be reckoned at another 100,000 at least. The Negro conscripts will serve three years, and two out of the three will be spent, according to the French military and colonial newspapers, *in France!*

This new development of French action in Africa raises a number of distinct issues of the gravest international concern. There is the moral issue as it affect Africa. It is not surprising that the native peoples of West Africa should look upon this conscripting and removal to distant countries of their young men in the light of the revival of the slave trade. It *is* the revival of the slave trade. The men are taken by force; must be taken by force, either through the instrumentality of native troops under French officers, or through the instrumentality of their own chiefs acting under French orders. True, once secured, they are not sent to work in plantations; they are not lashed and kicked and tortured They are sent to camps where they are taught to kill men—black men in Africa, white men in Europe; they are well fed and indulged. All the same they are slaves in every moral sense.

There is the issue of white government in Africa. The French example cannot fail to be imitated by other Powers with African possessions. Nothing is more certain than that British militarists will want to impose conscription upon the native peoples in the British Protectorates. And from their point of view they will be right. Reasons other than purely military ones will be evoked, and it will be difficult to oppose them. Should we be justified in leaving the hard-working, industrious, progressive native communities of Nigeria, surrounded on three sides by French possessions, at the mercy of a Power which could invade the country at any moment with a force of 50,000 first-class fighting black troops? Alliances are not eternal. Again, can we run the risk of leaving Nigeria open to the invasion by a French native army in rebellion against its French officers? Such a rebellion is only a matter of time. What could a handful of French officers and administrators do against tens of thousands of black troops thoroughly inured to scientific warfare, and many of them having opposed trained white troops on European battlefields—" blooded " with white blood! The white man has dug the grave of the " prestige " of his race in West Africa, by employing West Africans to kill white men in Europe, and by stationing them in European cities where they have raped white women. In applying conscription not only to French West Africa proper, but south of the Equator to the Congo forest region, the French are virtually compelling the Belgians to do the same in their neighbouring Congo. The spirit of the Leopoldian *régime* is not so dead that the measure would not meet with eager approval by a number of the Belgian officials. And the Congo abuts upon British territory, upon the confines of the Union of South Africa. French action is replete with immeasurable consequences in Africa, and for Africa.

And what of the distinctively European issue? For the European democracy, this militarising of the African tropics and this introduction of African troops upon European soil is a terrific portent. The French militarists, whose schemes in Europe are a menace to the world, inform us that they intend to have a standing army of 200,000 coloured troops in France, 100,000 of which composed of primitive Africans. They will be used by the French militarists all over Europe in pursuance of their avowed purposes. They will garrison European towns. They will be billeted in European homes. They will kill Europeans who object to the policy of the French militarists. They will be used, no doubt, to fire upon French working-men should these at any time come into collision with the ruling classes in France. These are some of the vistas which this policy uncovers. And this is the military machine with which the British people are to conclude an alliance! Negroes, Malagasies, Berbers, Arabs, flung into Europe by the hundred thousand in the interests of a capitalist and militarist Order. That is the prospect—nay, that is the actuality—which the forces of organised European Labour have got to face, squarely.

. . . . . .

What could a League of Nations do to protect the peoples of tropical Africa from these evils? Is any machinery provided in the Covenant for this purpose? Let us take the latter point first.

The Covenant postulates a measure of international control for Africa, both of a political and of an administrative kind. Politically, it professes to introduce what is termed the "mandatory system," although that expression is not found in the Covenant itself, which merely speaks of "mandatories." But the Covenant limits the applicability of this system to "those colonies and territories which, as a consequence of the late war, have ceased to be under the sovereignty of the States which formerly owned them, and which are inhabited by peoples not yet able to stand by themselves under the strenuous conditions of the modern world." The Covenant goes on to say that the well-being and development of such peoples forms a sacred trust of civilisation, and that their " tutelage " should be entrusted to " advanced nations," who would be the League's mandatories.

It seems to be widely assumed that the wording of the Covenant permits of the extension of this system of " mandatories " to the whole of Africa. I can find no justification whatever for the belief. There is nothing in the wording of the Covenant which suggests that the framers of this instrument contemplate submitting their political control in Africa, except as regards the additional territory they have acquired through the war, to the supervision of the League. The mandatory purpose is clearly limited to the territory formerly governed by the States recently at war with the States responsible for drawing up the Covenant.

So far as Africa is concerned those territories are the former German dependencies, viz., Togo and Kamerun, in Western tropical Africa; Damaraland or German South-West Africa; and German East Africa. In the case of German South-West Africa, it is laid down that that particular territory shall become an " integral portion " of the mandatory's territory. From the point of view of political control, then, all that the Covenant does is to provide that the African territories formerly administered by Germany shall be administered henceforth by the European States which have conquered Germany in arms. In point of fact this obvious design was promptly consummated, before the ratification of the Peace Treaty, of which the Covenant forms part, i.e., before the League —which is composed exclusively of the States formerly at war with Germany—acquired legal existence. German South-West Africa passed to the Union of South Africa. Britain and France divided the Kamerun and Togo between them, and Britain took German East Africa, subsequently presenting Belgium with a substantial slice of it. In other words the " mandatory system " was introduced into the Covenant as a device to distribute Germany's dependencies in Africa between such of

Germany's former enemies as were African Powers already.*

It should be clearly understood, therefore, that only the former German dependencies in Africa are subject to any kind of international control under the Covenant—i.e., 700,000 square miles of territory, the area of Africa being 11,500,000 square miles; and that the governing body of the League upon which that control will devolve, is composed of the particular States which have attributed the former German dependencies to themselves and to one another. It should be equally well understood that if this principle of international control is to be extended to the remaining 10,800,000 square miles of Africa, provision will have to be specifically made; for the Covenant neither allows of it nor hints at it.

So much for the political side.

What of the administrative side? We have observed that the government of the former German dependencies is to be regarded as a "sacred trust of civilisation." But why this differentiation in favour of the inhabitants of the former German dependencies? Why the responsibilities of Britain (for example) should be invested with a special moral significance when the well-being of the native races in German East Africa is concerned, is not apparent. The obligation is not less in the case of the native population of British East Africa, Nigeria, or Nyassaland. The moral obligations of the Belgians towards the peoples of the Congo are just as considerable as their moral obligations for the welfare of the inhabitants of that section of German East Africa, which we have graciously passed on to them, as if it were a bale of merchandise. And the same argument applies to the French.

Putting that aside, how is the "sacred trust" interpreted in the Covenant? Those called upon to exercise it shall do so under conditions guaranteeing "freedom of conscience and religion, subject only to the maintenance of public order and morals, prohibition of abuses such as the Slave trade, the arms traffic and the liquor traffic, with the prevention of the establishment of fortifications, or military and naval bases and of military training of

* I do not propose to discuss here the justice or the wisdom from the point of view of international peace of this wholesale appropriation of the German dependencies. I have expressed my views on that subject elsewhere ("Africa and the Peace of Europe": National Labour Press), and I have submitted arguments—which remain unanswered—that such a policy is both inequitable and unwise.

the natives for other than police services and the defence of territory, and will also secure equal opportunities for the trade and commerce of other members of the League." We will examine these conditions *seriatim*.

"Freedom of conscience and religion, subject to the maintenance of public order and morals." Here, indeed, is a prodigious safeguard for native rights! The phrase is merely an echo of the old *formulæ* of the Berlin Act of 1885. All that it means is that European Catholic missionaries shall not be favoured by the administrative Power at the expense of Protestant missionaries, and *vice versa*. It has nothing to do with the natives. "The prohibition of abuses such as the Slave trade, the arms traffic, and the liquor traffic." Here, again, is much solemn make-believe. The old-fashioned Slave trade is a thing of the past. The so-called internal Slave trade which the natives have to fear to-day does not arise from internecine warfare and the ensuing sale of prisoners of war, but from the acts of European governments. These are never, of course, described as " Slave trade ": we find other and less repulsive terms for them. Prohibition of the "arms traffic" is a measure of European, not of native interest; it naturally does not suit European Administrations in Africa that the native population should purchase weapons of precision, licitly or illicitly. But it does suit the French Government that hundreds of thousands of African natives should have rifles placed in their hands, and should be taught how to use them against the enemies of the French Government. As regards the liquor traffic, its prohibition is a salutary measure; but an ineffective one if the prohibition is not universally applied to whites as well as blacks. Where liquor has become by long usage a recognised article of trade and large revenues are raised by taxes upon the import, prohibition can only be just and salutary provided it be not accompanied by administrative measures of direct taxation to supply the equivalent revenue lost, calculated to provoke local wars with their attendant loss of life and destruction of food supplies. The whole problem of liquor in Africa is an immensely complicated one, and its brief dismissal in the Covenant by the blessed word "prohibition" is in the nature of an appeal to the gallery. "The prevention of the establishment of fortifications, or military and naval bases. . ."

PROTECTION FROM LEAGUE OF NATIONS

This, once more, is a question that concerns, primarily, European interests, not African interests. No doubt it is entirely satisfactory that in 700,000 square miles of African territory, the European "mandatories" should not erect fortifications and naval and military bases. But when one recalls that there are 10,800,000 square miles of African territory to which this preventive clause does not apply, and in which there are numbers of fortifications and military and naval bases, it is difficult to feel deliriously enthusiastic. The prevention of "military training of the natives for other than police purposes and the defence of territory." In this connection the natural comment is the same as in the case of military and naval bases. There is no reality in a policy which prevents the militarising of one-sixteenth of the African Continent, and which allows of it in the remaining fifteen-sixteenths. "Equal opportunities for the trade and commerce of other members of the League.' This would be an excellent provision were it not for the fact that considerably more than half the population of Europe is excluded from the League. When, and if, that population is included, the excellence of the provision will be unquestioned. But the spectacle (for example) of French administrators governing the Kamerun as mandatories of the League on free trade principles, and of French administrators governing the coterminous French territory as agents of a protectionist French Government, will assuredly be entertaining.

It is obvious that none of these stipulations, except, indirectly, the last, go to the heart of the problem of African administration even in the restricted and scattered area to which it is proposed to apply them. Outside that area the great mass of Africa, including about five-sixths of the tropical and sub-tropical zone, is left unprotected and untouched by the Covenant.

Hence we may say of the Covenant that it entirely fails to provide the requisite machinery to deal with the African problem, even of that part of Africa—the tropical region—where it is possible for an international standard of administrative conduct and policy to be evolved. Some method will have to be found by which such a standard can be created and internationally supervised. How is this to be done?

. . . . . .

We have seen that the mandatory system, such as the Covenant conceives it, is but a thinly disguised device to camouflage the acquisition by the African Powers of the Entente, of the African territories conquered by them from Germany. It is an attempt, not devoid of ingenuity, to reconcile the altruistic pronouncements of President Wilson with what is substantially a policy of imperialistic grab at the expense of the beaten foe on the familiar lines of the 17th and 18th century wars. But is a so-called "mandatory system" capable of becoming a genuine international instrument through which the equitable treatment of the African races shall be a recognised international concern? Is it the right sort of instrument to ensure that result? I confess to the gravest of doubts. People talk somewhat loosely of the extension of the system. Do they understand its implications? Are they prepared to abide by them? Are the European States which hold African territories to-day, either through the conquest of their indigenous inhabitants or through treaties of amity and commerce with the native rulers, prepared to recognise that in future they shall derive the powers they have hitherto exercised as sovereign States in Africa, from the League and as mandatories of that body? Is this a practicable proposition to-day when the League is, to all intents and purposes, merely the continued association of some of the States allied in the war? Would it be more practicable if the existing League became in due course a real League of Nations? Unless it pre-supposes a power of censure and even of revocation of the mandate, resident in the League, a "mandatory system" is a mere phrase. It is, of course, possible to conceive of a change so complete not only in the character and composition of European Governments, but in the ethics of nationalism, that European States which are also colonial Powers. would consent to subordinate their *status* as colonial Powers to the League, while preserving their own machinery of administration. But he would be an optimist, indeed, who would deem such a consummation achievable within a measurable period. And, meantime, what of these African peoples, whose interests are at stake, who have no one to represent them at the council boards of the European States and who are threatened with grave and ever-increasing dangers?. The difficulties of securing international sanction for a right policy in tropical Africa are great enough in all conscience. Why add to them a procedure which bristles with constitutional, legal and sentimental obstacles?

What is really needed is that certain definite principles by which administrative policy in tropical Africa should be guided, be worked out and laid down at an international Conference; and that this policy should have behind it the sanction of a real League of Nations, and the moral support of public opinion.

. . . . . .

I return to my original question. What could a League of Nations do to protect the peoples of tropical Africa from the evils of capitalistic exploitation and militarism?

So far as the militarisation of the African tropics is concerned, a League inspired by the purpose above mentioned, would recognise that anything short of cauterising the evil at its root was useless. So long as Europe persists in treating tropical Africa as a potential war zone, liable to be involved at any moment in European quarrels, and so long as France persists in treating her African dependencies as a reservoir of black cannon-fodder, the militarisation of the country is inevitable, and the conscription of its adult male population is bound to follow everywhere.

There is but one remedy: the exclusion of tropical Africa from the area of European conflict by international agreement. This can be accomplished only in one way. Tropical Africa should be placed under perpetual neutrality. It is, of course, perfectly true that its neutrality might be violated. But that applies to any provision enunciated by the League. The whole conception of a League of Nations is the subordination of selfish national interests to the major international interest. If the sanction of the League were obtained for the neutralisation of the African tropics, we should have the collective moral forces of civilisation arrayed in opposition to the Power, or Powers, which sought to infringe that neutrality: and there is no force carrying greater weight which humanity at its present stage of ethical development can invoke. If civilisation is incapable of rising to the height of a self-denying ordinance affecting the most helpless section of the human race, the hopes centred in a League of Nations are mere illusions.

There is nothing fantastic in the suggestion to neutralise tropical Africa. It is merely a proposal to extend the provisions of the Congo Act (Berlin Conference, 1884) which neutralised the Congo Basin, i.e., a considerable portion of the tropical region, to the whole tropical region. It is true that the Congo Free State was never really neutral because its Sovereign was perpetually using, and being used by, European States competing for African territorial mastery. But that competition no longer exists. It is also true that when the Great War broke out, the neutrality of the Congo Basin was definitely broken. But that was the consequence of the European anarchy which the League of Nations is founded to combat. If the conception of the League of Nations possesses significance at all, that significance is derived from the desire of civilised humanity to substitute something better for the anarchy which produced the war; and from faith in the possibility of doing so. The failure of the experiment to neutralise a portion of the African tropics before the war was due to the inherent vices of the international order which civilised humanity desires to change. It should not, therefore, be regarded as a deterrent to a further experiment on the same lines, under the new international order, which it is the object of the League to promote. The principle is sound and is not invalidated because the first attempt to apply it failed.

Short of neutralisation, I see but one alternative course of action to prevent the militarisation of the African tropics. It is that the stipulations of the Covenant affecting the former German dependencies, should be applied to the whole tropical region. There is neither rhyme nor reason in prohibiting the erection of fortifications, etc., and the military training of the native population in a relatively small area of the tropical region, and allowing these things in the remainder. It is absurd, for instance, that the League's mandatory in the Kamerun should be restricted to retaining a police force; while the *same Power* in contiguous territory, should be permitted to conscript the native population. Anyone can see at a glance how preposterous is such a notion. But in one vital respect the stipulations of the Covenant would need amendment. The Covenant speaks of the

PROTECTION FROM LEAGUE OF NATIONS 231

"military training of the natives for other than police purposes, *and the defence of territory.*" The italicised words leave the door wide open to the very evils which the Covenant professes to guard against. No State ever acknowledges that its military establishment is for other than "defensive" purposes. The phraseology used in the Covenant would permit of the military training of the adult male population in the former German dependencies by the mandatory State. Given an equitable administrative policy all that is required to maintain order in the tropical regions of Africa is a mobile, well disciplined force of a few hundred, or a couple of thousand or so, native police, at the disposal of each local Government. The number would vary, of course, with the size of the particular territory, and with the character and density of the native population. And this brings us to a consideration of the problem of administration itself.

. . . . . .

At this point, I venture upon a digression in order that subsequent remarks may not be misapprehended. If the purport of this volume has been in any sense fulfilled, I have succeeded in imparting the conviction I myself hold that a tremendous moral liability is laid upon Europe to do justice to the peoples of Africa; that recognition of this moral obligation should find expression, and that it can find such expression at an early date in concrete acts of policy as regards, at least, that very considerable section of the Dark Continent where the racial problem in its acute forms is non-existent. I am bold enough to hope that a perusal of these pages will have established that the moral obligation of repairing wrongs done to, and preventing further wrongs upon, the peoples of Africa, is the basis of the whole case I have sought to put forward here in behalf of these peoples.

I shall not, then, I trust be misunderstood when I say that unless the public opinion which admits this *moral* obligation and is anxious that it should be a powerful stimulus in the formation of policy, is prepared to face and examine with open eyes the *material* factors which influence and direct the relations of Europe with tropical Africa, there is little or no expectation that moral considerations will be able, in any appreciable degree, to affect policy. Mere negative criticism is useless. To denounce the material factors in Europe's relations with tropical Africa as necessarily evil, because they are material, is futile. *The real problem is to ensure that a material relationship, which is inevitable, shall not preclude just, humane, and enlightened government of tropical African peoples by European States.*

. . . . .

In elaborating what should be, in effect, a charter of rights for the peoples of tropical Africa, a League of Nations would begin by frankly recognising that the driving force which has conducted European States to undertake the experiment of direct government of the tropical African region, is neither altruistic nor sentimental, but economic. The League would then find itself confronted (as a League) with the problem which confronts every European State now ruling in tropical Africa, and the public conscience within every such State. Can this economic purpose of Europe in tropical Africa be worked out in such a way that the native peoples shall benefit from its accomplishment? To put the matter even more baldly, is it possible that Europe can become possessed of the natural riches of the African tropics and of the riches which the soil of tropical Africa can produce through the labour of tropical man, without degrading, enslaving and, in the ultimate resort, probably destroying the peoples of tropical Africa? The reply is in the affirmative provided that native rights in land are preserved, and provided the natives are given the requisite facilities for cultivating and exploiting the raw material which it is Europe's economic purpose to secure. The League, if convinced of the accuracy of this affirmative assertion, would then regard the preservation of this fundamental native right as the first step in the elaboration of its charter.

This would be an easy matter in a considerable area of the tropical region, where policy has either been directed to the preservation of the land rights of the native population—in Nigeria, for example—or where policy has not been directed to usurping them. But what should be the attitude of the League where this fundamental right has been set aside; where the governing European administration has allocated great stretches of country to syndicates and concessionaires; where the natives, divorced from their land and unable, in consequence, to improve their material conditions, or even to sustain themsleves, have already lost their economic independence and with it their freedom; where they have become the wage slaves of alien white men without any means of safeguarding their interests even as wage slaves; where, in short, capitalistic exploitation of the native population is in full swing?

Should the League take up the position that the evil has gone too far to be arrested, and content itself with devising means whereby the wage slaves can be protected against the worst abuses of alien exploitation? Or should the League recommend the cancelling of the private interests which have been created, with or without compensation to the beneficiaries—and a reversion to sound policy? The difficulty is a very real one. While it may be possible for a League in which the most important European States actually governing tropical Africa will presumably enjoy a dominating position for many years to come, to elaborate a general charter of native rights; it is a very different proposition to expect these States, which in any case would play the chief part in the drawing-up of such a charter, to sweep away, or to buy out, the vested interests established, with their sanction, in particular African dependencies. Nor is this the only point to be considered. Where the destruction of native rights in land has taken place and the native has become a helot, the edifice of native society has crumbled and cannot be repaired. Native life has been broken up. A community of free African landowners, cultivators and farmers has been converted into a landless proletariat, dependent upon alien enterprise for the wherewithal to feed and clothe itself. New conditions have been set up: certain consequences have resulted. The *central* mischief is done, and cannot be undone.

But that is no reason why an evil political and economic system should be allowed to grow, any more than a human disease. If it cannot be extirpated, its progress can be checked. If—to take a concrete case—a portion of the land of British East Africa has been handed over to European syndicates, that is no reason why the process should be continued. The remainder of the country can still be preserved for the native population. Nor is this all. Even where the evil has become implanted, it can be assailed indirectly. Labour legislation can be devised of such a character as will make it impossible for coercive influences to be brought to bear upon the native population in the unalienated areas, to give their labour to the corporations exploiting the alienated areas. It can also be made impossible for these corporations, or individuals, to prevent dispossessed natives from settling in the unalienated areas. The individual native in British East Africa inhabiting an alienated area can be placed by law in the position to acquire land in the unalienated areas sufficient in extent to support his family, and to enable him to cultivate valuable crops for sale and export; in which he, and the native population on the unalienated areas, should receive every encouragement and help from the Administration. Should these measures eventually bring about a state of affairs which would decrease the profits of the corporations or concessionaires by adding to the costliness of labour, this result need only perturb those who take a short view of the part which these tropical African dependencies ought to play in the economy of the world. And this, for reasons which have been indirectly touched upon already, and to which I now return.

. . . . .

As I have pointed out, the problem of tropical Africa is at bottom the problem of so moulding and directing an economic relation which is inevitable, that it shall not entail degradation and destruction upon the African peoples, and disgrace to Europe. What public opinion in the European States, which are governing States in Africa, must insist upon; what all the decent and humane influences in internationalism must exact, is that the economic purpose of Europe in the African tropics shall be carried out in such a way as will permit of the moral responsibilities of Europe for a righteous government of tropical Africa being fulfilled. In much of the most populous, and intrinsically the richest portion of the African tropics, the development of this economic purpose is proceeding on lines which do not substantially conflict with just and wise government. On the other hand, this is not the case in a considerable portion of the tropical region. Government is not there performing its proper function of trustee for, and protector of, the native peoples. Its power is exerted on behalf of enterprises which make for the exploitation and impoverishment of the native population. The welfare of the natives is subordinated to the exigencies of the alien capitalist. The evil must be attacked, nationally and internationally, without cessation.

But there is special need to impress upon those who are already won over to the moral side of the question, or whose traditions and outlook would naturally induce them to take that side, that the attack will not be successful in the ultimate resort if it confines itself merely to insistence upon the moral issue. *It must face the economic issue.* It must form a clear conception of what is sound, and what is unsound in the methods of economic development in these regions. It must persuade by economic reasoning as well as by appeals to ethical and humanitarian instincts and motives. *It must be in a position to demonstrate that what is morally right is also economically sound; that what is morally wrong is also economically unsound.* It must seek to convince the public mind that the economic purpose of Europe in tropical Africa is served by the individual and collective prosperity of the native population, not by its impoverishment; by the existence of native communities of agriculturists and abori-culturists producing for their own profit, not for the benefit of the shareholders of white syndicates and concessionaires. It must be at great pains to show that the policy of encouraging forms of European enterprise which convert African labour into a dividend-producing force for the individual European, is sheer economic waste of the potentialities of African labour: whereas the full potentialities of African labour can be secured for the economic purpose of Europe by encouraging forms of European enterprise in which the African figures, not as a hired servant, but as co-operator and partner.

The task is not an easy one, because all the tendencies of our European capitalist system incline to make the test of "prosperity" of a tropical African territory depend upon the number of European enterprises therein established which are acquiring profits out of the direct employment of African labour. And curiously enough there is a type of European Socialist mind that unconsciously reinforces these tendencies, of course from an entirely different standpoint. This type of mind visualises the mass of African humanity in terms of a dogmatic economic theory.

It would stand aside from any effort to preserve the native races from capitalistic exploitation, which it regards as a necessary and inevitable episode in human development. It would do nothing to safeguard native institutions, which it looks upon as archaic and reactionary. It would apply the same processes to all races (it refuses, apparently, to admit any other form of civilisation than the *European socialised* State) at whatever stage of cultural development. It would cheerfully, and with the purest of motives, assist at the destruction of African institutions, and assent to the conversion of African cultivators and farmers into wage-slaves, sublimely indifferent to the social havoc and misery thereby inflicted upon millions of living Africans and Africans yet unborn, content with the thought that in the fullness of time the wage-slaves would themselves evolve the Socialist *African* State. The only comment that I would venture to make upon the contentions of this school, is that the form of Socialism which Russia has evolved, and which, I suppose, is the most advanced form of European Socialism now available to study, approximates closely to the social conditions of an advanced tropical African community. The spinal column of both is a system of land tenure which ensures to the population a large measure of economic independence—in tropical Africa the degree of economic independence is necessarily greater; while the corporate character which the Soviet system imparts to all economic activities is substantially identical with the African social system. It seems a strange anomaly to laud advanced Socialism in Europe, and to assent to its destruction in tropical Africa.

. . . . . .

The ordinary business man's view of " prosperity " in relation to an African dependency, referred to above, is thoroughly fallacious. The true prosperity of a tropical African dependency is to be judged by altogether different standards, even from the standpoint we are now examining, that of Europe's utilitarian purpose in this part of the world. Flourishing towns and villages surrounded by well-kept fields, plantations and live stock (you may see thousands such in Nigeria): a happy and expanding population, self-supporting in the matter of foodstuffs, carrying on a brisk trade with its neighbours, cultivating products for export, becoming steadily wealthier, and in consequence—and here the European economic purpose comes in—providing an increasingly large market for the absorption of the manufactures of Europe, and an increasing revenue to the local European Government, which that Government, if it is in the hands of men of vision and commonsense, will spend upon improving means of communication and locomotion, water supply and sanitation, forestry and agricultural improvements: this is "prosperity." Take a concrete case. When I visited Nigeria a year or two before the war, some eight hundred villages in one particular district had been taught by the Forestry Department to start plantations of rubber. At that time the potential wealth of these native communities in their rubber plantations amounted already to several hundreds of thousands of pounds, and was, of course, increasing year by year. In due course they would gather and prepare that rubber. They would sell it to European merchants, and they would buy with the equivalent the merchandise of Europe. They would be purchasers of European goods on the basis of the intrinsic value of the article their labour had produced. A party of European capitalists came along one fine day, saw these flourishing native plantations, and proposed to the Administration that they should buy them up. They were told that the land belonged to the natives, not to the British Government, and that the plantations were the property of the owners of the land. Now what would have happened if these gentlemen had had their way, from the standpoint of the economic relationship of these particular native communities with Europe? Simply this —instead of being purchasers of European goods to the extent represented by the intrinsic value of the article they produced, they would have sunk to the level of wage earners on plantations henceforth owned by European concessionaires. Their purchasing capacity in terms of European goods would therefore have enormously declined, and the trade of the dependency would have suffered in the same proportion.

The economic purpose of Europe in tropical Africa, properly understood and judiciously directed, requires a free African labour, profiting from its activities, working under the stimulus which comes of the knowledge that the material reward of its labour is assured to it. That economic purpose requires that the African producer of raw material for the world's markets shall be encouraged to produce, by the consciousness that he will obtain the equivalent not only for his labour, but for the value of the article his labour has produced. It requires that the industrial classes of Europe shall find in tropical Africa an ever-widening market for the absorption of their output. This cannot be if African labour is exhausted and impoverished, because—if for no other reason—African purchasing capacity in the goods of Europe is thereby diminished. Other consequences are numerous and obvious: but that one is immediate.

Now consider the picture of a tropical African dependency—take British East Africa as typical—where policy is directed to ensuring that a dozen or so European concessionaires shall earn large dividends. The first call upon the labour of the country is for work on the plantations and estates of these concessionaires. As a result native villages decay. The population is unable to feed itself. The Administration has to import foodstuffs at great expense. The people sink immeasurably in the scale of their self-respect. They are reduced to a proletariat with no rights. There is no horizon before them: no honourable ambition to fulfil. Their capacities are arrested. Their condition becomes one of stagnancy. Add to this all the abuses incidental to labour thus economically forced, with their attendant discontents developing into sporadic outbreaks; the notorious inefficiency of African labour under such circumstances; the decrease in vitality consequent upon the introduction of an unnatural existence; the lowered birth rate; the increase in prostitution and venereal disease. Here is no constructive policy, but a destructive one. Nothing is being built up, except the ephemeral fortunes of a few white men. The future, viewed from the broad standpoint of both European and African interests, is being undermined all the time.

The folly of the conception is palpable. If it be true in an economic sense, as true it is, that the " asset " of a tropical African dependency is primarily, the native; a system which enfeebles and impoverishes the native is suicidal, always from the same utilitarian point of view. That is one side of the case. The other side is that in enfeebling and impoverishing the African, you are destroying the major economic interest of Europe in the African. Every penny taken from the national wealth of a European State for the purpose of bolstering up a system of that kind in tropical Africa, is flung into the sea. Every European nation which is a governing State in tropical Africa and which tolerates a system of that kind in its dependencies, is allowing the major national interest to be sacrificed for the temporary enrichment of a restricted number of individuals. And, from the point of view of economics, the national interest is also the international interest.

. . . . . .

Such, broadly, are some of the most important considerations which one might hope would guide a League of Nations approaching the problem of tropical African Government with the desire of promoting an international policy for this vast region, at once intelligent and humane. The foundation upon which it would work would be that the material prosperity of the native was the key-note to administrative success: that the exploitation of African labour for sectional European interests was an economic error; that the native communities of tropical Africa need protection, in the major European interest and to ensure the progressive development and expansion of the economic purpose of Europe, from the positive evils of a capitalist system which, bad for all Europe, is fatal for Africa.

Apart from these fundamental issues it would be the object of the League to ensure the " open door " for commercial enterprise throughout the tropical region of Africa. This would involve absolute trading equality for all nations within the tropical area, and the consequent disappearance of the differential tariff and the territorial concessionaire. The subjects of the various Powers adhering to the League would enjoy complete equality in all commercial transactions. The European States, members of the League, that were also governing States in tropical Africa, would be free to make their own fiscal arrangements; they would not be free to differentiate in favour of their nationals—a fertile cause of endless international friction in the past. It would be very desirable that the principle of the " open door " should be broadened so as to include capital enterprises such as the construction of railways, harbour works, dredging of rivers and kindred matters. In these cases the permanent tropical African Commission, referred to in the next paragraphs, could be empowered to form a special department which would act as an impartial adjudicating body for the placing of contracts for public works of this character on a system of open international tender.

. . . . . .

There would be created under the auspices of the League a tropical African Commission in permanent session at the headquarters of the League, employing special commissions which would be continuously engaged in visiting the tropical African dependencies and reporting upon conditions. Such a Commission would be a centre for the collation of all material relevant to the affairs of tropical Africa, for the classification and study of all *data* bearing upon tropical African ethnology, social customs, philology, economic resources—actual and potential. It would receive and consider the reports of its travelling commissioners, and make recommendations to the League. It would be open to receive all reports, grievances and representations from whomsoever emanating, within the limits of its jurisdiction. The cfficial papers of each Dependency would be regularly communicated to it by the respective Administrations—reports of Residents on political affairs, reports of Forestry Departments, Agricultural Departments, Native Affairs Departments, Treasuries, and so on. It would form, in effect, a permanent court of inquiry, investigation and scientific research. It would itself issue periodical reports and remain in close touch with universities, educational and agricultural institutions, labour organisations, scientific societies, and Chambers of commerce in every country adhering to the League. Through its instrumentality a link would be forged between the African tropics and the economic activities and requirements of the world of labour, commerce and affairs in Europe and elsewhere. It would help to create an international conscience with regard to tropical Africa which does not now exist, and would be the vehicle through which that aroused conscience would find expression.

. . . . . .

Were the problem of tropical African government approached in the manner indicated in this chapter, all that is good in European endeavour throughout that great region of the globe would be confirmed and consolidated, and would have free scope for increased usefulness. The men of vision and of humanitarian instincts, the men who regard the administration of these races as a high duty and a high privilege, would be encouraged by the thought that they were supported by progressive and coalesced international influences: that an organised international moral force had been created upon which they could rely. A halt would be called to manifold errors and injustices which the absence of an international mechanism making for just and wise government and ensuring international publicity for the affairs of the tropical Continent, had rendered possible in the past. It would be perceived that the duty and the legitimate interests of Europe in tropical Africa lay on the same path. It would come to be regarded not only as right in essence, but expedient in practice, that government in tropical Africa should aim at establishing the well-being, self-respect and intellectual advancement of the native population. Philanthropic effort directed to the welfare and progress of the tropical African peoples would everywhere be strengthened, and the public conscience in the various European States governing in tropical Africa could be more easily invoked for the remedy and removal of abuses.

And out of this awakening and purifying process would grow a wider concept of the latent mental powers and spiritual potentialities of these African peoples, and a keener realisation of the great and noble task which unselfish effort could undertake among them. We should look back with horror and shame at a past in which the African, arbitrarily sundered from his land, his social and family life, ground out a life of servile toil, with no beacon of hope, no incentive to rise, no other stimulus to labour than starvation and the lash. For the first time in the history of contact between the white races and the black, the black man's burden would be lifted from the shoulders which for five hundred years have bent beneath its weight.

MONTHLY REVIEW

an independent socialist magazine
edited by Paul M. Sweezy and Harry Magdoff

Business Week: ". . . a brand of socialism that is thorough-going and tough-minded, drastic enough to provide the sharp break with the past that many left-wingers in the underdeveloped countries see as essential. At the same time they maintain a sturdy independence of both Moscow and Peking that appeals to neutralists. And their skill in manipulating the abstruse concepts of modern economics impresses would-be intellectuals. . . . Their analysis of the troubles of capitalism is just plausible enough to be disturbing."

Bertrand Russell: "Your journal has been of the greatest interest to me over a period of time. I am not a Marxist by any means as I have sought to show in critiques published in several books, but I recognize the power of much of your own analysis and where I disagree I find your journal valuable and of stimulating importance. I want to thank you for your work and to tell you of my appreciation of it."

The Wellesley Department of Economics: " . . . the leading Marxist intellectual (not Communist) economic journal published anywhere in the world, and is on our subscription list at the College library for good reasons."

Albert Einstein: "Clarity about the aims and problems of socialism is of greatest significance in our age of transition. . . . I consider the founding of this magazine to be an important public service." (In his article, "Why Socialism" in Vol. I, No. 1.)

DOMESTIC: $13 for one year, $25 for two years, $10 for one-year student subscription.
FOREIGN: $16 for one year, $29 for two years, $12 for one-year student subscription. (Subscription rates subject to change.)

62 West 14th Street, New York, New York 10011

Selected Modern Reader Paperbacks

Accumulation on a World Scale by Samir Amin	$ 8.95
African Social Studies edited by Peter Gutkind and Peter Waterman	6.95
The Age of Imperialism by Harry Magdoff	3.95
American Radicals, edited by Harvey Goldberg	3.45
Armed Struggle in Africa: With the Guerrillas in "Portuguese" Guinea by Gérard Chaliand	2.95
Away With All Pests: An English Surgeon in People's China, 1954-1969 by Dr. Joshua S. Horn	3.95
Cambodia: Starvation or Revolution by George C. Hildebrand and Gareth Porter	3.25
Capitalism and Underdevelopment in Latin America by Andre Gunder Frank	5.95
Capitalist Patriarchy and the Case For Socialist Feminism, edited by Zillah R. Eisenstein	5.95
Caste, Class, and Race by Oliver C. Cox	7.95
China Shakes the World by Jack Belden	6.95
China Since Mao by Charles Bettelheim and Neil Burton	2.50
China's Economy and the Maoist Strategy by John G. Gurley	5.95
The Chinese Road to Socialism: Economics of the Cultural Revolution by E. L. Wheelwright and Bruce McFarlane	4.50
Class Struggles in the USSR. Part 1: 1917-1923 by Charles Bettelheim	7.95
The Communist Manifesto by Karl Marx and Friedrich Engels, including Engels' "Principles of Communism," and an essay, "The Communist Manifesto After 100 Years," by Paul M. Sweezy and Leo Huberman	2.25
The Communist Movement. From Comintern to Cominform by Fernando Claudín (2 vols.)	11.90
Consciencism by Kwame Nkrumah	2.95
Corporate Imperialism by Norman Girvan	5.95
Corporations and the Cold War, edited by David Horowitz	4.50
A Critique of Soviet Economics by Mao Tse-tung	4.00
Cuba: Anatomy of a Revolution by Leo Huberman and Paul M. Sweezy	3.95
The Economic Transformation of Cuba by Edward Boorstein	5.95
The End of Prosperity by Harry Magdoff and Paul M. Sweezy	2.95
The Energy Crisis by Michael Tanzer	3.75
The Formation of the Economic Thought of Karl Marx by Ernest Mandel	3.95
The Growth of the Modern West Indies by Gordon K. Lewis	6.95
Humanity and Society. A World History by Kenneth Neill Cameron	6.50
How Capitalism Works by Pierre Jalée	3.95
Imperial Brain Trust by Laurence H. Shoup and William Minter	6.50
Imperialism and Underdevelopment: A reader, edited by Robert I. Rhodes	6.50

Introduction to Socialism by Leo Huberman and Paul M. Sweezy	2.95
Karl Marx's Theory of Revolution. Part 1: State and Bureaucracy by Hal Draper (2 vols. in one)	9.50
Labor and Monopoly Capital by Harry Braverman	5.95
Latin America: Underdevelopment or Revolution by Andre Gunder Frank	6.50
Law and the Rise of Capitalism by Michael Tigar and Madeleine Levy	4.95
Lenin's Last Struggle by Moshe Lewin	5.95
Man's Worldly Goods by Leo Huberman	6.50
Marx and Modern Economics, edited by David Horowitz	3.45
Marxism and Philosophy by Karl Korsch	3.45
Marxist Economic Theory by Ernest Mandel (2 vols.)	11.90
The Military Art of People's War: Selected Political Writings of General Vo Nguyễn Giap, edited by Russell Stetler	5.95
Monopoly Capital by Paul A. Baran and Paul M. Sweezy	5.95
Notes on the Puerto Rican Revolution by Gordon K. Lewis	4.50
On the Transition to Socialism by Paul M. Sweezy and Charles Bettelheim	3.25
Open Veins of Latin America by Eduardo Galeano	5.95
The Political Economy of Growth by Paul A. Baran	5.95
A Political History of Japanese Capitalism by Jon Halliday	8.95
Politics and Social Structure in Latin America by James Petras	5.95
The Ragged Trousered Philanthropists by Robert Tressell	7.50
Selected Political Writings of Rosa Luxemburg, edited by Dick Howard	6.95
Socialism in Cuba by Leo Huberman and Paul M. Sweezy	4.50
Strategy for Revolution: Essays on Latin America by Régis Debray	2.95
The Sugarmill by Manuel Moreno Fraginals	10.95
The Theory of Capitalist Development by Paul M. Sweezy	5.95
The Third World in World Economy by Pierre Jalée	3.95
The United States and Chile: Imperialism and the Overthrow of the Allende Government by James Petras and Morris Morley	4.50
Unequal Exchange: A Study of the Imperialism of Trade by Arghiri Emmanuel	6.95
The Watchdogs: Philosophers and the Established Order by Paul Nizan	2.95
We, the People by Leo Huberman	5.95